*Lord,
Answer My Prayer*

NINA SMIT

Lord, Answer My Prayer

When Women Pray

*The Lord is near to all who call on him,
to all who call on him in truth.*

PSALM 145:18

STRUIK CHRISTIAN BOOKS

Published in Afrikaans under the title, *Here, hoor U my?*
by Struik Christian Books Ltd in 2001.

Struik Christian Books Ltd
(A division of New Holland Publishing (South Africa) (Pty) Ltd)
Cornelis Struik House
80 McKenzie Street
Cape Town 8001

Reg. No. 1971/009721/07

Text © Nina Smit 2001
This edition © Struik Christian Books Ltd 2001

This edition August 2001
Second impression March 2002

© Quotations from the Holy Bible, New International Version.
Copyright 1973, 1978, 1984 by International Bible Society.
Used with permission.

All rights reserved. No part of this publication may be reproduced
or transmitted in any form or by any means, electronic or mechanical,
including photocopying, recording, or in any information storage and
retrieval system, without the written permission of the publisher.

Translated into English by Lizel Grobbelaar
Edited by Lizé Lübbe
DTP by Petro Quinton
Cover design by Christian Jaggers
Cover photograph by Struik Image Library
Cover reproduction by Hirt & Carter Cape (Pty) Ltd
Reproduced, printed and bound by CTP Book Printers
PO Box 6060, Parow East 7501

ISBN 1 86823 454 1

Preface

According to Henri Nouwen, it is extremely difficult to write about prayer because, as soon as you do, you become aware of how far away you are from the ideal you are writing about (*Circles*, p. 20). This is only too true! However, should we truly wish to learn how to pray, we would have to pay attention to what the Bible teaches us about prayer because, without prayer, we can never reach God and communicate with him in a meaningful way.

It is true that you can learn to pray only by praying. When you really become involved with God, you discover that he himself teaches you how to communicate with him. In these daily readings we will learn about prayer month by month, and also discover how to pray. We will study the Bible lessons on prayer, look at how the various characters in the Bible prayed, and also look at the prayers of Jesus himself.

It is my prayer that your personal prayer life will be more intimate and fervent once you have completed this book.

The author

CONTENTS

January	Our Father …	9
February	How to worship God	41
March	The Holy Spirit and prayer	71
April	God is there whenever you call to him	103
May	Prayer in times of trouble	135
June	Jesus and prayer	167
July	Obstacles to prayer	199
August	Praying for others	231
September	Prayers from the Bible	263
October	Prayer is a joy	295
November	Answer to prayer	327
December	The power of prayer	359

January

Our Father ...

The Lord's Prayer is Jesus' model prayer which he himself used to teach his disciples to pray. To this day the Lord's Prayer is still the model which the children of God should use in their own prayers. In the phrases of the Lord's Prayer we learn how to talk to God, to address him as Father, to worship and glorify him, to lay our daily needs at his feet and to request him to deliver us from temptation and the evil one.

If you would like to learn how to pray correctly, you merely have to repeat the words in the Lord's prayer to your heavenly Father.

1 January
Lord, teach us to pray
Read: Luke 11:1–4

One day Jesus was praying in a certain place. When he finished, one of his disciples said to him, 'Lord, teach us to pray, just as John taught his disciples.'
Luke 11:1

Jesus' disciples soon noticed that prayer was of cardinal importance to him. No matter how busy he was, he always made time to communicate with his heavenly Father in prayer. His disciples envied this ease with which Jesus prayed and one of them therefore requested him to teach them to pray the way John had also taught his disciples.

Jesus then taught them his model prayer, the Lord's Prayer, and added a parable on the value of prayer (Luke 11:5–12), and appealed to them to pray (Luke 11:13). 'If you then, though you are evil, know how to give good gifts to your children, how much more will your Father in heaven give the Holy Spirit to those who ask him!' he promised them.

Like Jesus' disciples, many Christians have a problem with prayer. We would like to learn how to pray, yet our personal prayer life remains feeble and disappointing. Jesus wants to teach you to pray correctly – just ask him and then use the prayer he taught his disciples when you want to talk to him.

Lord Jesus, please teach me to pray, just as you taught your disciples to pray long ago. Thank you for the promise that you give your children good gifts when we ask you. Amen.

2 January
Go into your room …
Read: Matthew 6:5–8

*But when you pray, go into your room, close the door
and pray to your Father, who is unseen. Then your Father,
who sees what is done in secret, will reward you.*
Matthew 6:6

We read that Jesus often sent away the people who flocked to him and then went to an isolated place when he wanted to communicate with his Father. When he taught his disciples how to pray, he told them not to pray standing on the street corners like the hypocrites, but rather to go into their rooms, and pray to God alone, behind locked doors. The Authorised King James version of this passage reads, 'But thou, when thou prayest, enter into thy closet, and when thou hast shut thy door, pray to thy Father which is in secret …'

When you want to pray, you also need a room, a place where you can communicate with God alone, without anybody disturbing you. Prayer always involves personal, individual contact with God and you should therefore set aside a specific time and place for it for yourself. 'Prayer is an intimate conversation with God, and the privacy of your room is therefore the proper place,' writes *Die Bybellennium* (p. 1127). Find yourself such a private place and set aside a specific time where you can communicate with God daily.

*Heavenly Father, thank you for the incredible privilege of being able to
communicate with you in my room when I pray. Help me to set aside
enough time for this daily communication with you. Amen.*

3 January
Your Father knows what you need
Read: Matthew 6:5–8

> *And when you pray, do not keep on babbling like pagans,*
> *for they think they will be heard because of their many words.*
> *Do not be like them, for your Father knows*
> *what you need before you ask him.*
> Matthew 6:7–8

Some Jews in Jesus' time (particularly the Pharisees) tried to draw God's attention by their lengthy and frequent prayers and also tried to impress other people who were listening to these prayers. Jesus therefore warned his disciples against prayers which were actually a mere torrent of empty words.

Unfortunately the vast majority of Christians have a meagre prayer life. Some find it difficult to pray because they do not know how to pray eloquently. Fortunately eloquence is not necessary at all. God knows all about you. He knows you inside out and he knows exactly what you want to ask him even before you start praying. You therefore do not have to wrap your prayer requests in rhetorical phrases. Merely tell God exactly what you have on your mind. This is more than enough and is so simple that even a young child can do it.

When you start praying you should never think about how little you have to give God, but about how much God wants to give you, says Andrew Murray *(With Christ in the school of prayer, p. 27)*.

Heavenly Father, how wonderful that I do not have to use flowery speech to be able to pray. Thank you that you have so much to give me when I speak to you. Amen.

4 January
A Father's blessing
Read: Matthew 6:9–13

This, then, is how you should pray ...
Matthew 6:9

'The Lord remembers us and will bless us: he will bless those who fear the Lord,' the psalmist wrote (Psalm 115:12–13). Every teacher is aware of the importance of not only telling the pupils what to do, but of showing them how to do it as well. Jesus also followed this principle when he taught his disciples the Lord's Prayer. The fact that God loves his children and therefore enables them to pray, to talk to him with childlike faith, to share their needs with him the way a child would confide in his human father, is of prime importance in this prayer.

When you speak to God in prayer, you experience his blessings first-hand. Only God blesses. This does not depend on the feeling you experience when you pray, but is based on the unconditional love and wonderworking power of the Father in whom you are confiding. No-one always feels like praying every day. Do not wait until you feel like communicating with God. Make a regular appointment with him. Talk to him in prayer in any case so that you can experience his lasting blessing in your life every day.

Heavenly Father, forgive me for not always feeling like praying.
Thank you for the assurance that you will pour out your blessing
upon me when I talk to you. Amen.

5 January
Our Father in heaven ...
Read: Matthew 6:9–13

> *This, then, is how you should pray: Our Father in heaven ...*
> Matthew 6:9

In telling his disciples that they could address God as their Father, Jesus told them something they had never known before: their relationship to God was one of the most intimate and tender relationships ever; that of a child to its father. To the Jews God was so holy that they would not even write his Name, yet they could now address this holy God as 'Dad'! However, Jesus stressed the fact that this Father is in heaven – he is therefore not merely 'one of us' just because we may call him Father, he is still a holy God.

In Jesus God wants to be a Father to you, and you may therefore call him 'Father' in your prayers. You are also entitled to the love and care of your heavenly Father. He knows you personally, as intimately as a father knows his child. You are infinitely precious to him and he wants to care for you and meet all your physical needs.

Should you ever doubt God's fatherly love for you again, underline the wonderful promise in 2 Corinthians 6:18, 'I will be a Father to you, and you will be my sons and daughters, says the Lord Almighty ...'

> *Heavenly Father, it is incredible that you are my Father, that you love me unconditionally and that you want to care for me every day. I praise you for this! Amen.*

6 January
Hallowed be your name
Read: Matthew 6:9–13

*This, then, is how you should pray:
Our Father in heaven, hallowed be your name ...*
Matthew 6:9

God's Name and his Person are inseparable. The Name of God is much more than the name of Father used by his children to address him in prayer. God's Name also tells us that he is holy, it stands for everything he is and everything we know about him. When we pray that his Name be hallowed, we therefore mean that we will give him the honour and the place in our hearts and lives he is entitled to. We also mean that he will be the most important Person in our life, and we commit ourselves to honouring his Name in everything we say and do.

If you therefore pray this part of the Lord's Prayer, you have to be quite sure that you will glorify God's Name in everything you do and say. See to it that the One who bears this Name reigns in your life. 'You are my Lord; apart from you I have no good thing,' the psalmist confessed in Psalm 16:2. This should be the confession of everyone who prays that the Name of God be hallowed in his or her life.

*Heavenly Father, please enable me to glorify your Name in everything
I do and say, so that others will be able to see by my life that nothing
is more important to me than you. Amen.*

7 January
Your kingdom come ...
Read: Matthew 6:9–13

Our Father in heaven ... Your kingdom come ...
Matthew 6:9–10

A king is always involved whenever we refer to a kingdom. When Jesus therefore taught his disciples to ask that God's kingdom come, he was simultaneously telling them that their heavenly Father ruled over the whole of creation and that he should also rule their lives. Subjects obey their king – and likewise God expects his children to obey his word and law, and he expects us to exert ourselves to proclaiming his kingdom here on earth.

This part of the Lord's Prayer wants to teach you to acknowledge and obey God as King with regard to every aspect of your life. As your Father is the King, you are the daughter of a king, and you can live like one every day – even if it means that pain and suffering await you here on earth, which we unfortunately cannot escape. However, this heavenly King promises you that if you seek his kingdom and will on earth, he will give you everything else involved (Matthew 6:33).

What are you doing to spread this kingdom?

Heavenly Father, I worship you as the King of my life.
I pray that your kingdom will come. Please help me sacrifice everything
for your kingdom and to obey your instructions unconditionally. Amen.

8 JANUARY
Your will be done ...
Read: Matthew 6:9–13

This, then, is how you should pray: Our Father in heaven ...
your will be done on earth as it is in heaven ...
Matthew 6:9–10

In heaven everything is done according to the perfect will of God, but here on earth, God's will is often resisted. Jesus therefore teaches his disciples to pray that God's will be done on earth as it is already being done in heaven because, where people are willing to obey God's will, God himself gives them his peace and tranquillity in their hearts.

'Before we can pray: "Lord, Thy kingdom come", we must be willing to pray: "My kingdom go",' writes Alan Redpath (*Prayer can change my life*, p. 19). When you therefore pray that God's will be done in your life, you are actually confessing that you are prepared to let go of your own way and will so that God's will can be done in your life. This is not so easy, as everybody would like to do things his or her own way! However, if your prayers are in line with God's will, you know he *will* hear them: 'This is the confidence we have in approaching God: that if we ask anything according to his will, he hears us,' writes John (1 John 5:14).

Ask God to teach you to pray this way.

Heavenly Father, I pray that your will be done in my life.
Please make me willing to surrender my own way and will
so that I will obey your will unconditionally. Amen.

9 January
Give us today our daily bread ...
Read: Matthew 6:9–13

Give us today our daily bread ...
Matthew 6:11

The first three 'your' supplications which emphasise God's Name, kingdom and will, are followed by the three 'I' supplications which revolve around our daily, human needs. In this way Jesus wants to teach his disciples that they may make their daily needs known to their heavenly Father. He loves them and wants to meet all their physical needs, like an earthly father would do for his children.

God promises to take care of you – not only today, but also in the future. You may therefore pray with confidence that God will meet your material needs. You may ask God for your daily bread and know that he will give it to you – but you first of all have to acknowledge that all your material possessions come from God. You have received everything you possess from him. For this reason you should in turn be willing to meet the needs of those who have less than you, to share your crust of bread with those who probably have no bread at all. Ask the Lord to open your eyes and your purse to meet the need of others.

Heavenly Father, thank you very much that I may ask you with confidence to meet my human needs. Please make me willing to meet the needs of others as you meet mine. Amen.

10 JANUARY
Forgive us our debts ...
Read: Matthew 6:9–13

Forgive us our debts ...
Matthew 6:12

Everybody is a sinner by nature. We cannot have any doubt about this fact, as the Bible states it repeatedly and in no uncertain terms. All have sinned and fall short of the glory of God, declares Paul in Romans 3:23. When we therefore talk to the holy God, we soon discover the vastness of our burden of sin, and we then cannot but confess that sin before God, because sin always alienates us from God.

Fortunately God is always prepared to forgive your sin. 'If we confess our sins, he is faithful and just and will forgive us our sins and purify us from all unrighteousness,' John wrote (1 John 1:9). One of our computer friends recently said God 'deletes' our sin, and he has no 'back-up file'. Once God has forgiven your sin, he never even thinks about it again.

God wants to forgive all your sin, but he cannot do so until you have confessed them before him one by one (by name and not merely in general).

Don't postpone, do this straight away!

Heavenly Father, you know me inside out, you also know all my sins. Please forgive my sins and help me to turn away from my sin. Amen.

11 January
As we also have forgiven ...
Read: Matthew 6:9–13

Forgive us our debts, as we also have forgiven our debtors.
Matthew 6:12

It is true that God is always prepared to forgive your sin, but Jesus nevertheless attached a condition in Matthew 6:14–15, 'For if you forgive men when they sin against you, your heavenly Father will also forgive you. But if you do not forgive men their sins, your Father will not forgive your sins.' This verse seems to suggest that God's forgiveness depends on the extent to which we are prepared to forgive others. Fortunately this is not true. God's forgiveness is not a direct result of your forgiving others, or you would probably be the loser! God's forgiveness is based on the principle that you should understand what forgiveness means.

Unlike us, God is always prepared to forgive, while we sometimes battle to forgive those who offend us. Whenever you ask God to forgive your sin, you have to ask yourself whether you are in turn really prepared to forgive those who have offended or hurt you. If so, you may be confident that God will forgive you.

Lord Jesus, thank you that you – by bearing my sin on the cross – have made it possible for God to forgive my sin. Please help me to forgive those who have sinned against me. Amen.

12 January
Lead us not into temptation
Read: Matthew 6:9–13

And lead us not into temptation ...
Matthew 6:13

All of us are tempted every day. The devil will not leave a single stone unturned in his effort to lure God's children away from God's way. After all, he even tried to tempt Jesus in the wilderness (Matthew 4:1–11)! You will never be able to resist the devil in your own power. He knows exactly where the weak spots are in your spiritual armour, and he will target you particularly when you are at your weakest.

Fortunately God is much stronger than the devil and you can rely on his power to thwart the devil's plans.

Jesus therefore teaches his disciples to pray that God will not lead them into temptation. With God on your side, you are always stronger than the devil. He also promises in his word that he will not let you be tempted beyond what you can bear, but when you are tempted, he will also provide a way out so that you can stand up under it (1 Corinthians 10:13).

Here you should learn from Jesus. He put the devil to flight by using the sword of the Word. Know your Bible so well that you will be able to use it as a weapon when the devil tries to tempt you.

Heavenly Father, thank you that I am able to tackle the devil
by your power with the assurance that you will not let me
be tempted beyond what I can bear. Help me by your power
to stand firmly against temptation. Amen.

13 January
But deliver us from the evil one
Read: Matthew 6:9–13

And lead us not into temptation, but deliver us from the evil one ...
Matthew 6:13

God's children on earth are involved in an endless struggle against the evil one. The devil will not necessarily leave you alone once you belong to God, and you can win this warfare against the devil only by the power of God and by means of God's armour (read more about this in Ephesians 6:10–18).

Jesus is fully aware of the power of the evil one to which his children are subjected in this world. In the Lord's Prayer he therefore asks his Father to deliver them from the evil one. When Jesus prayed for his disciples shortly before his crucifixion, he repeated this supplication: 'My prayer is not that you take them out of the world but that you protect them from the evil one' (John 17:15).

'Be self-controlled and alert,' Peter warned in his letter. 'Your enemy the devil prowls around like a roaring lion looking for someone to devour' (1 Peter 5:8). Never lose sight of this fact. The devil will remain a very real danger, but Jesus is strong enough to deliver you from his clutches. He has already defeated him on the cross. Appeal to his power to deliver you when the devil knocks on your door again.

Lord Jesus, thank you that you have already defeated the devil
on the cross. Help me to be prepared and level-headed
so that I will be able to resist him by your power. Amen.

14 January
For yours is the glory ...
Read: Matthew 6:9–13

For thine is the kingdom, and the power, and the glory, for ever. Amen.
Matthew 6:13 (King James Version)

Although the concluding words of the Lord's Prayer are not included in the New International Version because they do not appear in the original source text, they form the perfect conclusion to Jesus' model prayer. These words were also generally used to conclude prayers in biblical times. By means of this phrase, the Lord's Prayer returns to where it starts – to the things of God: the power and the glory belong to that God to whom we are talking, for ever.

God's kingdom is not of this world – but if you seek his kingdom, he will give you everything else. His power is much greater than that which you can grasp with your human brain. And the glory which radiates from him must be reflected by you so that others will be able to see it in your life.

'The kingdom, the power and the glory belong to God who is the same God whom you may address as Father. As the *kingdom* belongs to him, he is able to establish his kingdom on earth. As the *power* belongs to him, he is able to accomplish his will on earth. As the *glory* belongs to him, he is able to see to it that his Name be honoured on earth. He is therefore also able to meet all the needs of his children,' says Dr Hennie Conradie (*ABC van gebed*, p. 129).

Heavenly Father, I praise you because yours is the kingdom and the power and the glory, for ever. Amen.

15 January
Sin forms a barrier
Read: Psalm 66:13–20

---

*If I had cherished sin in my heart, the Lord would not have listened;
but God has surely listened and heard my voice in prayer.*
Psalm 66:18–19

Sin in our lives always forms a barrier between us and God – a barrier which prevents him from listening to our prayers. 'But your iniquities have separated you from your God; your sins have hidden his face from you, so that he will not hear,' writes the prophet Isaiah (Isaiah 59:2).

Fortunately the sins Isaiah refers to here are not those sins which you have already confessed and renounced, but those you refuse to renounce. The Lord will not listen to your prayers if you still cherish habitual sin in your life which you are not prepared to renounce.

Before you kneel in prayer again, consider carefully whether certain things in your life have become more important than God. Usually this type of sin involves relationships. Resolve any disturbed relationships in your life and ask the Lord to make you aware of those things which are still separating you from him, those things which prevent him from listening to your prayers.

*Lord Jesus, please point out my sin to me – show me
what is still separating us, what is still serving as a barrier
to prevent you from listening to my prayers.
Grant that I will also be willing to renounce them. Amen.*

16 January
God wants to forgive your sin
Read: Psalm 85:1–9

You forgave the iniquity of your people and covered all their sins.
Psalm 85:2

When one reads the history of God's disobedient people, one cannot but be amazed at the love, patience and mercy of God. He was repeatedly prepared to forgive their sins and cover their iniquity.

The prophet Micah wrote as follows about this God who forgave again and again: 'Who is a God like you, who pardons sin … You will again have compassion on us; you will tread our sins underfoot and hurl all our iniquities into the depths of the sea' (Micah 7:18–19). God is not only prepared to forgive sin, he never even thinks about the sin again.

And this merciful God is also your God who sent his Son so that everybody can have their sin forgiven – the sin committed in the past as well as the sin still to be committed in the future. Jesus bore the punishment for your sin on the cross, once and for all – all you have to do on your part is to confess your sin before God. Since Jesus has already restored the relationship between you and God which had been disturbed by sin, you may place your hope for the future on him.

Lord Jesus, I praise you for having paid the price for all my sin on the cross. Thank you that I may now be free and place my hope for the future on you. Amen.

17 January
Go now and leave your life of sin
Read: John 8:1–11

*'Then neither do I condemn you,' Jesus declared.
'Go now and leave your life of sin.'*
John 8:11

One day a group of teachers of the law and Pharisees brought in a woman who had been caught in adultery and made her stand before Jesus. 'In the Law Moses commanded us to stone such women. Now what do you say?' Jesus did not fall into the trap they had set for him – nor did he judge the woman. 'If any one of you is without sin, let him be the first to throw a stone at her,' is his response (verse 7). Hereupon the accusers left one by one until only Jesus and the woman remained.

'Has no-one condemned you?' Jesus asked her. 'No-one, sir,' she said. Then Jesus returned his famous verdict comprised in the above-mentioned verse: 'Then neither do I. Go now and leave your life of sin.'

Jesus always has tremendous compassion for sinners, but he never condones sin. He is always prepared to forgive you, but there is a proviso: you may not continue living in sin, you must be willing to do your best to renounce the sin and, in turn, be willing to forgive others like God is doing in your case time and again.

Can you do that?

Lord Jesus, thank you for not judging me for my sin. Please help me not to live in sin any longer, but to serve you with my life. Amen.

18 January
God always forgives again and again
Read: Romans 7:15–24

I do not understand what I do. For what I want to do I do not do, but what I hate I do. Who will rescue me from this body of death? Thanks be to God – through Jesus Christ our Lord!
Romans 7:15, 24–25

All of us find ourselves quite frequently committing that habitual sin which we have just confessed. If you are in the same boat, you are in good company! Paul had exactly the same experience. In the above verse he confessed that he did not do the things he wanted to do, but that he in fact did the very things he hated.

Only one Person can deliver you from this life of falling and struggling to your feet again, and that is God himself. He does this by the intervention of Jesus who died on the cross to deliver you from sin. God is therefore prepared to forgive you again and again. 'You are forgiving and good, O Lord,' the psalmist wrote (Psalm 86:5).

In your own power you will never be able to obey God's law to the letter. However, the Holy Spirit can enable you to live so close to Jesus that, by his power, you will no longer have to be ruled by sin. Ask him to do this for you.

Heavenly Father, thank you that you are always prepared to forgive my sin. I now pray that you will enable me to resist the sin by your power and that I may live only for you in future. Amen.

19 January
Agreeing in Jesus' Name
Read: Matthew 18:15–20

Again, I tell you that if two of you on earth agree about anything you ask for, it will be done for you by my Father in heaven.
Matthew 18:19

Although Jesus frequently prayed alone, and also encourages us to go to our room when we pray, he says here that believers should at times agree in prayer. 'Just as a tree needs roots in the ground as well as a trunk which grows in the sunlight, prayer requires secrecy ... as well as public fellowship with fellow believers who come together in fellowship in the Name of Jesus,' writes Andrew Murray *(With Christ in the school of prayer,* p. 111).

Writers of books on prayer agree that where believers pray together, their prayers have even more power than when they pray individually. When Christians pray together, they share their problems and come to love one another. When people pray together it also becomes easier to share one's own crises and problems and pray about them. I still remember clearly how much it meant to me when we experienced a crisis in the family and my Bible study group started praying for us spontaneously.

Should you have a serious prayer request again, ask a couple of your friends to pray with you about the problem. If two people agree about a matter and pray about it, God *will* do it for them.

Heavenly Father, you know that I find it difficult to pray with others. Teach me to agree with other believers when I pray so that our prayer requests can be answered. Amen.

20 January
Ask, seek and knock
Read: Matthew 7:7–8

Ask and it will be given to you; seek and you will find; knock and the door will be opened to you. For everyone who asks receives; he who seeks finds; and to him who knocks, the door will be opened.
Matthew 7:7–8

In this verse Jesus wants to teach his disciples that it is important to pray without ceasing. Next to the revelation about the Father's love, this is the most important lesson in the school of prayer, according to Andrew Murray (*With Christ in the school of prayer*, p. 39). The person who is prepared to persevere in prayer has the assurance that God will listen to his prayers. For this very reason, the three verbs used here – ask, seek and knock – are used in the continuous tense in the Greek text. The literal translation here would therefore be to keep on asking, keep on seeking, and keep on knocking.

Sometimes you do not receive answers to your prayers immediately. When this happens, you simply have to keep on praying. To get to know God requires effort, writes *Die Bybel in praktyk* (p. 1390). However, Jesus assures you that your prayer effort will always be rewarded and you must therefore never stop seeking God. Keep on asking him to give you more wisdom, patience, knowledge, hope and understanding.

He *will* do this for you.

Lord Jesus, you know I soon get tired of asking, seeking and knocking when my prayers are not answered immediately. Enable me to keep on praying until you have answered me. Amen.

21 January
When you ask and you do not receive
Read: James 4:1–6

When you ask, you do not receive, because you ask with wrong motives, that you may spend what you get on your pleasures.
James 4:3

You sometimes pray earnestly – you also do what was said in yesterday's daily reading – you keep on praying, and yet God does not answer that prayer. When this happens to you, you have to double-check whether your prayer could perhaps be selfish. If you pray merely to have your own selfish desires gratified, God will not answer your prayers.

When Moses asked to be allowed to enter the promised land, God did not grant his prayer request. When David prayed that the life of his little boy should be spared, the child died. God's response to your prayers is sometimes 'no' because the things you desire will not be good for you. At other times the things which you ask may not be according to his will.

If you therefore pray and your prayer request is not granted, you may rest assured that God's response is always the right one for you, even if it differs from the answer you desired. Accept God's will for your life, and his answer to your prayer request.

Heavenly Father, I am sorry that I sometimes insist on an answer when I ask you something. Teach me that your answers sometimes differ from what I would like to receive and grant that my prayers will never be selfish. Amen.

22 January
Good gifts to his children
Read: Matthew 7:9–13

If you, then, though you are evil, know how to give good gifts to your children, how much more will your Father in heaven give good gifts to those who ask him!
Matthew 7:11

Just as an earthly father gives good gifts to his children, God will give his children good things in response to prayer. However, just as God is greater than an earthly father, he will respond to our requests – and give us much more than we ask or imagine. 'Now to him who is able to do immeasurably more than all we ask or imagine … to him be glory …,' writes Paul in Ephesians 3:20–21.

God is therefore able to give you much more than you ask of him in prayer, provided you will always remember that the promises in his Word apply to his children only. Your prayers will therefore be answered only if you are in the right relationship to your heavenly Father. Just as an earthly father sometimes withholds privileges from a disobedient child, you cannot expect to have your prayers answered if you refuse to obey God.

Therefore, before you kneel to pray, check whether your relationship with God is right.

Heavenly Father, I praise you because you are able to give me much more than I ask – grant that I will obey you so that you will answer my prayers. Amen.

23 January
The love of God
Read: 1 John 4:7–16

And so we know and rely on the love God has for us. God is love. Whoever lives in love, lives in God, and God in him.
1 John 4:16

When you pray, you always have to remember to whom you are talking. The God to whom you are praying *is* love and he loves you unconditionally. Not because you are so cute, but because he is your Father. He does not hesitate to demonstrate his love either. 'For God so loved the world that he gave his one and only Son, that whoever believes in him shall not perish but have eternal life,' Jesus told Nicodemus (John 3:16).

However, this loving Father asks something of you: if you love him he wants you to demonstrate your love for him – the way he has already demonstrated his love. This is done by your loving others. This is probably one of the most difficult commands in the Bible, but you cannot be God's child unless you do this. 'Dear friends, let us love one another, for love comes from God. Everyone who loves has been born of God and knows God,' John wrote (1 John 4:7).

When you spend time with God again, ask him to give you his love in your life.

Heavenly Father, thank you that you are love, that you loved me when I was still a sinner. Grant that I will be able to love others as much as you love me. Amen.

24 January
Jesus reveals the Father to us
Read: Hebrews 1:1–5

*The Son is the radiance of God's glory
and the exact representation of his being ...*
Hebrews 1:3

Jesus is not only God's Son and his spokesman, he is God himself. As he is the One closest to the Father, he reveals the Father to us. In the Old Testament, no-one could see God and remain alive, because he was too holy. However, when God sent his Son to the world, Jesus introduced his Father to us. When you look at the Son, you actually see God himself and you see how wonderful he is. The Son mirrors God, says *Die Boodskap* translation of our verse (p. 719).

One day Philip asked Jesus to show them the Father, and Jesus said, 'Don't you know me, Philip, even after I have been among you such a long time? Anyone who has seen me has seen the Father' (John 14:9).

In Jesus it is also possible to know the Father and talk to him. Jesus not only reflects God's glory but his Father's unique attributes are reflected in everything he does and says.

In Jesus God also draws close to you. While he walked on earth, he obeyed his Father unconditionally. If you therefore pray in Jesus' Name, your heavenly Father will grant your prayer requests.

*Lord Jesus, I praise you for showing me the Father
and for enabling me to pray in your Name so that the Father
can grant my prayer requests. Amen.*

25 January
Workers in the harvest field
Read: Matthew 9:35–38

Then he said to his disciples, 'The harvest is plentiful but the workers are few. Ask the Lord of the harvest, therefore, to send out workers into his harvest field.'
Matthew 9:37–38

The Bible mentions several instances where Jesus taught his disciples that they should pray, and also how to pray. In Matthew 9 he also told them what they should pray for. God's children must pray for workers in his harvest field so that a rich harvest will be harvested for his kingdom.

There are about 1 739 population groups consisting of more than 10 000 people each that still have no churches. Millions of people have never heard Jesus' good tidings. The 'harvest fields' which Jesus refers to have never been so ready for the harvest as right now and there has never been such a desperate need for workers as in the 21st century.

You also have to pray that the Lord will send out workers. Perhaps the Lord wants you to do more than merely pray – perhaps he wants you to be willing to become a worker yourself – to proclaim Jesus' gospel to people who have never heard of him.

Lord Jesus, forgive me for not praying more for workers to be sent out into the harvest field. Grant that I will be willing to become a worker myself, should it be your will. Amen.

26 January
Let go and let God!
Read: Psalm 31:19–24

Be strong and take heart, all you who hope in the Lord.
Psalm 31:24

The literal meaning of our verse for today is: 'Be brave and courageous, you who are looking forward to what the Lord is going to do.' When we pray we should already be looking forward to that which God is going to do for us in response to our prayers. However, few of us manage to do this! To quote the American expression – to 'Let go and let God' – is one of the main problems in praying. We pray about something which is a matter of concern to us – and yes, we are sometimes even prepared to leave the matter in God's hands – but the very next day we take it all back and start worrying about it again!

The Bible frequently refers to people who were not content to leave their anxieties with God, but tried to find their own solutions to their problems. Their own solutions invariably caused greater problems.

When you pray again, leave your problems with God. Let go and allow God to solve the problem for you. Be strong and courageous while you rely on God. You will then be able to look forward to that which God is going to do for you!

Heavenly Father, forgive me for often leaving my problems with you and then snatching them back again immediately. Please enable me to allow you to handle them on my behalf. Amen.

27 January
Share your anxieties with God
Read: 1 Peter 5:5–7

Cast all your anxiety on him because he cares for you.
1 Peter 5:7

The Christians to whom Peter addressed his letter were suffering. As foreigners they were rejected by the heathen society and discriminated against in various ways. The situation was so bad, many of them were at times ready to give up. Peter encouraged these afflicted people to cast their anxieties on God because he would care for them.

In our modern setup we also have many anxieties. We no longer feel safe and our economic prospects are pathetic. Sometimes we even feel we no longer have a future. Sometimes we even feel ready to give up. However, Christians do not have to feel like this. We merely have to share all our anxieties with God.

If you have tried to cope with your own daily stress and anxieties in the past, you have obviously not yet put your life in God's hands completely. Follow Peter's advice and cast your anxieties on God. He is omnipotent, he wants to care for you because he loves you, and he is also fully in control of those circumstances which cause you so much anxiety.

Heavenly Father, thank you that you are aware of all my anxieties. I submit all of them to you. Thank you that you are fully in control of my circumstances and that you want to care for me. Amen.

28 January
Praying and doing
Read: Ecclesiastes 9:7–10

Whatever your hand finds to do, do it with all your might,
for in the grave, where you are going, there is neither working
nor planning nor knowledge nor wisdom.
Ecclesiastes 9:10

Some people pray earnestly and then feel that God will solve everything without their lifting a finger. While a new church building was being inaugurated in Malawi, the congregation prayed earnestly for funds to buy pews for the new church. In his sermon the minister then said, 'Would you like to know where the pews are at the moment? The pews are still in your pockets!' Sometimes we pray for a particular matter while the money to accomplish what we are praying for is in our pockets!

'How many of us who pray for others are prepared to be the instrument with which God can accomplish that prayer?' Billy Graham asked in one of his radio sermons. These words really made me think, because it is only too true that when one prays about a certain situation, one's heart as well as one's purse is opened with regard to the situation.

God does not merely want you to pray, but he also wants you to be prepared to work in his kingdom. That you will pray as well as do. That you will be willing to put your hand deep into your pocket so that God's kingdom will come here on earth.

Heavenly Father, thank you for the privilege of being able to pray and
to know that when we pray, God moves. Help me not to be lazy but to
pray as well as work so that your kingdom can be proclaimed. Amen.

29 January
Prayer and gratitude
Read: Luke 17:11–19

One of them, when he saw he was healed, came back, praising God in a loud voice. He threw himself at Jesus' feet and thanked him ...
Luke 17:15–16

One day Jesus healed ten lepers, but only one of the men turned back to thank him. And this man was not even a Jew – he was a Samaritan, someone the Jews despised.

We often act like the nine ungrateful lepers. We pray – and receive what we have asked God – merely to forget that we should thank the Lord for answered prayers. The Bible repeatedly urges us to be grateful. 'And be thankful,' Paul writes in Colossians 3:15.

See to it that you live a life of gratitude in future – that you never fail to praise God for his love and mercy in your life. By expressing your gratitude towards God, you acknowledge what he does for you.

Any grateful thought directed towards heaven is in itself a prayer, writes Ephraim Lessing. Let this also be true of you!

Heavenly Father, I want to thank you for every time you answered my prayers in the past. Please forgive me for so often having been ungrateful. Amen.

30 January
To the glory of the Father
Read: John 17:1–10

After Jesus said this, he looked towards heaven and prayed: 'Father, the time has come. Glorify your Son, that your Son may glorify you.'
John 17:1

The main objective of Jesus' prayers was to glorify his Father. By his life and prayers he wanted to show his disciples how important and powerful his Father really was. His prayers were therefore never selfish or self-centred, but always focused on his Father. The very first supplication in his model prayer was therefore 'Hallowed be thy name'. Shortly before his crucifixion, he again prayed: 'Father, the time has come. Glorify your Son, that your Son may glorify you' (John 17:1).

What are the contents and objective of your prayers? The objective of your prayers should primarily be to glorify God and not be an accumulation of selfish requests. Do you glorify God in your prayers yet? You should live in such a way that the Father will be glorified by your life as well as your prayers. Jesus himself gives away the secret as to how to succeed in this regard: 'This is to my Father's glory, that you bear much fruit, showing yourselves to be my disciples' (John 15:8). 'Ultimately the conduct of the believer is merely a manifestation of the greatness and power of God. The believer should also see the meaning of his life in this,' writes *Die Bybellennium* (p. 1357).

Lord Jesus, teach me to pray like you so that the Father will be glorified by my prayers and by my life. Help me to bear much fruit for you and be your disciple. Amen.

31 January
Worship God
Read: Matthew 4:8–11

Jesus said to him, 'Away from me, Satan! For it is written: "Worship the Lord your God, and serve him only."'
Matthew 4:10

Matthew reported that when the devil tried to persuade Jesus to worship him by offering him all the kingdoms of the world and their splendour, Jesus answered him without mincing his words, '"Worship the Lord your God, and serve him only." Then the devil left him, and angels came and attended to him' (Matthew 4:10–11).

True prayer should primarily be worship, and only God is worthy of our worship. When you pray, God's honour and glory should be your most important reason for prayer – not the things you want to ask God. You must not worship anybody else either. John once fell on his knees before an angel, but the angel immediately responded, 'Do not do it! I am a fellow-servant with you … Worship God!' (Revelation 22:9).

'Worship is more than a holy fear. Worship is acknowledgement of the majesty of God and his awe, reverence and love,' writes Dr Hennie Conradie *(ABC of prayer*, p. 3).

Your prayers should include these three elements.

Heavenly Father, I praise you as the Lord of my life. Help me to acknowledge your majesty at all times, to stand in awe of you, to glorify and love you with my whole heart. Amen.

February

How to worship God

The Bible provides us with various guidelines for prayer. Firstly you have to realise that it is God's will that his children worship him, that he wants to be worshipped in spirit and in truth, that God often answers your prayers in a different way and that he sometimes expects you to be patient, to persevere in prayer and to wait upon him. Before God listens to your prayers, you should renounce your sin.

When you pray you also need faith – he answers your prayers only when you firmly believe that he will do so. Naturally he answers the prayers only provided the prayer requests are in line with his perfect will for your life and you pray in the Name of Jesus.

When people pray, God comes close to them – your prayer can make a huge difference in your own life and the lives of others and when you pray, you may remind God of his promises with confidence.

1 February

Living water

Read: John 4:4–19

---

*'Sir,' the woman said, 'I can see that you are a prophet.
Our fathers worshipped on this mountain, but you Jews claim
that the place where we must worship is in Jerusalem.'*
John 4:19–20

Initially the Samaritans had wanted to build the temple in Jerusalem with the Jews, but the Jews refused since they looked down upon the Samaritans. They therefore worshipped at Shechem as that was the first place where Abraham had built an altar. Now Shechem was the very place where Jesus met the Samaritan woman at the well.

As Jews never spoke to Samaritans, the woman found it odd that Jesus should ask her for a drink of water. However, Jesus used his conversation with her to show her that he could give her living water which would quench one's thirst for ever. The woman said to him, 'Sir, give me this water so that I won't get thirsty and have to keep coming here to draw water' (verse 15).

Hereupon Jesus told her that the whole way of worship was going to change for ever. Sacred places would no longer be required – people who worshipped God in the right way (in spirit and in truth) would be able to worship him anywhere.

You do not have to seek God in temples and churches either. If you are his child, God himself lives in you by his Holy Spirit – you always have him with you and you can talk to him at any time.

*Heavenly Father, thank you that I do not need a special place
to worship you, because you are always present in my life
by your Holy Spirit. Amen.*

2 FEBRUARY
God is seeking worshippers
Read: John 4:19–26

'Yet a time is coming and has now come when the true worshippers will worship the Father in spirit and in truth, for they are the kind of worshippers the Father seeks.'
John 4:23

God is seeking worshippers. 'Our worship pleases his loving heart and fills him with joy,' Andrew Murray writes *(With Christ in the school of prayer*, p. 17). When the Samaritan woman asks Jesus where one should worship, he answers, 'You Samaritans worship what you do not know; we worship what we do know, for salvation is from the Jews' (John 4:22).

However, the most important lesson Jesus wants to teach the woman is how God should be worshipped, that is 'in spirit and in truth' (verse 23). This means that those who worship God have to be believers, and that he himself will live in people by his spirit so that they will have direct access to him.

I find it incredible that the omnipotent Creator who knows full well what we want to ask him is patiently waiting for his children to communicate with him. God is looking for worshippers. He wants you to talk to him! And it remains a miracle that God listens to people and that our feeble prayers can make a tremendous difference in the world.

Heavenly Father, I praise you for looking for worshippers, that my stammering prayers fill you with joy. Teach me to worship you sincerely by your Holy Spirit. Thank you that I may know that you are always ready to listen to me. Amen.

3 February
Pray in spirit and in truth
Read: John 4:21–26

God is spirit, and his worshippers must worship in spirit and in truth.
John 4:24

There are three types of worshippers, according to Andrew Murray:

- those who pray without actually knowing what they are asking; their prayers are not always answered.
- those who pray with their hearts and minds, but fail to experience the full blessings of worship by the Spirit and in truth.
- and those who worship God in spirit and in truth (*With Christ in the school of prayer*, p. 17).

Only Jesus is able to teach people (by means of his Holy Spirit) to pray in the way mentioned in the third point. According to *Die Bybel in praktyk* p. 1594), 'Choosing Christ means that our prayers are directed by the Holy Spirit'. Only the Spirit of God is able to lead us into the full truth and make our stammering prayers acceptable to God. In order to pray for others in this way there should be perfect harmony between God and his worshippers and their lives should be committed to the rulership of the Holy Spirit.

Which category applies to you? Do you still battle to pray, do you pray without sharing the true blessings of prayer, or has the Holy Spirit taught you how to worship God in spirit and in truth?

Spirit of God, you know that I often battle to pray in Spirit and in truth. Please teach me the right way to communicate with God himself in prayer. Amen.

4 February
Jesus teaches you to pray
Read: John 4:21–26

---

*The woman said, 'I know that Messiah' (called Christ) 'is coming.
When he comes, he will explain everything to us.'*
John 4:25

The Samaritan woman still does not quite understand what Jesus means when he says that God has to be worshipped in spirit and in truth. I know that Messiah is coming, she tells Jesus. When he comes, he will explain everything to us. Although she is spot on, she misses the mark at the same time! The Messiah will explain everything to his followers, but Jesus *is* the Messiah – only those who believe in him can worship him in spirit and in truth, because only he can reveal the Father to us. 'The worship in spirit is only possible for those to whom the Son has revealed the Father and who have received the spirit in Sonship. It is only Christ who opens the way and teaches the worship in spirit,' Andrew Murray writes *(With Christ in the school of prayer,* p. 20).

Jesus wants to teach you to get in touch with his Father, how to worship God in spirit and in truth. He himself is also the way, the truth and the life, and no-one comes to the Father except through him (John 14:6). For this reason you may pray with confidence in the Name of the Father, and know that the Father will answer your prayers.

*Lord Jesus, thank you that you not only teach me to pray,
but that you enable me by your death on the cross
to reach God without any other mediator. Amen.*

5 February
Keep on praying
Read: Luke 18:1–8

*And will not God bring about justice for his chosen ones,
who cry out to him day and night? Will he keep putting them off?
I tell you, he will see that they get justice, and quickly.*
Luke 18:7–8

This parable deals with the judge who 'neither feared God nor cared about men.' A widow kept coming to this judge with a plea. At first the judge refused, but eventually he relented because she continued asking. Even such an unjust person who does not care about others at all, will eventually listen even if only to keep her from bothering him!

Jesus tells this parable to teach us that we have to be willing to keep on asking if we do not receive an answer to our prayers immediately. Luke spells it out clearly: 'Jesus told his disciples a parable to show them that they should always pray and not give up' (Luke 18:1).

If you ask God for something again and he does not answer immediately, do not become discouraged – keep on asking like the widow in this parable. Jesus promises his disciples that God will bring about justice to his disciples who call to him day and night, that he will help, and that he will not delay.

*Heavenly Father, thank you for the assurance that you will always hear
when your children pray, and that you are ready to help me,
provided I am willing to keep on praying. Amen.*

6 February
Wait upon the Lord!
Read: Psalm 131

I do not concern myself with great matters or things too wonderful for me. But I have stilled and quietened my soul; like a weaned child with its mother ... put your hope in the Lord, both now and forever more.
Psalm 131:1–3

When you pray there is no room for emotions such as haughtiness and pride in your life. One who prays sincerely prays in childlike dependence and such a person is then also willing to wait upon the Lord.

Sometimes the Lord does in fact make one wait for his answer. Should this happen, follow the advice of the psalmist. Acknowledge your total dependency upon the Lord and your own inability to change your circumstances. Stop whining, stop being concerned about matters which you cannot change in any case. The psalmist uses the beautiful picture of a contented baby cuddled against its mother's breast. Be still with God and share your problems with him.

A friend of my grandmother's prayed all his life that his daughter who was not a believer would receive the Lord. He died without experiencing God's positive response to his prayer. However, his daughter was converted at his funeral. God is faithful: he will answer your prayers, provided they are in line with his will. All you have to do is wait patiently until he answers.

Heavenly Father, forgive me for sometimes being so impatient. Grant that I will be at peace and remain calm with you – and be prepared to wait for your answer. Amen.

7 FEBRUARY
God is planning prosperity
Read: Jeremiah 29:8–14

'For I know the plans I have for you,' declares the Lord, 'plans to prosper you and not to harm you, plans to give you hope and a future. Then you will call upon me and come and pray to me, and I will listen to you.'
Jeremiah 29:11–12

Jeremiah wrote this letter to the exiles who had been carried into exile to Babel by King Nebuchadnezzar. The people had been carried into exile through their own fault, as a result of their disobedience to the Lord, yet the prophet feels sorry for them. He advises them to continue worshipping God in the heathen country.

Instead of rebelling against their difficult circumstances, Jeremiah encourages the people to remain positive and to keep on praying. He promises them that God was planning to prosper them and not to harm them, that he would shortly give them a future, a hope, again.

While Jeremiah was writing this letter, the people were not yet experiencing any of God's promises of prosperity, but history proves that God kept his promises – he brought his people back from exile and they worshipped him in Jerusalem again.

God is planning prosperity for you too, he wants you to get to know him and seek his will. He wants to give you hope, a hope of eternal life, provided you will serve him and call upon him.

Heavenly Father, thank you that you only plan prosperity for your children, that you sent your Son into the world so that those who call upon you would one day have eternal life. Amen.

8 FEBRUARY
You must have faith in God
Read: Mark 11:12–14 and 20–25

'Have faith in God,' Jesus answered. 'Therefore I tell you, whatever you ask for in prayer, believe that you have received it, and it will be yours.'
Mark 11:22, 24

Praying without believing is useless. God expects each person who prays to believe in him. When Jesus announces that nobody would ever eat the fruit of the unfruitful fig tree again, his disciples were nevertheless very surprised the following morning when they saw that the fig tree had been withered down to its roots. Hereupon Jesus said: Have faith in God!

'Now faith is being sure of what we hope for and certain of what we do not see,' said the writer of Hebrews (Hebrews 11:1). Faith is the ability to hold on to the promises of God and accept them for yourself although they have not yet been realised. If you are unable to pray and believe in this way, you may take Jesus' above-mentioned promise literally and then pray knowing that God will answer your prayer requests, provided they are in line with his will.

God always keeps every one of his promises. Ask him to increase your faith to such an extent that you will be able to believe in this way when you pray.

Heavenly Father, I often pray without actually believing that you will give me the things I ask for. Give me the ability to distinguish between what to ask for and the faith that you will give it to me. Amen.

9 February
Believe that you have already received
Read: Mark 11:20–25

Therefore I tell you, whatever you ask for in prayer, believe that you have received it, and it will be yours.
Mark 11:24

In Mark 11:24 Jesus makes an incredible promise to his disciples: should they, while they are praying, be able to believe that they have already received the prayer request concerned, God would give it to them. And God always keeps his promises. He has the power to fulfil every promise in his word. 'Praise be to the Lord, the God of Israel, who with his hands has fulfilled what he promised with his mouth to my father David,' Solomon said in 2 Chronicles 6:4.

Jesus' promises regarding prayer are therefore true literally. However, one has to know one secret before one prays this type of prayer: first of all check whether that which you ask God is his will for your life. You may know God's will by living close to Jesus, and submitting your whole life to be controlled by the Holy Spirit. Your prayers should always meet three requirements:

- If you pray in the Name of Jesus
- to the glory of God, and
- directed by the Holy Spirit

you may be confident that you will receive the things you ask of God.

Heavenly Father, it is incredible that I may receive everything I ask of you, provided I pray according to your will, to your glory and in the Name of Jesus. Teach me to pray in this way. Amen.

10 February
Prayer and forgiveness
Read: Mark 11:20–25

And when you stand praying, if you hold anything against anyone, forgive him, so that your Father in heaven may forgive you your sins.
Mark 11:25

Before you pray, you first of all have to forgive those against whom you hold a grudge. You cannot expect God to forgive you again and again if you refuse to forgive others. God will not forgive someone who is praying for forgiveness with a selfish attitude, because answer to prayer is usually linked to relationships. If your relationship with God is not right, he will not listen to your prayers either, and if your relationship with your neighbour is not right, this fact will likewise sink your prayer life.

Love for God and love for your neighbour are linked inextricably. For this reason Jesus teaches his disciples to pray: 'Forgive us our debts, as we also have forgiven our debtors' (Matthew 6:12).

Perhaps many of your prayers have in fact not yet been answered because you do not yet love others enough. God's unconditional forgiveness of you should be the model on which you have to base your forgiveness of others. 'Our forgiving love toward man is the evidence of God's love in us,' Andrew Murray writes *(With Christ in the school of prayer,* p. 107).

Are you willing to forgive others in love because Jesus has forgiven you?

Heavenly Father, forgive me because I have always merely assumed that you will forgive my sin while I have not been willing to forgive others. Help me to forgive like you. Amen.

11 February
Pray according to the will of God
Read: 1 John 5:14–17

> *This is the confidence we have in approaching God:*
> *that if we ask anything according to his will, he hears us.*
> 1 John 5:14

Sometimes it is quite difficult to know exactly what God's will is. Although the Bible highlights certain aspects which are not according to God's will (for example, that a believer not marry an unbeliever) and specifies other matters clearly as God's will (for example, that everybody be saved and that we love one another), many things are not perfectly clear.

God's children must seek his will in his word. We may also pray that he reveal his will in our lives by the Holy Spirit. Another way of knowing God's will is to discuss it with other believers.

If you have doubts about whether the things you are asking God are in line with his will, see what your Bible says about these things and ask the Holy Spirit to explain God's will to you.

> *Heavenly Father, I pray that you will explain your will to me*
> *by your word and Spirit when I pray so that my prayer requests*
> *will always be in line with your will for my life. Amen.*

12 February
Ask with confidence!
Read: 1 John 5:14–17

And if we know that he hears us – whatever we ask –
we know that we have what we asked of him.
1 John 5:15

In the last verses of his letter, John reminds the believers of everything they have received because they have become children of God. Based on Jesus' expiatory death on the cross, they have the confidence to go to God in prayer and know God will hear their prayers. However, those prayers must be in line with God's will. If they pray in this way, they know they will receive what they ask God. According to *Die Bybellennium*, p. 1754, 'Prayer answered by God is the highest form of an intimate personal relationship with him.'

You may also ask things of God with confidence, but you first of all have to check whether you are in the right relationship with God, and that your prayer requests are according to his will. If you make your wishes and desires known to God in this way, he will fulfil them for you, because God loves you and has a personal interest in you.

C.S. Lewis once wrote that although God has so many children who pray thousands of prayers to him daily, he nevertheless treats your prayer as if you are the only one praying. God always has time for you. The psalmist writes that he neither slumbers nor sleeps (Psalm 121:3–4). You may therefore submit your requests to him with confidence.

Heavenly Father, thank you that you always listen when I pray,
that you are always within call. Teach me to pray in such a way
that my requests will be according to your will. Amen.

13 FEBRUARY
Develop a new way of thinking!
Read: Romans 12:1–8

Do not conform any longer to the pattern of this world, but be transformed by the renewing of your mind. Then you will be able to test and approve what God's will is – his good, pleasing and perfect will.
Romans 12:2

In Romans 12 Paul describes someone who has been transformed by the new life in Jesus. Such a person knows the will of God because he no longer conforms to the sinful world but permits God to change his way of thinking and teach him a new way of thinking, so he will be able to distinguish the will of God in all things.

If you do the will of God, you will have to be prepared to submit your own will to God's will. You will therefore no longer be able to do exactly as you please, and you will not be able to follow the example of others either – you are now a new creation and should live like a new creation. You will therefore no longer be able to do the things which your old, natural temperament dictated to you.

God in fact changes you by renewing your mind. This change starts on the inside and changes every aspect of your life. Likewise you should be prepared to set aside your own desires until God's will is revealed in your life and prayers.

Lord Jesus, thank you for renewing my will. Teach me to develop a new way of thinking and praying so that your perfect will can be manifested in my life. Amen.

14 FEBRUARY
The righteous may pray!
Read: James 5:13–18

The effectual fervent prayer of a righteous man availeth much.
James 5:16 (King James Version)

If you are experiencing an emotional low because you are battling, James recommends that you pray. The RIV reads: The prayer of a righteous man is powerful and effective. Sometimes it is very informative to use several translations of the Bible in Bible study. In the King James Version, James stipulates two conditions for a powerful prayer life: our prayers must be fervent – not weak and lukewarm as is often the case – and the person who is praying must be righteous.

What exactly does righteous mean? Webster's defines it, among other things, as being free from guilt or sin (*Webster's Third New International Dictionary*, p. 1956).

Psalm 18:21–23 describes such a righteous person beautifully: 'For I have kept the ways of the Lord … All his laws are before me; I have not turned away from his decrees. I have been blameless before him.'

When you therefore pray fervently, obey God's will, allow yourself to be led by his decrees and do right to others, you may be confident that God will answer your prayers. What is more, you may also assume that your prayers will have a powerful effect on your own life as well as the lives of others.

Heavenly Father, I confess that my prayers are often feeble and powerless. Teach me to pray fervently, and show me how to live righteously daily by the power of your Spirit. Amen.

15 February
Bear fruit and ask
Read: John 15:9–17

You did not choose me, but I chose you and appointed you to go and bear fruit – fruit that will last. Then the Father will give you whatever you ask in my name.
John 15:16

Here Jesus asks his disciples to go out and bear fruit so that their prayers could be answered. When we live in obedience to God's commands in such a way that the fruit of the Holy Spirit can be manifested in our lives, it shows that we take our faith seriously. This condition to have our prayers answered does not exclude God's mercy at all, in fact, we do the things God asks out of gratitude for his mercy in our lives.

Obedience and service are two very important aspects in the life of every Christian, Andrew Murray writes. When we are perfectly obedient to the word of God in our lives, the Holy Spirit lives within us, he introduces the Son to us and the Father dwells within us. Those who obey inherit the indwelling Triune God *(With Christ in the school of prayer,* p. 171–173).

A fruitful life and answer to prayer are therefore also within your reach if you are willing to obey God's will faithfully from today. This is the only way you will be able to take the promises in your Bible and use them effectively in your prayers.

Lord Jesus, thank you for having selected me specially to bear fruit for you. Please enable me to do this in obedience to your word and Spirit. Amen.

16 February
God's words must remain in you
Read: John 15:1–7

---

*If you remain in me and my words remain in you,
ask whatever you wish, and it will be given you.*
John 15:7

By means of his illustration of the vine and the branches, Jesus wants to explain to his disciples that it is important for his children to remain in him. Without the vine, it is impossible for the branches to bear fruit. Likewise we will not be able to bear fruit for God unless we remain in Jesus and have an intimate relationship with him. However, should we in fact do so and his words remain in us, he gives us a wonderful promise here: we will be able to ask anything we wish, and receive it.

This does not concern a self-centred prayer, but the things asked according to the will of the Lord. According to *Bybelkennis* (p. 1357), 'you will be saturated with his will if you are in Jesus and his Word is in you. His will becomes your will. If you therefore ask something it would actually be his will expressed in words of prayer.' You may therefore appropriate the above promise for yourself: if you pray according to the will of God, he will answer your prayer – all you have to do is remain in Jesus and allow his words to remain in you.

*Lord Jesus, I want to remain in you, be as close to you
as the branch to the vine, so that I will be able to bear fruit for you.
Grant that your words will also remain in me so that I will ask you
for the right things. Amen.*

17 February
Pray in Jesus' Name
Read: John 14:12–15

And I will do whatever you ask in my name, so that the Son may bring glory to the Father. You may ask me for anything in my name, and I will do it.
John 14:13–14

This fact is so important to Jesus that he asks the disciples five different times to pray in his Name (John 14:13–14, 15:16 and 16:23–24). To pray in Jesus' Name also means that what we ask will be based on Christ's work and be in accordance with the will of God, says *Die Bybel in praktyk* (p. 1620).

When we think of the name of a person, it encompasses his whole person. When we refer to a well-known person, everybody immediately knows whom we are referring to. Even the little ones in grade one will be able to tell you exactly who Nelson Mandela is.

The Name of Jesus also tells you everything he has done for you. God therefore gives you those things which you ask in the Name of his Son. However, you should not merely pray in Jesus' Name, you should also live and walk as he did for his Father to take your prayer requests really seriously. On the cross Jesus earned his Father's 'ear' for you when you pray. Pray therefore as Jesus would have done, and you will receive whatever you ask.

Lord Jesus, thank you that by your death on the cross you have enabled me to ask things of the Father in your Name. Please help me to live and pray like you. Amen.

18 February

Pray in faith

Read: Hebrews 11:1–6

Now faith is being sure of what we hope for and certain of what we do not see. And without faith it is impossible to please God.
Hebrews 11:1, 6

The Bible emphasises the fact that prayer without faith does not have much power. According to the writer of Hebrews, faith implies two things, that is, you may be sure of the things you are hoping for and be convinced of the things you cannot see yet. Should you believe in this way that God will answer your prayers, he will give you what you ask.

However, it does not always happen exactly like this. Even if you firmly believe that your prayers will be answered, you may still not receive everything you ask, just as you will not give your own children everything they ask you. Sometimes God withholds things we desperately want because he knows what is good for us. He will never give you anything which could harm you or which is not in his will for you.

God always answers your prayers. However, he sometimes does this in his own way and in his own time and his answers may sometimes differ from your desires. You may nevertheless rest assured that the answers will always be the right answers for you, provided you pray in faith.

Heavenly Father, grant that I will be sure of the things I hope for, and certain of the things which I cannot see. Amen.

19 February
Pray for strength
Read: Psalm 138

When I called, you answered me; you made me bold and stout-hearted.
Psalm 138:3

All of us experience times in our lives when we come to the end of our tether. Should you, right now, be in a position where you have no strength left to continue, you could be still with God, and ask him to give you the strength you need. When the psalmist did that, he was able to testify as follows after his prayer: 'When I called, you answered me; you made me bold and stout-hearted' (verse 3). At the end of the psalm he then said, 'you stretch out your hand against the anger of my foes, with your right hand you save me. The Lord will fulfil his purpose for me' (verse 7–8).

Even if you are in the midst of a crisis at the moment, you have the assurance that God will give you strength and everything – even the negative things in your life – will eventually work together for good in your life. 'The Lord is the everlasting God, the Creator of the ends of the earth ... he gives strength to the weary and increases the power of the weak ... those who hope in the Lord will renew their strength. They will soar on wings like eagles; they will run and not grow weary, they will walk and not be faint,' writes the prophet Isaiah (Isaiah 40:28–31).

If you ask him to give you strength, God will do it for you too!

Heavenly Father, you know how little strength I have left today.
I feel as if I cannot carry on, but I rely on you.
Please give me new strength. Amen.

20 February
Prayer and confession of guilt
Read: Psalm 32

When I kept silent, my bones wasted away through my groaning all day long.
Then I acknowledged my sin to you and did not cover up my iniquity.
Psalm 32:3, 5

The writer of Psalm 32 gives a vivid description of the suffering of people who refuse to confess their sin – but he also states that God will forgive our sin if we confess it to him. Verse 6 reads, 'Therefore let everyone who is godly pray to you while you may be found.'

In the world in which you live society sees very few things as really wrong. We have become so used to things which are in direct conflict with God's law and will, such as murder, violence, robbery, adultery and abortion, that we hardly bat an eyelid when we are confronted with these on television night after night and in the media day after day.

Perhaps it has become time for you to realise the seriousness of sin again before you kneel in prayer – and that you will particularly pray that God will forgive your burden of sin. 'Blessed is he whose transgressions are forgiven, whose sins are covered,' says the psalmist in verse 1. Do not postpone confession of your own sin – then God will bless you again.

Heavenly Father, I pray that you will make me sensitive
to the sin in my life, and that you will forgive my sin
so that I can be blessed again. Amen.

21 February
God is always ready to answer you
Read: Isaiah 65:17, 21–25

Before they call I will answer; while they are still speaking I will hear.
Isaiah 65:24

In this chapter Isaiah sketches a wonderful picture of the new heaven and the new earth which the Lord promises his people. God wants to create a brand-new beginning for his people – he wants to establish a new Jerusalem for them – and recommit himself to his people. On this new earth creation will once again be in harmony as in the beginning.

The Lord furthermore promises that he will answer his people even before they call, he will respond to their prayers even while they are still speaking. God is still ready to hear and respond to the prayers of his children. He loves you so much that he is really interested in you and wants to meet all your needs.

'For the eyes of the Lord range throughout the earth to strengthen those whose hearts are fully committed to him', reads 2 Chronicles 16:9. God searches everywhere to see where his children may need his help. If you are able to trust God and to hold on to his promises, he will help you and answer all your prayers. Hold on to this promise when you pray.

Heavenly Father, it is wonderful to know that you are always ready to listen to my prayers – that you have undertaken to answer me while I am still speaking. Amen.

22 February
Prayer is contact with God
Read: Psalm 86:1–10

Hear, O Lord, and answer me, for I am poor and needy.
Have mercy on me, O Lord, for I call to you all day long.
Psalm 86:1, 3

The psalmist deals with his grief by being in touch with God by prayer all day long. He pleads with God to answer him, to hear his supplication. God's children may feel free to communicate with him all day long. You may also talk to God all day long. You do not pray only when you are alone in your room, but also when you are driving your car, queuing in a supermarket, drinking tea at the office. God is always available to you, not only in the morning before rising or in the evening before going to bed.

Prayer is always deliberate contact. Married couples are in touch all day long, even if the husband is in his study and the wife in the kitchen, but when they look each other in the eye and talk, they have contact on another level. This contact is deliberate communication, conscious conversation.

God is with you all day long, but when you pray, you draw closer to God in a special way. Do not hesitate to be in contact with God all day long.

Heavenly Father, thank you that prayer, deliberate contact with you, has become a way of life to me. I praise you for being able to talk to you at any time, day or night. Amen.

23 February
Prayer as an incense-offering
Read: Psalm 141:1–4

*May my prayer be set before you like incense;
may the lifting up of my hands be like the evening sacrifice.*
Psalm 141:2

The psalmist describes his prayers as an incense-offering before God. As the smoke of incense ascends ... so his prayer reaches out to God in total dependence and he trusts that God will answer him.

In Exodus 30 we are told how a special altar had to be built in the tabernacle to burn incense before the Lord. This incense-offering was a mixture of spices and herbs and was used for sacrifices only. The incense-offering was regarded as so holy that the Israelites were forbidden to prepare the mixture merely to sniff it themselves.

In Revelation 8:3–4 the prayers of the believers are also compared to incense: 'He was given much incense to offer, with the prayers of all the saints, on the golden altar before the throne. The smoke of the incense, together with the prayers of the saints, went up before God from the angel's hand.'

Your prayers are like incense to God – they are an offering which pleases him. He likes listening when you call out to him and responds to you when you stretch out your hands to him in prayer.

*Heavenly Father, I pray that my prayers will ascend to you
like sweet-smelling incense – and that they will please you,
because praying to you fills me with joy. Amen.*

24 February
Prayer and resignation
Read: Psalm 130

*Out of the depths I cry to you, O Lord; I wait for the Lord,
my soul waits, and in his word I put my hope.
My soul waits for the Lord more than watchmen wait for the morning.*
Psalm 130:1, 5, 6

When the psalmist prays this prayer, he is praying in the midst of a crisis in his life. He calls to God 'out of the depths'. He feels as if God is far away from him at that moment, yet he firmly believes that God will help him again; he still depends on the Lord, and declares himself ready to wait upon the Lord.

All of us experience a time in our lives when we have to be still before God and resign ourselves to circumstances which we cannot change ourselves. Should God delay in changing our negative circumstances, solving our problems or answering our questions as to the reason why. We have to learn to wait on God like the psalmist, and still trust God during this time of waiting.

Sometimes situations such as illness and financial problems make you feel as if you are far from God. Try the good advice of the psalmist if you land in dark depths again. Resign yourself to your circumstances, wait upon God without demanding instant answers from him. He is aware of your crises – entrust them to him.

Heavenly Father, thank you for the assurance that you are aware of all my crises. I am prepared to wait upon you and to trust you to solve them. Amen.

25 February
Who may pray?
Read: Isaiah 1:12–18

When you spread out your hands in prayer, I will hide my eyes from you; even if you offer many prayers, I will not listen. Your hands are full of blood; wash and make yourselves clean. Take your evil deeds out of my sight! Stop doing wrong!
Isaiah 1:15–16

The prophet Isaiah reveals a shocking fact in the first chapter of his prophecy: religion can become sin if it is not accompanied by sincere commitment to God. God's people tried to worship him with unclean hands and hearts, but he himself says, 'Even if you offer many prayers, I will not listen. Take your evil deeds out of my sight!' (verse 15). They have to renounce their sin before God is prepared to listen to their prayers.

The Bible spells it out repeatedly that we try in vain to approach God if our hearts are full of sin and unrighteousness. Before you can even pray, you have to wash your hands and confess your sin. Take Isaiah's invitation in verse 18 personally: 'Come now, let us reason together,' says the Lord. 'Though your sins are like scarlet, they shall be as white as snow …'

God wants to wash away all your sins because the blood of Jesus has been shed for you on the cross. Ask him to do this for you.

Lord Jesus, thank you that I may accept God's invitation because my sins which are like scarlet have been washed as white as snow by your blood on the cross. Amen.

26 February
Pray fervently
Read: Hebrews 6:12

We do not want you to become lazy, but to imitate those who through faith and patience inherit what has been promised.
Hebrews 6:12

God wants his children to persevere in prayer. He wants them to continue serving him and to pray fervently until he has done everything he has promised.

Sometimes we become discouraged when we pray and we feel God does not hear our prayers. At such times we want to give up and stop praying altogether, or prayer is no longer a priority because we feel God does not listen to us anyway.

Even men of God like Job, Jeremiah and David wrestled with this problem. Many psalms also start with the complaint that God does not listen, but practically each one of these psalms is concluded with the testimony that God was nevertheless present and that he had in fact delivered the one who had been praying. 'How long, O Lord? Will you forget me for ever? How long will you hide your face from me?' David asks in Psalm 13:1. And then he testifies in verse 5: 'But I trust in your unfailing love; my heart rejoices in your salvation.'

Do not become apathetic in your prayers. Keep on praying, even if it takes long before God answers your specific prayer. Ultimately he will always deliver you.

Heavenly Father, I have prayed for such a long time and still receive no answer from you. Forgive me for thinking like the psalmist that you have forgotten me. Thank you for the promise that you will deliver me. Amen.

27 February
Seek the presence of God
Read: Psalm 105:3–4

Let the hearts of those who seek the Lord rejoice.
Look to the Lord and his strength; seek his face always.
Psalms 105:3–4

Throughout their history God's people could testify to the fact that his presence had brought them joy and protection.

When you pray, God wants to do the same for you and by your prayers he draws close to you. 'The Lord is close to all who call on him, to all who call on him in truth,' the psalmist says in Psalm 145:18.

If you seek the Lord's presence in prayer, he will allow you to find him. He is always available and you should therefore make enough time to be still with him, to listen to his voice and meditate about his glory. The busier your day, the more you need this quiet time in God's presence.

Those who dwell in God's presence receive a gift from him: his joy which fills and enriches their lives. 'You will fill me with joy in your presence' (Acts 2:28), and '[you] have made him glad with the joy of your presence,' says the psalmist in Psalm 21:7. This is also the only guarantee you have to experience God's joy in your life in the midst of struggles and crises.

If you make time for him, God promises to bless you: 'The same Lord is Lord of all and richly blesses all who call on him,' reads Romans 10:12. Do not delay to seek the presence of God!

Heavenly Father, thank you for your blessed presence in my life,
for the joy I experience merely by spending quiet times with you
and for the joy of your presence. Amen.

28 February
Prayer makes a difference
Read: Philippians 4:1–6

Do not be anxious about anything, but in everything, by prayer and petition, with thanksgiving, present your requests to God. And the peace of God, which transcends all understanding, will guard your hearts and your minds in Christ Jesus.
Philippians 4:6–7

Paul advises the church in Philippi to pray more if they wanted less anxiety. This is invaluable advice which you would do well to follow. Tell God the things you need and realise once again that he is fully in control of your life and the world around you.

When you pray, give God your anxieties and trust him to solve your problems for you. Sometimes prayer reminds me of the before and after pictures one sees in certain advertisements: before you prayed you were probably an example of a discouraged, weary person with sagging shoulders and drooping mouth. After prayer you usually feel happy and refreshed. When you speak to God and he speaks to you, you are always encouraged. When you make your requests known to him and you trust him, he will always give you his lasting peace. Try it!

Heavenly Father, it is wonderful that I may present all my requests to you with thanksgiving when I pray. Please give me your peace. Amen.

29 February
Remind God of his promises
Read: Isaiah 62:1–6

I have posted watchmen on your walls, O Jerusalem; they will never be silent day or night. You who call on the Lord, give yourselves no rest.
Isaiah 62:6

The prophet Isaiah reminded the watchmen on the walls of Jerusalem that they had to pray day and night and remind God of his promises until God intervened and Jerusalem had been restored. Literally hundreds of promises are made in the Bible. When we pray we may remind God of his promises and you may also claim each one of them.

However, in order to do this you would have to know the Bible. You cannot remind God of his promises unless you know what those promises imply. Start making a list of your favourite promises today. Write them on slips of paper and put them up in places where you can see them regularly. Learn these promises by heart and make them your own – and 'repeat' them to the Lord when you pray. God is faithful – he has never made a promise which he has not fulfilled to the letter.

Walter Luthi writes: 'Where the improbable becomes the impossible, God's promises become reality' (*Abraham-avontuur*, p. 85).

It is also at this stage where your faith in God's promises is really proved.

Heavenly Father, thank you for each promise in the Bible. Thank you that I know that I may remind you of these promises and that you will fulfil each of them in my life. Amen.

MARCH

The Holy Spirit and prayer

Only the Holy Spirit can teach human beings to communicate with God in such a way that they know that what they are asking of God is in fact God's will. God therefore gives us what we ask when we are led by the Holy Spirit. 'No-one can lay down fixed rules for prayer, not even for himself. Only the Holy Spirit can guide us in prayer from moment to moment,' writes Onbekende Christen *(Die Christen en gebed,* p. 80).

You would therefore have to learn to obey the guidance of the Holy Spirit with regard to your prayer life as well as to address him in your prayers directly.

It is also the Holy Spirit who gives God's gifts to his children and who helps you to manifest the fruit of the Spirit in your life so that other people who are watching you can see clearly to whom you belong.

Think carefully – do you obey the voice of the Holy Spirit in your life?

1 March
Ask for the Holy Spirit
Read: Luke 11:5–13

*If you then, though you are evil, know how to give good gifts
to your children, how much more will your Father
in heaven give the Holy Spirit to those who ask him!*
Luke 11:13

God's willingness to give his children the things they ask, is the focal point of this parable. An earthly father wants to give his children good gifts, but our heavenly Father even more so, and the very best gift we can receive from God is the Holy Spirit. 'And I will ask the Father, and he will give you another Counsellor to be with you for ever,' Jesus promises his disciples (John 14:16). This promise of Jesus was in fact fulfilled on the very first day of Pentecost when the Holy Spirit was poured out (Acts 1:14).

The Holy Spirit is a gift of God one has to pray for, after the first Pentecost as well. You have to ask God personally to pour out his Spirit in your life. 'Although every child of God already has God's Spirit in his life, we should pray to be better equipped and be even more committed to the Holy Spirit' (John 16:13).

God wants to give you more of his Holy Spirit. If you ask him for the Holy Spirit, God will give you his Spirit!

*Heavenly Father, thank you for all the good things which you give me.
I pray that you will give me your Holy Spirit in my life in such a way
that my whole life will be controlled by him. Amen.*

2 March
Receive the Holy Spirit!
Read: John 20:19–23

Again Jesus said, 'Peace be with you! As the Father has sent me,
I am sending you.' And with that, he breathed on them and said,
'Receive the Holy Spirit.'
John 20:21–22

When Jesus appeared to his disciples for the first time after his resurrection, he told them that, just as the Father had sent him, he would send them out into the world to proclaim his good news. Then Jesus did something very odd: he breathed on the disciples and asked them to receive the Holy Spirit. In this way he wanted to tell them that they would not have to carry out his instructions in their own power. He equipped them with his Holy Spirit to enable them to do so.

Jesus' instruction in John 20:21 still applies to every child of his to this day. He still sends us out to proclaim his gospel, but he gives us his Holy Spirit to equip us with power. 'The mission of Jesus in this world is continued by the power of his Holy Spirit and the willingness of the believer. An active follower is a Spirit-filled follower,' writes *Die Bybellennium* (p. 1368).

If you have the Holy Spirit in your life, you also have the equipment to enable you to carry out every instruction you receive from God. All you have to do is to acknowledge the rule of the Holy Spirit in your life.

Lord Jesus, thank you that you have offered me your Holy Spirit
to equip me to carry out your command to be a witness for you.
Thank you for the assurance that I will be able to do all things
by means of the power he gives. Amen.

3 March
The Holy Spirit teaches you to pray
Read: Romans 8:24–29

*In the same way, the Spirit helps us in our weakness.
We do not know what we ought to pray for, but the Spirit
himself intercedes for us with groans that words cannot express.*
Romans 8:26

When we are in deep trouble, it is easy to sigh in despondency! However, the Bible assures you that God hears your sighs. What is more, the Holy Spirit takes your sighs close to God and pleads for you with the Father. 'Our greatest weakness is that we do not always know what to pray. But … at such times, the Spirit himself prays for us. He translates all our troubles into heavenly language and takes it straight to the throne of God,' reads *Die Boodskap* version of this verse.

When you pray it is always with the Holy Spirit's support and inspiration. It is he who gives you the right words to communicate with God. He also arranges the stammering words you pray to be in line with God's will. This verse always reminds me of the spell check on my computer. It corrects spelling errors without my even noticing it.

However, the Holy Spirit not only helps you with your prayer language, he also makes you keen to pray. Ask him to do this for you.

*Holy Spirit, please give me the right words so that all my prayers will be
in line with God's will for my life. Thank you for also making me keen
to communicate with God in prayer. Amen.*

4 MARCH
When you lack words
Read: Hebrews 4:12–16

Nothing in all creation is hidden from God's sight. Everything is uncovered and laid bare before the eyes of him to whom we must give account.
Hebrews 4:13

God knows all about you. He knows what you need, he knows what you are thinking. He also knows what you are asking of him when you pray. Nothing is invisible to God – you cannot hide anything from him either. 'He sees and knows everything as if we have spread it out before him on a table. Likewise we will have to give account of what is going on in our lives,' writes *Die Boodskap* (p. 726).

Sometimes you do not know what to say to God – you do not have the right words to express your feelings. The Holy Spirit sometimes also prays with 'groans that words cannot express', according to our verse for yesterday. Fortunately it is not necessary to pray eloquently. The Lord knows everything you have in your heart. He knows what you want to share with him and what you want to ask him even before you speak to him.

When your own words run out, you may ask him with confidence to send his Holy Spirit to give you the right words in order to talk to him.

Holy Spirit, thank you that I do not even need words to communicate with you because you know everything, but that you nevertheless give me the right words when I lack the necessary words. Amen.

5 March
The Holy Spirit prays according to the will of God
Read: Romans 8:9–14, 27

---

*And he who searches our hearts knows the mind of the Spirit,
because the Spirit intercedes for the saints in accordance with God's will.*
Romans 8:27

The Holy Spirit is the great creator of order, writes Dr Hennie Conradie in the *ABC van gebed* (p. 38). While the earth was still formless and empty and dark, he was hovering over the waters and giving life.

God's Spirit wants to recreate you as well so that you can be the person God wants you to be. For this reason he helps you when you want to communicate with God. For the sinful human being it is very difficult to put his prayer requests in the right words, but the Holy Spirit turns your confused thoughts into order.

Even when you do not know what to say to God, when you do not understand your own heart, the Holy Spirit knows the deepest desires of your heart. He can therefore create order despite the chaos of the confused thoughts, take your clumsy words and rearrange them so that what you are led by him to say to God will be in accordance with his will. As God knows that the intention of his Spirit is always in line with his will, he answers every prayer which you pray according to the Holy Spirit's guidance.

*Holy Spirit, thank you that you turn the chaos of my prayer requests
into order and that you also steer my prayers in the right direction so
that they conform to God's perfect will for my life. Amen.*

6 March
How can you know God's will?
Read: Colossians 1:91–14

We have not stopped praying for you and asking God to fill you with the knowledge of his will through all spiritual wisdom and understanding.
Colossians 1:9

In his prayer for the church in Colosse, Paul prayed that they be filled with the knowledge of his will through the wisdom and understanding the Holy Spirit would give them. However, sometimes it is very difficult to understand God's will clearly. The Bible is clear about certain matters: for example, it is not God's will that we sin or that a believer marries an unbeliever. On the other hand, we also know that it is God's will that we study his Word, that we pray to him, that we proclaim his gospel.

However, in some areas God's will is not crystal-clear in his Word.

In Ephesians 1:9 Paul writes that God wants to make the mystery of his will known to us. Jesus came in order to show us God's will in detail and the Holy Spirit makes this will of God known to us. He gives you the right insight so that you will really know God's will, and he also enables you to do God's will.

Holy Spirit, I pray that you will help me to be filled with the knowledge of God's will through the wisdom and insight which only you can give. Amen.

7 MARCH
The Holy Spirit makes God's will known
Read: Matthew 12:15–21

*I will put my Spirit on him, and he will
proclaim justice to the nations.*
Matthew 12:18

Here Matthew quoted from Isaiah 42:1 (NIV) where the prophet spoke about the servant of God: 'Here is my servant, whom I uphold, my chosen one in whom I delight; I will put my Spirit on him and he will bring justice to the nations.' In our verses for today, he applies the prophecy of Isaiah to Jesus.

Jesus is the One God has sent, the One on whom his Holy Spirit rests in a special way. At the time when Jesus was baptised in the river Jordan by John the Baptist, God let the Holy Spirit descend on his Son like a dove (Matthew 3:16). Because he had been sent by God, it was Jesus' objective to proclaim the justice of God to all the nations (and not only to God's original people).

When Jesus returned to his Father, he sent his Holy Spirit to continue his work on earth. The Spirit of God is still proclaiming God's will to his children. He guides you by means of your thoughts to focus closely on God's will and he also gives you the necessary insight to distinguish between right and wrong so that you will know as well as do the will of God.

Holy Spirit, I pray that you will give me the necessary insight so that I will distinguish between the things which are in line with God's will and the things which are contrary to his will. Please make me obedient to your voice. Amen.

8 March
Pray in the power of the Holy Spirit
Read: Jude 17–20

*But you, dear friends, build yourselves up in your
most holy faith and pray in the Holy Spirit.*
Jude 20

The Holy Spirit is the Spirit of prayer. He teaches us to pray, he also stirs the desire to pray in our hearts. When we pray, he endues us with his Divine power so that our prayers will have more power. When you pray in this power, that which you desire in prayer will no longer merely be focused on your own will, but on the kingdom of God. Before you can pray in the power of the Spirit, you should therefore be willing to set aside your own desires and pray for the things God desires.

You can comply with this calling to pray in the Holy Spirit only if you are willing to hand the control of your whole life to the Holy Spirit. 'Since we live by the Spirit,' Paul continued after he had explained the fruit of the Holy Spirit to the church in Galatia, 'let us keep in step with the Spirit' (Galatians 5:25).

People who pray in the power of the Spirit, live in such a way that others can see by their lives to whom they belong. Is this true about you yet? If so, you may rely on the Holy Spirit to fill your prayers with his wonder-working power.

*Holy Spirit, I would like to live in such a way that others
will be able to see you in my life. Help me to submit my will
to the will of God and pray in your power at all times. Amen.*

9 March
Remain in God's love
Read: Jude 20–23

Keep yourselves in God's love as you wait for the mercy of our Lord Jesus Christ to bring you to eternal life.
Jude 21

Besides encouraging the believers to build their lives on their faith and always pray in the power of the Holy Spirit, Jude makes two more recommendations in his letter, that is:

- Remain in the love of God, and
- wait for the mercy of Jesus Christ to bring you to eternal life.

Just as you will never be able to live by faith in your own power, you will never be able to pray in the right way by yourself either. Fortunately God does not expect that of you. He sends his Holy Spirit to help you with this. The Holy Spirit enables you to remain in God's love and to wait for the mercy of Jesus because you know he has made eternal life possible to you by his death on the cross.

When you pray, ask God to give you faith by his Spirit and teach you how to pray. Ask the Holy Spirit to help you to feed on the unselfish love of God daily so that you will be able to see the need of others and expect the return of Jesus every day.

Holy Spirit, please help me to love other people the way God loves me and help me to notice their need. Let me wait for the mercy of Jesus to bring me to eternal life. Amen.

10 March
The Holy Spirit makes God your Father
Read: Romans 8:9–17

You received the Spirit of sonship.
And by him we cry 'Abba, Father'.
Romans 8:15

The role of the Holy Spirit in prayer is closely linked to his role in God's plan of redemption. He makes us children of God, he convicts us of our faith and tells us that God wants to be a loving Father to us so that we may address him as 'Abba' (Father) with confidence. Now you can live in a personal relationship of love and joy with God daily, but you should also live in such a way that you will please your Father in heaven every day.

The presence of the Holy Spirit in your life is therefore your proof that you are God's child just as your birth certificate is proof that you are your parents' child. However, the Holy Spirit also assures you that you are not only God's child, but also his heir together with his Son Jesus!

This inheritance consists of two parts, that is, suffering and glory. Like Jesus, you will often experience suffering on earth as God's child, but you will nevertheless have the assurance that you will one day also share God's glory (see verse 17).

Holy Spirit, I praise you for having made the holy God my Father.
Thank you for the assurance that I am now God's child
and heir for ever. Amen.

11 March
The Spirit of prayer
Read: Zechariah 12:9–14

And I will pour out on the house of David and the inhabitants of Jerusalem a spirit of grace and supplication.
Zechariah 12:10

It is interesting to know that although the Holy Spirit was poured out in the New Testament only, he was already seen as the Spirit of prayer in the Old Testament.

The prophet Zechariah prophesied in our verse that God wanted to do something great for his people: he wanted to deliver them by destroying their enemies. However, in order to do that, they first had to learn to pray. Thereupon he poured out the Holy Spirit, the Spirit of 'grace and supplication' on them, as Zechariah put it.

Only the Holy Spirit can teach people to pray. 'God is Spirit,' Jesus told the Samaritan woman, 'and his worshippers must worship in spirit and in truth' (John 4:24).

God wants you to talk to him in prayer, therefore he sent his Son to enable you to pray, and his Spirit to teach you how to pray. 'The One who hears prayer provides the One who Mediates in prayer as well as the One who Accomplishes prayer,' writes Dr Hennie Conradie *(ABC van gebed,* p. 72).

The Holy Spirit wants to establish a spirit of prayer in your life as well – ask him to do this for you.

Holy Spirit, I worship you as the Spirit of prayer who encourages people to pray and who teaches them to talk to God. Please do this for me as well. Amen.

12 March
Filled with the Holy Spirit
Read: Acts 4:23–31

*After they prayed ... they were all filled with the Holy Spirit
and spoke the word of God boldly.*
Acts 4:31

The actual pouring out of the Holy Spirit occurred only after Jesus' group of followers had gathered in Jerusalem and prayed together earnestly for ten days. Prayer is also one of the most important ways in which you are able to acknowledge the rule of the Holy Spirit in your own life.

However, there is a difference between the pouring out of the Holy Spirit and being filled with the Holy Spirit. The people Luke refers to in the above passage of Scripture were believers and they therefore already had the Holy Spirit in their lives. However, they prayed to be filled with the Holy Spirit and God answered these prayers by once again filling them with the Holy Spirit.

The event described here was therefore not a new pouring out of the Holy Spirit, but the Spirit already dwelling in them ruled them to a greater extent. When that happened they were no longer timid but spoke the word of God boldly.

If you desire a more abundant spiritual life, pray more. You are strengthened spiritually by prayer, and you gradually become more and more prepared to surrender your life to the Holy Spirit.

*Spirit of God, I pray that you will fill me more and more, that I will
surrender my life to you more and more, so that I will be able to
proclaim the message of God more boldly. Amen.*

13 March
The Holy Spirit guides you into all truth
Read: John 14:16, 16:12–15

And I will ask the Father, and he will give you another Counsellor ... the Spirit of truth. When he ... comes, he will guide you into all truth.
John 14:16–17, 16:13

When Jesus' time on earth was drawing to a close, and he noticed that this fact upset his disciples, he comforted them by promising to send them another Counsellor – the Spirit of truth. This Spirit, he said, would guide them into all truth. 'When the Holy Spirit comes, he will take you by the hand and guide you into all truth. After all, he is the Spirit who knows all truth,' reads *Die Boodskap* version (p. 358).

The Holy Spirit knows the truth. He always guides us back to those things which Jesus said. He reminds us of the things which Jesus did, and he builds on that. He guides us by the truth according to the will and nature of God and he gives us this guidance by means of his word.

God still wants to guide you by his Spirit and his word when you pray. Concentrate carefully on the voice of the Holy Spirit and obey the guidelines which he gives you in his word unconditionally.

Holy Spirit, I praise you as the Spirit of truth. Please guide me by the word into truth so that I will know how to discern between right and wrong. Amen.

14 March
Free access to the Father
Read: Ephesians 2:13–19

For through him we both have access to the Father by one Spirit.
Consequently, you are no longer foreigners and aliens,
but fellow-citizens with God's people and members of God's household.
Ephesians 2:18, 19

Although Jesus is the only door to heaven, the Holy Spirit has made it possible for you to have access to the Father. He makes you a member of God's household, Paul wrote in the above verse. 'Jesus prepared the way to God for everybody (Jews and non-Jews) and by the Spirit we now also experience how close God has really come to us,' says *Die Boodskap* version (p. 626).

Dr Hennie Conradie expresses this beautifully in *ABC van gebed*: 'The part played by the Holy Spirit in fervent prayer is not completed once he has brought the prayer to the point where he addresses God as "Father". He not only tunes the one who is praying into the correct wavelength and then leaves him to his own designs; he is the wavelength on which the prayer remains tuned in to God' (p. 75).

The Holy Spirit also makes it possible for you to go to God's throne of grace boldly with the assurance that God will hear and answer your prayers. Furthermore, because of him you are now a member of God's household! By the Spirit you form part of the believers who are linked to him by the blood of Jesus.

Holy Spirit, thank you for the great privilege of making it possible
for me to communicate freely with God and for making me
a member of God's household. Amen.

15 March
Pray that the Spirit will explain the word
Read: Psalm 119:129–136

---

*The unfolding of your words gives light;
it gives understanding to the simple.*
Psalm 119:130

Only the Holy Spirit can explain God's word to us. Have you ever had the experience of reading your Bible and suddenly a specific verse – which you have often read before – takes on a completely new meaning? Or you are reading your daily reading for a specific day and you find in this message from God exactly what you need for that particular day? When this happens, it is the Holy Spirit who highlights the word so that you are able to hear God's voice speaking to you even more clearly.

'The Holy Spirit controls your life by the word of God, not by emotions, dreams or visions,' says *Die Bybellennium* (p. 1473).

You can cooperate with the Spirit by studying the Bible faithfully. Read your Bible every day as if it has been written for you personally. Always pray that God will illuminate his will for your life and your personal relationship with him by means of your Bible study. Always check your understanding of a particular passage of the Bible against that of other believers who are led by God's Spirit. You will then hear God speaking to you from his word.

Holy Spirit, thank you that you enable me to hear God's voice with a message addressed to me personally whenever I open my Bible. Amen.

16 March
The Holy Spirit helps you to witness
Read: Acts 1:4–8

But you will receive power when the Holy Spirit comes on you; and you will be my witnesses in Jerusalem, and in all Judea and Samaria, and to the ends of the earth.
Acts 1:8

The disciples were fairly nervous when they heard that Jesus was going to leave them. They did not quite understand him either when he told them they would be baptised with the Holy Spirit a few days later. 'Lord, are you at this time going to restore the kingdom to Israel?' they asked him. After Jesus' resurrection they again hoped that the Messiah King would deliver them from Roman rule. However, Jesus' kingdom is a heavenly kingdom. He would return to his Father, but would send his Holy Spirit to the world and his children would then be his witnesses. 'You will receive power when the Holy Spirit comes on you, and you will be my witnesses,' he promised his timid disciples. He also explained to them that his kingdom had to be proclaimed all over the world.

The Holy Spirit still makes his immense power available to you when you want to witness to others. You never have to rely on your own power to be a witness. Ask the Spirit to equip you to be a dynamic witness just as he equipped the disciples.

Holy Spirit, you know I find it difficult to talk about God to other people. Please equip me with your power so that I will be able to proclaim Jesus' message to others with confidence. Amen.

17 March
Power, love and self-discipline
Read: 2 Timothy 1:3–9

*For God did not give us a spirit of timidity,
but a spirit of power, of love and of self-discipline.*
2 Timothy 1:7

Sometimes you are afraid to witness because you are too concerned about what others would think. Our passage of Scripture seems to indicate that the young Timothy also doubted his abilities as a witness. However, Paul encouraged 'his son in the faith'. When God gives us his Holy Spirit, he gives us power, love and self-discipline as well, he writes. Timothy therefore did not have to be ashamed to testify about the Lord. Paul continues in verse 9 that God has saved and called his children for one purpose only, that is, to be committed to him.

Once you know this secret – that the Holy Spirit likewise wants to perfect you with power, love and self-discipline so that you will be able to proclaim God's good news successfully as a result of the effect he has on your life, and that he will help you to live a life committed to God every day – your Christianity will fill you with greater joy daily. Before you shy away from testifying again, concentrate on the qualities the Holy Spirit will give you and live a life of commitment to God from today.

*Holy Spirit, please fill me with power, love and self-discipline
so that I will be a powerful witness, and help me to live a life
committed to God every day. Amen.*

18 March
Pray to receive the gifts of the Spirit
Read: 1 Corinthians 12:1–11

There are different kinds of gifts, but the same Spirit ...
All these are the work of one and the same Spirit,
and he gives them to each one, just as he determines.
1 Corinthians 12:4, 11

God gives each of his children a unique, specific gift by the work of his Holy Spirit. The purpose of these gifts is that we have to use them to glorify God and serve our neighbour. Each of us has received a specific gift although our gifts are not the same. The Holy Spirit distributes the gifts and he gives them as he determines.

However, the Holy Spirit also gives gifts which are shared by all believers. The most important of these gifts are set out in detail in 1 Corinthians 13. All of us should have the love of God in our lives and this love – according to Paul – is poured out into our hearts by the Holy Spirit whom he has given us (Romans 5:5).

When you pray, ask the Holy Spirit to show you your specific gift clearly, and to equip you to use it in God's kingdom in the best possible way. Also pray that the Spirit will pour God's love into your heart – and then pass it on to every person who crosses your path.

Holy Spirit, thank you for the specific gifts you have entrusted to me.
Help me to use them to your honour. I also pray for the gift of love
in my life. Amen.

19 March
A temple of the Spirit
Read: 1 Corinthians 3:16–17

Don't you know that you yourselves are
God's temple and that God's Spirit lives in you?
1 Corinthians 3:16

'Your body is the temple of God. God himself lives in you by his Spirit. You obviously realise that God lives in you in a very special way – as if you were a temple. God's Spirit lives in you as one would live in a house,' says *Die Boodskap* version of our verse.

Never lose sight of this fact, because it means that you do not belong to yourself – you can no longer merely do as you please and do those things you enjoy. You belong to God – your body is the temple of his Spirit. You are therefore expected to live a holy life, to act the way God expects of you, to obey the guidance of his Spirit unconditionally every day, to keep your body and life pure.

It is practically impossible to do this in your own power because inherently all of us are sinful. Pray that the Holy Spirit will enable you to be a temple worthy of him.

Holy Spirit, forgive me for sometimes being such an unworthy temple, and enable me by your presence in my life to live according to the will of God. Amen.

20 March
Pray for the fruit of the Spirit
Read: Galatians 5:16–26

The fruit of the Spirit is love, joy, peace, patience, kindness, goodness, faithfulness, gentleness and self-control.
Galatians 5:22

A believer who really lives a life controlled by the Holy Spirit bears the fruit of the Holy Spirit as described in the above verse. The purpose of this fruit is to glorify God in our lives, to show others the greatness and glory of God by the way we act and to testify to the incredible things he is able to do in our lives.

Jesus selects each child of his Father specially to bear fruit for him. 'This is to my Father's glory, that you bear much fruit,' he said to his disciples shortly before his crucifixion (John 15:8). He then added, 'You did not choose me, but I chose you and appointed you to go and bear fruit – fruit that will last' (John 15:16). To this fruit-bearing he then added: 'Then the Father will give you whatever you ask in my name' (the last part of John 15:16).

Check the list in our verse once again and tick the qualities which you still need in your life. If your prayers are not answered, check whether the fruit of the Holy Spirit is present in your life.

Holy Spirit, today I pray for your fruit in my life.
Make me loving, full of joy, peace-loving, patient, kind,
good, faithful, gentle and self-controlled. Amen.

21 March
The fruit of love
Read: Ephesians 3:14–19

The fruit of the Spirit is love ...
Galatians 5:22

'And to know this love that surpasses knowledge – that you may be filled to the measure of all the fulness of God' (Ephesians 3:19).

When love is described as part of the fruit of the Spirit, Paul is not referring to ordinary human love which always expects something in return, but to the way God loves us – a love which surpasses knowledge. God's love never changes and is unconditional. It is a love which always gives and never expects anything in return. A love which is patient and kind, which does not envy or boast, which is not proud. A love which is not self-seeking, easily angered and which does not keep any record of wrongs. A love which always protects, always trusts, always hopes and always perseveres (1 Corinthians 13:4–7). This is what your love for others should be like.

Unfortunately this is impossible! In your own power you cannot love others with the same love God has for you. This is totally contrary to your sinful human nature. Yet the Holy Spirit can give you this love in your life. 'God has poured out his love into our hearts by the Holy Spirit, whom he has given us,' Paul writes to the church in Rome (Romans 5:5). If you ask him, he will do this for you, too.

Heavenly Father, I pray that you will give me the fruit of love in my life – please pour out your love into my heart and life by the Holy Spirit who lives in me. Amen.

22 March
The fruit of joy
Read: John 15:9–11

The fruit of the Spirit is joy …
Galatians 5:22
*'As the Father has loved me, so have I loved you.
Now remain in my love. I have told you this so that my joy
may be in you and that your joy may be complete.'*
John 15:9, 11

God's children have a quality by which they can be recognised immediately: the joy on their faces and in their eyes.

However, the fruit of joy implies that we will always be joyful – even during bad times. It implies that we will be able to look up to God and still radiate joy despite hurts and troubles. This joy which has nothing to do with outward circumstances is likewise from the Holy Spirit. Only the Holy Spirit in your life enables you to be joyful at all times, because the flame of joy which cannot be lit by your circumstances comes from the heart, from God himself.

And this joy cannot be separated from love.

You may therefore be filled with joy and live each day to the full and joyfully because you are assured of Jesus' love, knowing that nothing will ever separate you from God's love and that his Holy Spirit lives in you.

*Holy Spirit, I am still unable to be joyful at all times.
Sometimes others cannot see your joy in my life.
Please give me your lasting joy in my life. Amen.*

23 March
The fruit of peace
Read: John 14:25–28

The fruit of the Spirit is peace ...
Galatians 5:22
'Peace I leave with you; my peace I give you. I do not give to you as the world gives. Do not let your hearts be troubled and do not be afraid.'
John 14:27

The Jewish leaders in Jesus' time tried to find human peace. They were concerned with self-preservation in the light of power on earth. Jesus was not referring to this type of peace. He always meant peace with God. When Jesus told his disciples that the Holy Spirit would be with them always, he simultaneously promised them his peace. Like the love of Jesus, this peace is not like the peace of the world. The nature and content of this peace differ from the peace of the world we know, which is usually little more than a cease-fire. This godly peace asks us to see others through the eyes of God and develop a completely new perspective on life.

Before you will find true peace in your life, you will have to make peace with God. Once you have done this, the Holy Spirit will enable you to live in peace with everybody else. Only then will you be able to find peace and hand all your troubles to God.

Holy Spirit, my life is so filled with strife. I pray that you will enable me to make right with God and others so that your lasting peace will rule in my life. Amen.

24 March
The fruit of patience
Read: Ephesians 4:1–6

The fruit of the Spirit is patience ...
Galatians 5:22
*Be completely humble and gentle; be patient,
bearing with one another in love.*
Ephesians 4:2

You teach best what you most need to learn, one of my professors used to say. As I grow older, this becomes more and more evident in my own life. I must have been absent on the day when patience was handed out! Patience is definitely that part of the fruit of the Spirit which I lack most in my own life.

However, God expects his children to be patient in their relationships with one another. 'Bear with each other and forgive whatever grievances you may have against one another,' Paul writes in Colossians 3:13. The Greek word in Galatians 5:22 which is translated as 'patience' actually means 'to give someone another chance'.

How patient are you with other people? At home with your children who try your patience, at work with your colleagues who frustrate you, with your (sometimes difficult!) husband you have to live with daily?

The Holy Spirit is prepared to give you the fruit of patience in your life so that you will be able to give others another chance in future – as God gives you another chance repeatedly.

*Heavenly Father, thank you for your tremendous patience with me.
Please enter this patience into my own life by your Holy Spirit who lives
in me. Make me willing to give others another chance. Amen.*

25 March
The fruit of kindness
Read: 2 Corinthians 6:1–7

The fruit of the Spirit is kindness ...
Galatians 5:22

'We commend ourselves in every way ... in purity, understanding, patience and kindness; in the Holy Spirit and in sincere love; in truthful speech and in the power of God' (2 Corinthians 6:4, 6–7).

Paul attaches special value to kindness. He groups it with understanding and patience when he describes his own conduct to the church in Corinth. The *Collins English Dictionary* defines 'kind' as having a friendly or generous nature or attitude, being helpful to others, pleasant, agreeable. To be kind therefore means to treat others the way you would like to be treated yourself. Oswald Chambers writes that being kind means to look at others with the Lord's attitude (from *My utmost for his highest*).

Unfortunately your facial expression can convey your kindness or lack of it. What do others see when they look at you? Some people are born good-natured. Others go through life with morose expressions. However, kindness is free and contagious – all of us can learn to cultivate this part of the fruit of the Holy Spirit in our lives. Start today with the good advice of 'if you see somebody without a smile, give him one of yours!' Make a point of greeting everybody with a smile, even when you do not know them.

Holy Spirit, please enable me to see others with your attitude.
Help me to be pleasant and kind to others. Amen.

26 March
The fruit of goodness
Read: Acts 9:36–42

The fruit of the Spirit is goodness ...
Galatians 5:22

'In Joppa there was a disciple named Tabitha, who was always doing good and helping the poor' (Acts 9:36).

Goodness usually concerns our relationship with others. It means that we will 'feel' for others, but also stretch out our hands to help them.

Tabitha, the widow referred to in Acts 9:36, appears to have been the woman in the Bible in whose life goodness was manifested the most. This Tabitha was always doing good and helping the poor. When she died all the widows she had helped were very sad. They asked Peter to come and showed him the clothes she had made for them. When Peter raised Tabitha from the dead, all the people in Joppa rejoiced and many of them believed in the Lord.

At present many people are battling financially in our own country. If you want the fruit of goodness to grow in your own life, you have to be willing to help them – not only by prayer and money, but also by doing something concrete to demonstrate your goodness towards them.

Are you going to try?

Holy Spirit, please make me aware of the despair of people around me and make me willing to reach out to them with an attitude of goodness. Amen.

27 March
The fruit of faithfulness
Read: Philippians 4:1–5

The fruit of the Spirit is faithfulness …
Galatians 5:22
Therefore, my brothers, … that is how you should stand firm in the Lord.
Philippians 4:1

'Moments of weakness, mistakes, laziness and shortcomings in your ministry are manifestations of faithlessness,' writes *Die Bybellennium* (p. 1651). This sounds so familiar, doesn't it? God's children are often unfaithful – regarding him as well as one another. Once Peter promised faithfully that he would never forsake Jesus yet shortly afterwards he denied him three times. The other disciples left Jesus when he needed them the most.

To be faithful means to decide to be reliable in everything you say or do. To keep your promises to God and to others to the letter. To be a woman who keeps her word so that others will be able to rely on you. I find it quite remarkable how easily people make promises without keeping them. Unlike us, God is absolutely faithful. 'If we are faithless, he will remain faithful, for he cannot disown himself,' Paul writes to Timothy (2 Timothy 2:13).

God is perfectly faithful to you – won't you try to be faithful to him as well as to others from this day on?

Holy Spirit, thank you for always being faithful.
Please forgive me for so easily making promises – to you as well
as to others – and then conveniently forgetting these promises.
Make me perfectly faithful and reliable. Amen.

28 March
The fruit of gentleness
Read: Luke 14:7, 11

The fruit of the Spirit is gentleness ...
Galatians 5:23
Everyone who exalts himself will be humbled,
and he who humbles himself will be exalted.
Luke 14:11

Once when Jesus noticed that the Pharisees picked the places of honour at the table, he told them a parable to teach them that when you seek your own gain, you invariably miss it. When someone invites you to dinner, rather take the least important place, he said, so that the host himself can invite you to take the place of honour.

The Bible points out in various passages that gentleness or humility is very important to God. Those who want to be first will in fact be last, Jesus warns in his parable; those who are proud, will be humiliated and those who are humble or gentle will be exalted.

Jesus is the perfect example of humility or gentleness – he was always prepared to put others first, even though he was God himself. Paul then concludes the chapter on the fruit of the Spirit with the words, 'Let us not become conceited, provoking and envying each other' (Galatians 5:26).

Regardless of how much we resist it, most people are proud and selfish by nature. Only the Holy Spirit can teach you to place yourself in the second place because you regard others as more important than yourself. Only his influence in your life can turn you into a sincerely humble person.

Holy Spirit, you know that I regard myself as very important – forgive me and make me humble like Jesus. Help me always to consider others better than myself. Amen.

29 March
The fruit of self-control
Read: Titus 2:11–15

The fruit of the Spirit is self-control.
Galatians 5:23
The grace of God ... has appeared to all men.
It teaches us to say 'no' to ungodliness and worldly passions,
and to live self-controlled, upright and godly lives ...
Titus 2:11–12

It is interesting to note that the Greek word translated as self-control in Galatians 5:23 is actually used in the case of a wild animal that has been broken in or tamed. Self-control therefore means that you will no longer behave 'wildly', dictated to by your sinful nature and doing as you please, but that you will allow God to 'tame' you by his Holy Spirit so that you will live according to the guidelines in his word. 'Self-control' as used here actually means the direct opposite, that is, a life controlled by the Holy Spirit!

'Like a city whose walls are broken down is a man who lacks self-control', says Solomon (Proverbs 25:28). People who lack self-control often land in trouble because they do not have control over themselves or their circumstances. The Holy Spirit in your life wants to turn you into a consistent, self-controlled woman. Ask him to do so.

Holy Spirit, forgive me for so often being temperamental and for embarrassing others in the process. I want my life to be controlled by you from this moment. Please give me your self-control. Amen.

30 March
Walking in the Spirit
Galatians 5:16–26

If we live in the Spirit, let us also walk in the Spirit.
Galatians 5:25 (Authorised King James version)

'Live by the Spirit, and you will not gratify the desires of the sinful nature,' Paul wrote in Galatians 5:16. God cannot redeem anyone according to his deeds because we have all sinned from birth. The only way you will succeed in saying 'yes' to the Holy Spirit and 'no' to your sinful nature in future is to have your whole life controlled by the Holy Spirit – once you realise that a continuous war between the Spirit and your flesh is being waged in your life.

If you really want to live 'in the Spirit', you will have to allow him to determine your behaviour, you will have to walk with him daily and listen carefully to his voice all the time and follow his guidance. If you want to walk in the Spirit from this day, you will have to resolve to make the right decision for the Spirit and against your sinful nature time and again and day by day – obviously with God's help. Are you willing to be led by the Holy Spirit moment by moment from this day?

Holy Spirit, you know how I still like following my own mind and doing my own thing. Please make me willing to obey you unconditionally and follow your guidance. Amen.

31 March
The pouring out of the Holy Spirit
Read: Acts 2:17–21, 37–39

I will pour out my Spirit on all people ... And everyone who calls on the name of the Lord will be saved.
Acts 2:17, 21

When the Holy Spirit was poured out on the first day of Pentecost, it was accompanied by strange phenomena. The believers on whom the Spirit was poured out started praising God – and they did so in other tongues, so that the Jewish pilgrims from various countries who were listening to them heard how God's Name was being glorified in their own languages.

Part of the crowd was amazed about this, but others thought the believers were intoxicated. In his speech, Peter gave the correct facts regarding the pouring out of the Holy Spirit. He explained that the people were not drunk, but that God had 'poured out his Spirit on them' as prophesied by the prophet Joel long ago (Joel 2:28–32). As a result of the pouring out of the Holy Spirit, each believer could now share in his power and mercy.

The Holy Spirit still makes a vast difference in the lives of people. If the Spirit has already been poured out on your life (on the day when you surrendered your life to God), you should live in such a way that others will notice his rule in your life daily.

Holy Spirit, thank you that you have already been poured out on my life. Help me to live in such a way that others who see my actions will be able to see you in my life. Amen.

April

God is there whenever you call to him

'When you pray something tremendous happens: earth and heaven meet, insignificant man comes into contact with the living God. The mere thought fills one with awe,' writes Dr Hennie Conradie *(ABC van gebed –* Preface). Although we are so used to praying that we sometimes pray almost involuntarily, it is incredible to know that when you pray God is there – that he listens to your prayers and that he is waiting impatiently to have mercy upon you. The depth of your spiritual life and your service to God is therefore in a direct relation to your prayer life.

Consider God's holiness and glory carefully before you start praying. Use the words in the Bible to talk to God – this will give you a new dimension. Be specific, make time to pray with other believers. However, the real reason why mortals talk to a holy God is not so much to verbalise their personal prayer requests, but primarily to glorify God himself by their prayers.

1 April
An early morning appointment
Read: Psalm 5

*In the morning, O Lord, you hear my voice; in the morning
I lay my requests before you and wait in expectation.*
Psalm 5:3

The psalmist makes time in the morning to wait upon God and talk to him. We also read that Abraham used to rise early to stand before the Lord (Genesis 19:27) and that Jesus got up 'very early in the morning, while it was still dark ... and went off to a solitary place, where he prayed' (Mark 1:35).

You also need a set time to pray. We are often so tired in the evening that we practically fall asleep on our knees. Early morning is therefore the very best time to set aside to talk to God, even if it means that you have to rise earlier to fit your prayer time into your busy daily schedule.

This early morning appointment with God is your most important appointment of the day because this is where you find the necessary energy and wisdom which you need to handle with confidence all the responsibilities which await you during the rest of the day. Decide right now how early you will get ready to talk to God – and then write your prayer time in your diary. God wants to hear your voice in the morning!

Heavenly Father, please impress on me the importance of my early morning appointment with you. Make me willing to rise earlier in future to have more time to spend with you. Amen.

2 April
Pray in the morning and in the evening
Read: 1 Chronicles 23:27–32

They [the Levites] were also to stand every morning to thank and praise the Lord. They were to do the same in the evening.
1 Chronicles 23:30

In the days of the Old Testament the Levites had a series of important functions which they had to perform faithfully. They had to perform the temple rituals, help with the sacrifices and care for the holy objects. One of their most important assignments was to meet at the temple every morning and evening to thank and praise the Lord. The people could listen to the songs of praise of the Levites morning and evening and be reminded of God's mercy.

Although early morning is the best time for your appointment with the Lord, it is as important that you conclude your day with him. One finds two types of people: those who rise early and those who rise late. My husband always rises at five o'clock and he brings me coffee in bed by seven. In the evening he is ready for bed much earlier than I am! If you go to bed late, you might find it easier to have your quiet time in the evening. However, never miss this daily appointment with God, keep it faithfully like the Levites of old.

Heavenly Father, I find it exciting that I may have a daily appointment with you. Thank you for the joy of your presence. Please make me faithful so that I will not miss a single appointment with you. Amen.

3 April
Be still ...
Read: Psalm 46:9–12

Be still, and know that I am God; I will be exalted among the nations, I will be exalted in the earth.
Psalm 46:10

God is great and holy and therefore you should not rush into his presence and start talking to him. Prayer requires the necessary respect. You should never start praying without thinking to whom you are talking. Before you start praying, you should be in the right frame of mind, be still, as recommended by our verse. Relax completely, forget the things which make you anxious and tense and concentrate on God. Eastern religions frequently use meditation, therefore some Christians are afraid to use Christian meditation, but it could become one of the most wonderful experiences in your prayer life – being still for a few minutes every day and considering God's omnipotence and greatness.

While Eastern meditation means that you have to empty yourself of everything, Christian meditation means that you fill your thoughts with God. Do this by forgetting everything around you and focusing only on God's presence. Fill your thoughts with God's attributes: think about his love for you, about the miracles of his creation, about his omnipresence, his omnipotence, faithfulness and mercy.

Bow before him and worship him – in this way you will be in the right frame of mind to talk to him.

Great is the Lord God! I want to be still in your presence, consider your attributes and focus only on you. Help me to forget everything else and fill my thoughts with yourself. Amen.

4 April
Meditate on God's word
Read: Psalm 1

Blessed is the man ... [whose] delight is in the law of the Lord, and on his law he meditates day and night.
Psalm 1:1–2

Here the psalmist writes that the man who meditates on the word of God – who thinks about this word day and night and is inspired by it – is blessed.

Christian meditation is a deliberate decision. You resolve to make an appointment with God. You deliberately grow still in God's presence, until you are so aware of his love for you that it practically washes over you and envelops you. However, meditation takes time – you cannot merely rush in and rush out when you become involved with God. To meditate means that you will focus on learning a new way of thinking.

To meditate correctly requires that you use your Bible in this thinking process. Take a short passage from your Bible which deals with God, and think about it. 'Mull it over' as it were, and make it part of your thought processes. You could also read a passage of Scripture until a specific verse strikes you personally and then spend some time considering this particular verse. Make yourself vulnerable and become teachable until you know exactly what God himself wants to say to you through his word.

Heavenly Father, thank you for your word in which I may find joy, on which I may meditate day and night. I now want to be still and listen, until I can hear you yourself talking to me through your word. Amen.

5 April
Draw near ...
Read: James 4:7–10

Submit yourselves, then, to God. Resist the devil, and he will flee from you. Come near to God and he will come near to you. Wash your hands, you sinners, and purify your hearts, you double-minded.
James 4:7–9

Prayer is fellowshipping with God, drawing near to him. However, before you draw near to God, you have to send the devil away and wash your hands and your heart. When you deliberately draw near to God, you have the assurance that he will allow you to find him – that he will also draw near to you.

When I entered a medieval cathedral for the first time about twenty years ago, it was an incredible experience. I could sense the presence of God so strongly that I wanted to wish away the tour group around me – I desired to kneel in a corner and talk to God. Perhaps I was so aware of God's presence because thousands upon thousands of prayers had been prayed in the centuries-old cathedral.

'The Lord is near to all who call on him, to all who call on him in truth,' writes the psalmist (Psalm 145:18). You may claim this promise for yourself when you kneel in prayer. God is always near you when you call on him.

Lord, it is incredible that you draw near to me when I want to talk to you. I praise you for being close to everybody who calls to you in truth. Amen.

6 April
Seek God's presence
Read: Psalm 105:1–7

Glory in his holy name; let the heart of those who seek the Lord rejoice.
Psalm 103:3

When you grow still with God, it becomes time to set aside everything else and focus on God only. The psalmist is familiar with the joy found in the presence of God and he knows how wonderful it is to praise God in prayer for the things he does and gives you. Prayer always brings joy.

You do not have to seek God's presence only during your quiet time. He promises to be with you every day, at home doing household chores, in the office, when you are playing sport or even just relaxing. He supports you from day to day. He promises to give you his power when you are tired, his protection when you are in danger, his faithful love when you are in the wilderness. You should therefore seek his presence at all times.

'Pray continually,' Paul advised the church in Thessalonica. Always be connected to God by means of a prayer line. Remember that you can talk to him at any time and in any place. God is impatiently waiting to have mercy on you – do not postpone but draw near to him.

Lord, it is so good to know that I may draw near to you in prayer at all times, that you are waiting to be merciful to me, that I have a hot line to you all the time. Amen.

7 April
Search your heart
Read: Psalm 139:1–4; 23–24

Search me, O God, and know my heart; test me and know my anxious thoughts. See if there is any offensive way in me, and lead me in the way everlasting.
Psalm 139:23–24

The Bible emphasises in several passages that we cannot enter the presence of God when we have sinned. God knows you inside out. He knows each hidden sin which you have tried to hide from everybody (even yourself!). Before you start praying, you should therefore ask God to search your heart, to test you to see whether you have not perhaps strayed from his way.

Evelyn Christenson shares how she and a group of friends once decided to meet weekly to pray for their church and that the Lord then made it clear to them that they first had to search their own hearts. He made them aware of things that were wrong in their own lives for six months before they were 'ready' to start interceding for their church.

Ask the Lord to search your heart and point out your sins to you before you start talking to him.

Heavenly Father, sometimes it is hard to know that you know me so well that you are aware of every wrong deed or thought which hampers my fellowship with you. Please point out my sin to me. Amen.

8 April
Praying is listening
Read: Isaiah 50:4–10

The Sovereign Lord has given me an instructed tongue …
He wakens me morning by morning, wakens my ear to listen
like one being taught. The Sovereign Lord has opened my ears.
Isaiah 50:4–5

The American journalist Dan Rather once asked Mother Teresa, 'What do you say when you pray?' 'I listen,' she answered. Baffled, Rather tried again, 'And then, what does God say?' 'He listens,' Mother Teresa smiled.

Prayer is a conversation with God. A conversation can never be a soliloquy – it consists of talking and listening. When you tune in to talk to God, you should also be prepared to listen to the voice of God.

God talks to you by his Holy Spirit and also by his word. Bible study should therefore be an inseparable part of your appointment with God. Prepare yourself to listen carefully to the specific message which God has for you every day. Pray before you start reading your Bible and also afterwards. First ask the Holy Spirit to reveal God's word to you, and when you have finished reading your Bible, you in turn respond to God's word.

Heavenly Father, please teach me to listen carefully to your special
message for me every day. Thank you that prayer not only means
talking to you but also listening to your voice. Amen.

9 April
Use the words in your Bible
Read: Hebrews 4:12–16

For the word of God is living and active. Sharper than any double-edged sword, it penetrates even to dividing soul and spirit ...
Hebrews 4:12

Children who cannot hear, cannot speak either. The same applies to prayer. If we do not listen to God's words and make them our own, it is difficult to reach him in prayer. Once you have learnt to 'repeat' God's word to him, you have discovered a secret which will intensify your prayers tremendously.

My husband often says one should read the Bible while praying and pray while reading. The two should, as it were, occur simultaneously. When you listen to God's voice in his word, you respond to that word by praying. And when you pray, you use the words of his word to speak to him.

When you are sad, you could use the penitential psalms as well as the lamentations of Jeremiah and Job to tell the Lord of your despair. When you are full of joy, you could repeat the songs of praise in the psalms to him. God's word is alive and powerful – you cannot communicate with him better than by using the words of his word.

Heavenly Father, today I want to praise you for your word – thank you that I may pray using the words of my Bible and know that you hear my prayers because the Bible contains your own words. Amen.

10 April
Be joyful, pray and give thanks!
Read: 1 Thessalonians 5:14–24

Be joyful always; pray continually; give thanks in all circumstances,
for this is God's will for you in Christ Jesus.
1 Thessalonians 5:16–18

There are three things you should know with regard to persevering in prayer: you have to be patient when you pray, you have to believe that God will answer and also be prepared to wait for this answer, and still remain joyful and give thanks to God while waiting!

If you are sure that your prayer request is in line with the guidelines of the Bible and in line with the guidance of the Holy Spirit (for example, if you are praying for someone's conversion), do not despair. Give God time and persevere in prayer and believe.

The command to pray continually does not mean that you have to spend all day on your knees, but that you have to live prayerfully all the time. Practise talking to God continuously, listening to his voice in his word and then communicating with him throughout the day. People who live close to God are also full of the joy which only he can give, and they have learnt to give thanks in all circumstances – even for the things they would rather have had differently, because they know that God will always give them only the best.

Heavenly Father, please help me to live prayerfully, to radiate
your joy, even under difficult circumstances, and to give thanks
in all circumstances. Amen.

11 April
Be specific
Read: Mark 10:46–52

'What do you want me to do for you?' Jesus asked him.
The blind man said, 'Rabbi, I want to see.'
Mark 10:51

When the blind Bartimaeus asked Jesus to have mercy on him, Jesus knew very well what the blind man wanted. He nevertheless asked him in so many words: 'What do you want me to do for you?' He wanted the blind man to verbalise his prayer request. 'It is God's will that we should be specific when we pray. Our prayers must be a distinct expression of definite need, not a vague appeal to his mercy or an indefinite cry for his help,' writes Andrew Murray *(With Christ in the school of prayer*, p. 74).

All of us are sometimes guilty of praying vague prayers: 'Have mercy on us, forgive our sin, bless our loved ones,' we ask God. Make a point of being specific in future. Specify the sins you want God to forgive and in which area you need his mercy. Name the people you are praying for and tell God exactly what you would like him to do for each of them. In this way you will learn to understand and verbalise your own needs better. Always remember to compare your desires with the will of God and to believe that you will receive what you have asked.

Heavenly Father, I apologise for sometimes exhausting you with strings
of vague requests. Teach me to pray specifically and by name. Thank
you that you already know what I need, even before I ask. Amen.

12 April
Speak to God face to face
Read: Exodus 33:9–17

As Moses went into the tent, the pillar of cloud would come down ...
while the Lord spoke with Moses. The Lord would speak to Moses
face to face, as a man speaks with his friend.
Exodus 33:9,11

In the days of the Old Testament, the people could not speak to God face to face. They needed a mediator in the form of a priest. The priest then spoke to God on their behalf and confessed their sin on their behalf. However, it was different in the case of Moses: God spoke to him face to face, as a man would speak with his friend. Moses and God had a personal relationship of trust which did not require a mediator.

Jesus makes it possible for you to talk to God directly, even though you are a sinner and he the holy God. Jesus is your Mediator – he stands between you and God and by his death on the cross he earned personal contact by prayer for you with his Father. When you pray you may therefore now speak to the holy God directly. And God also speaks to you directly. He does this through his word. When you read your Bible, it contains God's personal message to you. When you have finished reading, it is your turn – you can then respond to God in prayer.

Lord Jesus, I praise you that you have made it possible for me
to speak to God personally, and that I can also hear him speaking
to me when I read his word. Amen.

13 April
Pray with others
Read: Acts 1:9–14

They all joined together constantly in prayer, along with the women and Mary, the mother of Jesus, and with his brothers.
Acts 1:14

The very first lesson on prayer which Jesus teaches his disciples is that prayer is a personal conversation with a Father who loves you. The second lesson is that believers sometimes have to pray with other Christians. 'If two of you on earth agree about anything you ask for, it will be done for you by my Father in heaven,' he promised in Matthew 18:19.

Praying with other believers is important if you want to grow in faith.

The Holy Spirit reveals his full power where people pray. The Spirit was also poured out for the first time while the early Christians in Jerusalem were praying together after Jesus' ascension. Our verse reads, 'They all joined together constantly in prayer.'

Two things are required when you pray with other believers: you have to agree in the Name of Jesus about the things you would like to receive; and secondly, you have to persevere in prayer. When you pray together in this way, God will grant your prayer requests.

Heavenly Father, it is not always easy for me to pray with others. Teach me that it is your will that your children should agree in prayer. Thank you for the promise that you yourself will be present with us and that you will grant our requests. Amen.

14 April
It will be done to you according to your faith
Read: Matthew 9:27–31

When he had gone indoors, the blind men came to him, and he asked them, 'Do you believe that I am able to do this?' 'Yes, Lord,' they replied. Then he touched their eyes and said, 'According to your faith will it be done to you.'
Matthew 9:28–29

Two blind men followed Jesus and asked him to have mercy on them. Jesus was willing, but he wanted to know whether they believed that he could heal them. When they answered in the affirmative, Jesus said, 'According to your faith will it be done to you.' Jesus himself stipulated that faith is a condition for prayers to be answered. He actually wanted to know whether the two blind men believed that he was the Messiah. When they addressed him as the 'Son of David' they had in fact already answered his question.

If you pray as well as believe, God answers your prayers – provided they are in line with his will. However, if you pray while you doubt that the Lord will answer your prayers, that which you believe will happen. This event does not mean that faith is always a prerequisite for healing. The recognition of Jesus as the Son of God, the true Son of David, is highlighted in this passage of Scripture. Those who approach him with this conviction and expectation will experience his mercy, writes *Die Bybellennium* (p. 1134).

Lord Jesus, I believe that you are the Son of God, I believe that you have paid for my sin on the cross and that you have made eternal life possible to me. Thank you for the assurance that you hear when I pray in faith. Amen.

15 April
Be reconciled!
Read: Matthew 5:21–25

Therefore, if you are offering your gift at the altar and there remember that your brother has something against you, leave your gift there in front of the altar. First go and be reconciled to your brother; then come and offer your gift.
Matthew 5:23–24

Most sins have something to do with our relationships. Before we pray we have to check whether our relationships are right, and if not, we have to be prepared to take the first step to be reconciled. Our verse does not say 'if you have something against someone else', but 'if your brother has something against you'.

God expects you to be the peacemaker, to be prepared to reach out to the other person, even if the breach was not your fault.

It is not so easy to forgive somebody when you are innocent, but the Lord nevertheless asks you to do so. If you fail to do this, you are disobeying him. Remember that God is always prepared to forgive you. You should therefore also be prepared to forgive those who have something against you. Ask the Lord to sow this forgiveness in your heart.

Heavenly Father, thank you for always being prepared to forgive me. Please help me to reach out to those who have something against me, and to be reconciled before I kneel to talk to you. Amen.

16 April
Persevere in faith!
Read: Hebrews 10:32–39

So do not throw away your confidence; it will be richly rewarded. You need to persevere so that when you have done the will of God, you will receive what he has promised.
Hebrews 10:35–36

The Bible frequently illustrates that we should not lose courage when our prayer requests are not answered immediately. It is God's will that we keep on asking and believing until he responds.

When the Canaanite woman came to Jesus and asked him to heal her child, he refused at first. However, the woman persevered until Jesus eventually said to her that it was not right to take the children's bread and toss it to their dogs. Even then she did not give up. 'Yes, Lord,' she said, 'but even the dogs eat the crumbs that fall from their masters' table.' Then Jesus answered, 'Woman, you have great faith! Your request is granted.' And her daughter was healed from that very hour (Matthew 15:21–28).

It is easy to lose courage when you pray without seeing any results. When you pray again and God delays, persevere in prayer until you receive an answer.

Lord Jesus, you know that I sometimes become discouraged when I pray without seeing any results. Make me willing to persevere in prayer and to believe until your promises for me have been fulfilled. Amen.

17 April
Be faithful in prayer
Read: Romans 12:9–15

Be joyful in hope, patient in affliction, faithful in prayer.
Romans 12:12

One of the 'guidelines for the Christian life' indicated by Paul in Romans 12, is that Christians have to persevere in prayer. When we succeed in persevering in prayer, it is easy to be joyful in hope and patient in affliction. Sometimes it is difficult to understand why we occasionally have to ask repeatedly before God answers some of our prayers. It is likewise difficult to continue believing when we persevere in prayer and nothing happens.

When your faith is tested, keep on praying. I think Andrew Murray describes this in a very striking way: 'Prayer must often be "heaped up" until God sees that its measure is full. Then the answer comes' *(With Christ in the school of prayer,* p. 119).

If you feel you have really prayed long enough, just persevere a little longer. Perhaps your prayer pyramid is not yet high enough, perhaps God wants you to continue praying only for the next week or month – and then he will grant your prayer requests.

You can be assured of one thing when you pray – sometimes God takes long to answer you, but he always answers you.

Heavenly Father, thank you for the assurance that although you sometimes keep me waiting for an answer, you always answer when I pray. Help me to persevere in prayer and not to lose courage. Amen.

18 April
Devote yourself to prayer!
Read: Colossians 4:2–6

Devote yourselves to prayer, being watchful and thankful.
And pray for us, too ...
Colossians 4:2,3

It is God's will that his children should persevere in prayer even when we do not receive the answers to our prayers immediately. It is interesting to note that it has been proved time and again that we pray much more in bad times than when all is well. Problems cultivate that very perseverance Paul refers to in our verse for today:

'We also rejoice in our sufferings, because we know that suffering produces perseverance; perseverance, character; and character, hope. And hope does not disappoint us, because God has poured out his love in our hearts by the Holy Spirit, whom he has given us,' Paul wrote to the church in Rome (Romans 5:3–5).

Therefore, take courage and pray more when the going is hard. You may even rejoice in the suffering because when you suffer, you are forced to your knees – it teaches you to persevere in prayer, because you realise that you cannot change anything with regard to your circumstances yourself. And this persevering prayer in turn strengthens your faith and makes you hold on to the hope in your heart, because God has poured out his love in your heart by his Holy Spirit.

Lord Jesus, today I want to thank you for the difficult times in my life, because they teach me to persevere in prayer, strengthen my faith and make me hold on to my hope in you. Amen.

19 April
Be watchful and thankful!
Read: Colossians 4:2–6

Devote yourselves to prayer, being watchful and thankful.
And pray for us, too …
Colossians 4:2,3

When you are praying, you should not only persevere in prayer, but also be watchful and thankful.

Watchfulness means to be wide awake, on your guard with regard to the traps the devil will most probably set for you. Thankfulness requires that you be aware of God's grace in your life at all times. You should also thank God sincerely every day for all these unmerited gifts which you receive from the hand of God.

Therefore, be watchful and thankful when you pray! Every Christian is involved in spiritual warfare – unless you are on your guard with regard to the temptations which the devil will bring your way, you will easily fall into one of his traps. Always remember that you cannot do anything against the devil on your own, but that Jesus has already defeated him on the cross.

When you pray, focus on all the blessings you receive from God as well, and remember to thank him for each of them.

Heavenly Father, please make me watchful and on my guard regarding the wiles of Satan. I also want to thank you for everything you give me daily by your grace. Amen.

20 April
Pray without fear
Read: 1 John 4:15–21

There is no fear in love. But perfect love drives out fear, because fear has to do with punishment. The one who fears is not made perfect in love.
1 John 4:18

Where there is love, there is no room for fear, particularly not for fear of God's final judgment, John wrote. Perfect love simply drives out all fear.

Sometimes we dread revealing to the Lord the things in our innermost being. However, you have to open your heart before the Lord when you pray. Henri Nouwen writes: 'The more we dare to reveal our trembling self to him, the more we will be able to sense that his love, which is perfect love, casts out all our fears' (*Circles of love*, p. 12).

You may therefore approach God without fear when you pray. You never have to run away from God or give up, you merely have to persevere in praying with confidence, even when it feels as if God is not listening to your prayers. You may continue hoping in the Lord without fear, even when you feel your prayers are a waste of time. You may ask him anything because he loves you unconditionally, and someone who loves unconditionally and so deeply, will only give you the best.

Heavenly Father, thank you for the privilege of being able to bring all my fears to you without fear. I praise you for your unconditional love for me which makes short work of my fears. Amen.

21 April
Pray with hope
Read: Psalm 138:3–8

When I called, you answered me; you made me bold and stout-hearted.
The Lord will fulfil his purpose for me.
Psalm 138:3, 8

It is easy to lose hope when you pray and you cannot see that the Lord is answering your prayers. However, when you pray, you should also continue hoping. 'My splendour is gone and all that I had hoped from the Lord,' Jeremiah lamented while he was suffering (Lamentations 3:18). Yet, only three verses later, he wrote, 'Yet this I call to mind and therefore I have hope: Because of the Lord's great love we are not consumed, for his compassions never fail. They are new every morning; great is your faithfulness' (Lamentations 3:21–23).

If you continue hoping in God when you pray, it also implies that you will believe that he will give you the things which are best for you, even if his answer does not always correspond to your wishes. Hope also means that you will be willing to wait for the fulfilment of God's promises, even if you do not know when they will be fulfilled. It should suffice to know that God will ultimately work out all things for your good.

Heavenly Father, it is wonderful to be able to pray with hope in my heart, because I have the assurance that you will ultimately cause all things to work together for my good. Amen.

22 April
Pray with joy
Read: Psalm 105:1–5

Let the hearts of those who seek the Lord rejoice.
Psalm 105:3

A certain Brother Laurence wrote: 'In this world no joy is sweeter and more delightful than that of a continuous conversation with God.'

When you seek God's presence in prayer, it always brings joy, because you cannot meditate on the attributes of God without being impressed by his omnipotence, mercy and love for you. Once you realise this, you will also know that God is far greater than your problems. No matter how serious your problems, when you pray and surrender your problems to God, a ray of light will always penetrate the darkness which surrounds you. You will discover time and again that you can always rely on God's help, assistance and protection.

Unfortunately this does not mean that all your problems will disappear immediately, but even if all your problems are still present in your life, the power of prayer will equip you so much better to solve them (or come to terms with them!).

For this reason you can kneel next to your bed with frowns of worry on your forehead and shortly afterwards rise from your knees; for this reason you can look up to God and still radiate joy despite your problems.

*Heavenly Father, I praise you for the joy of prayer.
I praise you for reassuring me time and again that you are far greater than my problems, and that you enable me to retain my inner joy despite times of crises. Amen.*

23 April
Pray in humility
Read: Psalm 51:8–19

Surely you desire truth in the inner parts; you teach me wisdom in the inmost place. The sacrifices of God are a broken spirit; a broken and contrite heart, O God, you will not despise.
Psalm 51:6, 17

In David's beautiful song of penitence after he had committed adultery with Bathsheba, he bowed low before God and confessed his sin. He pleaded for mercy and prayed that God would take away all his transgressions and wash his sins away. He told God that he had nowhere to hide and lay his heart full of humility and contrition before God.

The definition of 'contrite' is 'full of guilt or regret; remorseful; remorseful for past sin and resolved to avoid future sin' *(Collins English Dictionary)*. This is the attitude God desires of you when you pray. Like David in Psalm 51, you are also guilty of sin before God. However, when you go to God in prayer with a contrite heart with the assurance that you cannot do anything about your situation and that only God can help you, you are exactly where he wants you.

Praying with a contrite heart, means standing before God with empty hands, like a beggar. And God always responds to the prayers of people who kneel before him in humility and with contrite hearts. He will wash away your sins on account of his love.

Heavenly Father, I now want to lay my contrite and humble heart before you. Like David I want to pray that you will forgive my sin and give me a pure heart again. Amen.

24 April
Pray when you lie awake
Read: Psalm 63

On my bed I remember you; I think of you through the watches of the night. Because you are my help, I sing in the shadow of your wings.
Psalm 63:6–7

When David wrote this Psalm, he was verbalising his longing for God: 'O God, you are my God, earnestly I seek you; my soul thirsts for you, my body longs for you, in a dry and thirsty land where there is no water,' he wrote in verse 1. He desired to be with God in the sanctuary, because God's love meant more to him than life. David seemed to have suffered from insomnia, because he wrote in our verse that he remembered God through the watches of the night and knew that God was his help and protection.

Many women today suffer from insomnia. I, too, frequently lie awake at night and my brain refuses to 'switch off'. When you go to bed tense, you usually wake up after a few hours' sleep and then cannot fall asleep again.

If you know these wakeful hours, stop trying to fall asleep again. You never succeed. Rather talk to God and tell him about the things which keep you awake. Follow Evelyn Christenson's good advice: 'If you can't fall asleep, don't count sheep – talk to the Shepherd' *(Journey into prayer*, p. 56).

Heavenly Father, thank you that I may talk to you when I lie awake at night. Lord, you know all my anxieties – thank you that you are a help and a protection to me as you were to David. Amen.

25 April
Pray until you can!
Read: Hebrews 4:14–16

Let us then approach the throne of grace with confidence, so that we may receive mercy and find grace to help us in our time of need.
Hebrews 4:16

'If you cannot pray, pray until you can,' Spurgeon wrote. Prayer is almost like learning to write your name. Just at first it is quite an effort, and eventually you do it practically automatically. One only learns to pray one way, and that is by praying. The more you pray, the easier it becomes to communicate with God. The more you want to pray, the more precious the time set aside for prayer will become.

No athlete will ever attain success unless he is prepared to spend long hours training. Prayer is an art – and the more you practise that art, the better you will be at it. You will have to set aside enough time for prayer every day. Five minutes before rising and five minutes before going to bed are definitely not enough if you really want to communicate with God in prayer.

If you are still battling to pray, pray more. Make enough time for prayer, use the words in your Bible as prayers and you will soon discover that you have mastered the art of prayer (with the help of the Holy Spirit).

Holy Spirit, please teach me to pray correctly according to the will of God. Give me the right words and make me keen so that I will set aside enough time to learn how to pray. Amen.

26 April
You may argue with God!
Read: Job 23:1–15

If only I knew where to find him; if only I could go to his dwelling!
I would state my case before him and fill my mouth with arguments.
I would find out what he would answer me, and consider what he would say.
Job 23:3–5

Job could not understand why God was afflicting him, therefore he would have liked to find God to state his case and get some answers from him. However, God's answers which he eventually gave Job (Job 39–41) differed completely from the answers Job had expected. In the end Job had to admit his own impotence and acknowledge God's omnipotence.

If you badly want something, you may tell God why you feel so strongly about it. You may even give him reasons why he should answer this particular prayer request. You may also ask the Lord questions if you cannot understand him. Sometimes men of God like Job, David and Jeremiah did not hesitate to pelt God with questions as to the reason why. And they eventually got their answers – even when the answers were not what they had expected.

Although you will definitely not receive answers to all your questions, you will gradually discover that God himself is the answer – that he always knows best and that what he gives you is always beautiful.

Heavenly Father, thank you for the privilege of being able
to submit to you my questions as to the reason why,
until I discover that you yourself are the answer. Amen.

27 April
Pray in the Name of Jesus
Read: John 16:16–24

I tell you the truth, my Father will give you whatever you ask in my name. Until now you have not asked for anything in my name. Ask and you will receive, and your joy will be complete.
John 16:23–24

Before his crucifixion, Jesus told his disciples that their grief of the moment would turn into joy when they saw him again. He then asked them to pray in his Name so that his Father would answer their prayers and their joy could be complete.

Your life will have power and your prayers will be strong if you live and speak in the name of your Master, writes Joni Eareckson *(Seeking God*, p. 89). On the cross Jesus earned you the privilege of standing in a new relationship to God, of having direct access to his Father in his Name.

Praying in the Name of Jesus means that you will pray like Jesus. Study Jesus' prayers recorded in the Bible carefully – he was always praying for others, he rarely asked anything for himself. He was always ready to submit his will to God's will.

And God listens to and answers your prayers because the Name of his Son is precious to him.

Heavenly Father, thank you that you answer all my prayers when I pray in the Name of your Son. Make me willing to pray unselfishly like Jesus and to submit my will to yours. Amen.

28 April
Reveal your dependence on God in prayer
Read: Matthew 5:3–12

Blessed are the poor in spirit, for theirs is the kingdom of heaven.
Matthew 5:3

Access to God is never obtained by eloquent prayers or a long history of church attendance or religiosity, writes Maretha Maartens. Access to God is possible only via God himself, the Mediator Jesus Christ and the Advocate the Holy Spirit *(Gebed kan jou lewe verander,* p. 47).

To reach God when you pray, you first of all have to realise your own bankruptcy. You have to reach the point where you realise that you do not deserve to receive anything from God, because what he gives you is mercy only. He listens and responds to your prayers only when you are totally dependent on him. Nobody enjoys being dependent on anybody else – or on God. We prefer to solve our own problems. If you still think you can cope by yourself, you have not yet learnt the meaning of dependence.

Dependence means that you will admit that you cannot continue without God; that you are willing to ask and accept his help. Have you reached the stage where you are ready to confess your own dependence on God when you pray? If so, he promises that the kingdom of heaven will be yours!

Heavenly Father, forgive me for wanting to be self-sufficient and independent. I now confess my absolute dependence on you. Thank you for your promise that you will give me the kingdom of heaven. Amen.

29 April
Pray for a miracle
Read: Psalm 4

*Know that God has set apart the godly for himself;
the Lord will hear when I call to him.*
Psalm 4:3

Believers who are desperate should relax in the knowledge that they worship a God of miracles. The psalmist also resigned himself knowing that God would intervene in his desperate situation. He believed that the Lord could indeed perform miracles – as he had experienced in the past.

When we pray and God does not answer, we sometimes think he cannot help us. However, we must remember that God can perform miracles – that nothing is impossible with God. The psalmist had learnt this lesson well. 'Answer me when I call to you, O my righteous God,' he prayed in verse 1. 'Give me relief from my distress; be merciful to me and hear my prayer.'

In Mark 11 Jesus talked to his disciples about the incredible things which could be wrought by prayer. 'I tell you the truth, if anyone says to this mountain, "Go, throw yourself into the sea," and does not doubt in his heart but believes that what he says will happen, it will be done for him' (Mark 11:23).

You may pray for a miracle, provided you believe that God will answer your prayer and provided your prayer request is in line with God's will. He can work a miracle for you, too.

Heavenly Father, I praise you as the God of miracles with whom nothing is impossible. Thank you that you are always able to help me in emergency situations and that you can perform miracles in my life, too. Amen.

30 April
Be filled with God
Read: Ephesians 3:14–20

---

*For this reason I kneel before the Father ... that you may
be filled to the measure of all the fulness of God.*
Ephesians 3:14, 19

The real reason why we pray is to glorify God and not to ask him to give us the things we want. You should therefore praise and glorify God when you pray but also guard against turning your prayers into a long list of requests.

It is impossible to grow spiritually without prayer. When we pray, Paul wrote to the church in Ephesus, we are filled with the fulness of God. He then mentioned the things he requested for them: he prayed that the Father would enable them by his Holy Spirit to have power, together with all the saints, to grasp the love of Jesus. He also asked that they would be filled with the power of the Holy Spirit, with the love of Christ and the fulness of the Father.

Consider the contents of your prayers again. If you had to write down your prayers of the past week, would you be able to show them to your friends with confidence? See to it that your prayers glorify God in future. Refer to Paul's prayers for the Ephesians.

Heavenly Father, forgive me for asking so many things and for so rarely remembering that the real reason for my prayers should be to glorify you. I pray that you will be glorified by my prayers in future. Amen.

May

Prayer in times of trouble

In times of suffering, the best you can do is to pray. 'Call upon me in the day of trouble; I will deliver you, and you will honour me,' God himself said speaking through the psalmist (Psalm 50:15). Not a single child of God will escape hard times, but we also learn our most precious lessons in times of trouble.

Suffering is never the will of God, but he permits it because he wants to teach you and keep you close to him. In times of crisis it sometimes feels as if God is not hearing your prayers, but that is always impossible. He is always there for you. However, he has a purpose with those crises you are experiencing, and in the end he will make all things work together for your good. Trust him to do this and hold on to his promise in Revelation 3:10: 'Since you have kept my command to endure patiently, I will also keep you from the hour of trial …'

1 May
Verbalise your suffering
Read: Job 7:11–17

Therefore I will not keep silent; I will speak out in the anguish of my spirit, I will complain in the bitterness of my soul.
Job 7:11

Job's three friends were trying their best to convince him to confess his sin before God and repent, but Job refused to keep silent about his anguish, he wanted to verbalise his pain and submit it to God. He then also blamed God outright for his distress.

When you are suffering, you do not have to keep your doubts and pain to yourself – you may talk to God about it. God knows you better than you know yourself, and he knows exactly what you are thinking.

It is not wrong to pray about the things which trouble you or the things you cannot understand. Men of God like Jeremiah, Job and David knew how to complain to God and verbalise their suffering.

'I cry aloud to the Lord,' the psalmist wrote in Psalm 142. 'I lift up my voice to the Lord for mercy. I pour out my complaint before him; before him I tell my trouble' (verses 1 and 2).

It not only brings you relief to tell the Lord about your pain and suffering; you may also be assured that he will give you relief as he gave relief to Job, David and Jeremiah – even if you have to wait a long time for his answer.

Heavenly Father, thank you that you know all about my suffering and misery. Lord, I want to tell you about it again. I pray that you will end this suffering. Amen.

2 MAY
Life abounds with thorns
Read: 2 Corinthians 12:6–10

> *To keep me from becoming conceited ... there was given*
> *me a thorn in my flesh ... Three times I pleaded with the Lord*
> *to take it away from me. But he said to me, 'My grace is sufficient for you,*
> *for my power is made perfect in weakness.'*
> 2 Corinthians 12:7–9

Paul prayed three times that the Lord should take away his 'thorn', but God's answer seemed to differ from Paul's request: he promised Paul that his power was made perfect when his children were weak.

Each of us has such a thorn. It could be poor health, problems in the family or financial problems. Perhaps you are also praying that the Lord should take away your personal 'thorn', and he does not answer your prayer. Sometimes God uses the thorns in your life to draw you closer to him. In fact, he wants to use these very thorns to teach you that you cannot cope without him.

Paul found it difficult to accept that God did not want to remove his thorn, but eventually that thorn made him more productive in God's kingdom and also revealed to him God's grace in his life.

Pray about your thorns, but remember that when the Lord does not remove them he might want to use those thorns to reveal his power in your life. Use your thorns as an opportunity to witness like Paul did.

> *Heavenly Father, I cannot understand why you refuse to take away*
> *the thorns in my life. Please teach me that those very thorns are being*
> *used to reveal your power. Amen.*

3 MAY
The best Comforter
Read: 2 Thessalonians 2:13–17

May our Lord Jesus Christ himself and God our Father,
who loved us and by his grace gave us eternal encouragement and good hope,
encourage your hearts and strengthen you in every good deed and word.
2 Thessalonians 2:16–17

After Paul had explained to the church in Thessalonica the terrible fate awaiting the unbelievers, he encouraged them by reminding them of all the things God was doing for them by his grace. He told them that God loved them very much and that he wanted to comfort them with the good news – that they were on their way to a wonderful future.

This message is still addressed to you today. Regardless of how bad your circumstances are at present, you may be comforted with the knowledge that the troubles will not last for ever, and you may also be assured of the fact that God is aware of your problems. 'Nothing in all creation is hidden from God's sight. Everything is uncovered and laid bare before the eyes of him to whom we must give account,' the writer to the Hebrews said (Hebrews 4:13).

God knows you inside out. You cannot hide anything in your life from him, and since he knows you so well, he is the perfect Comforter. Allow him to do this for you!

Heavenly Father, thank you that you are aware of everything in my life
which is hurting me and that you want to comfort me with the
wonderful promise of a future with you. Amen.

4 May
Prayer brings peace
Read: Philippians 4:4–9

Do not be anxious about anything, but in everything, by prayer and petition, with thanksgiving, present your requests to God. And the peace of God, which transcends all understanding, will guard your hearts and your minds in Christ Jesus.
Philippians 4:6–7

All of us tend to be anxious when we are troubled. You lose your appetite as well as your energy, you suffer from sleeplessness – and your anxious thoughts all mulled over in your mind.

There is a simple solution to this problem: tell God about them! Hand those anxieties to him. He wants to take responsibility for each one, but you have to undertake to leave them with him instead of immediately taking them up again and dragging them along. 'Do not worry about things or be anxious,' writes *Die Boodskap*. 'Talk to God about them. Discuss them with him. You will then feel relieved and content because you know that since you belong to Jesus, you will no longer feel upset' (p. 646).

Once you have reached the stage where you have handed your anxieties to God, he gives you his peace in exchange. With God's peace in your life, you have the assurance that he is in control and that you are safe in his hands. This is the best trade you can ever make!

Heavenly Father, I no longer want to postpone exchanging my anxieties for your peace. Thank you that I may know that you are in control of my life, and that you will make all things work together for my good. Amen.

5 May
Pray in times of trouble
Read: James 5:13–18

> *Is any one of you in trouble? He should pray. Is anyone happy? Let him sing songs of praise. The prayer of a righteous man is powerful and effective.*
> James 5:13, 16

If you are experiencing an emotional low, you have to pray, James advised his readers. If you are happy, you should sing songs of praise to God's glory, because the prayer of a righteous man is powerful and effective. 'The way you handle suffering and joy indicates whether God's wisdom has placed you in the right relationship to God. Somebody who is not in the right relationship to God could either be broken by suffering or be driven to unjustifiable and excessive action,' writes *Die Bybel in praktyk* (p. 1942).

If you are at present trapped in a period of suffering, your best move is to consult God about the matter. 'For the Lord gives wisdom, and from his mouth come knowledge and understanding,' the wise writer of Proverbs wrote (Proverbs 2:6). Tell God about everything you find difficult to handle, and ask him to give you the necessary wisdom for each day, so that you will be able to resolve your troubles in the right way.

Heavenly Father, I pray that you will give me the wisdom to discern between right and wrong so that I will be able to handle my problems in the right way with your help. Amen.

6 May
Prayer changes you
Read: Habakkuk 3:17–19

Though the fig-tree does not bud and there are no grapes on the vines, though the olive crop fails and the fields produce no food, though there are no sheep in the pen and no cattle in the stalls, yet I will rejoice in the Lord, I will be joyful in God my Saviour.
Habakkuk 3:17–18

The prophet Habakkuk was praying earnestly to the Lord to do something about the situation in the country. The situation looked desperate: the Chaldeans were destroying the land, but the Lord remained silent …

At the end of the book, the situation was still unchanged, but Habakkuk's prayers had changed him. He could testify: even if the fig-tree failed to bud and there were no grapes to harvest, even if all the livestock were dead, I will still be joyful in the Lord.

You do not always receive what you pray for either. 'It is not a bad sign when we receive exactly the opposite to what we have asked as answer to our prayers,' Martin Luther wrote. 'Likewise it would not be a good sign if we received everything we ask. The reason for this is that God's counsel and will are much higher than our counsel and will.'

You may nevertheless be assured of one thing: God's answer to your prayers will always be what is best for you, even if it differs from what you had asked initially.

Heavenly Father, please enable me to continue believing in you, even when you do not change my circumstances, so that I will be able to rejoice like Habakkuk despite the circumstances. Amen.

7 May
God never changes
Read: Psalm 77:1–11

*I cried out to God for help; I cried out to God to hear me.
To this I will appeal: the years of the right hand of the Most High.
Psalm 77: 1, 10*

The writer of Psalm 77 felt as if God had turned his back on him. Although he called out to God, he was not comforted. He lay awake at night, but to no avail. Worst of all was that he felt God had changed, he felt God was no longer the same as in the past. Then he pelted God with questions: will he never have mercy on him again, has he rejected him for ever, has he forgotten his promises?

In times of trouble you sometimes also feel as if God no longer wants to help you, as if he is no longer the loving Father who used to care for you. Fortunately this can never happen. God never changes – he still loves you as much as ever. 'Jesus Christ is the same yesterday and today and for ever', the writer to the Hebrews says (Hebrews 13:8).

When you pray again and receive no answers, consider the things God has done for you in the past. He is still the same God who works miracles. He can (and will!) help you now like he has always done in the past.

Heavenly Father, forgive me for sometimes thinking that you have changed, that you no longer hear my prayers and that you no longer want to help me. Thank you for the assurance that you remain the same, now and for ever. Amen.

8 May

God cares!
Read: Psalm 39

Hear my prayer, O Lord, listen to my cry for help; be not deaf to my weeping. For I dwell with you as an alien, a stranger.
Psalm 39:12

In Psalm 39 David at first tried not to complain to God, but gradually his suffering overwhelmed him and as had happened so often before, he had to beseech God to help him. 'My heart grew hot within me, and as I meditated, the fire burned; then I spoke with my tongue,' he wrote in verse 3. He pleaded with God to help him, because he was his only hope. 'Be not deaf to my weeping, for I dwell with you as an alien,' he pleaded in our verse.

However, David did not have to be anxious that God was not aware of his tears. The Bible assures us time and again that God really cares for his children. He loves each one of us as if each of us were an only child. He is aware of your suffering – that is when he carries you, calls you by name, when he is always with you to help and support you.

'Record my lament; list my tears on your scroll – are they not in your record?' David confessed in Psalm 56:8. When you look to the Lord in times of trouble, you may be sure of one thing: God does not ignore your tears. He is aware of every single tear.

Heavenly Father, thank you that you care for me, that you see my pain and that you are aware of every tear I shed. Please comfort me today. Amen.

9 May
When you are ill
Read: 2 Kings 20:1–11

This is what the Lord says: 'I have heard your prayer and seen your tears; I will heal you. On the third day from now you will go up to the temple of the Lord.'
2 Kings 20:5

When King Hezekiah fell seriously ill, he prayed to the Lord – and God heard his prayer and not only healed him, but added another fifteen years to his life. As a sign, Hezekiah asked that the Lord make the shadow go back ten steps, which it did. Hezekiah prayed for a miracle and he asked the Lord for a sign, and God answered both prayers.

Unfortunately our prayers are not always answered to the letter as in the case of Hezekiah's prayers. When you are ill, and you pray for healing, you have to be grateful if the Lord answers your prayer. However, not everybody is healed after praying. When you pray and still remain ill, try to find out what the Lord wants to teach you by your illness. Ask him to show you how your illness could bring you closer to him and make you a better witness for him.

Catherine Marshall had to spend months in bed. At first it was very difficult for her to accept this, but she gradually realised that she had much more time to spend with the Lord so that her illness eventually became a plus because it brought her closer to the Lord.

Heavenly Father, I pray that you will heal me, but if this is not your will, that you will use this illness to teach me valuable lessons for life so that I will draw closer to you. Amen.

10 May
Illness to God's glory
Read: John 11:1–11

When he heard this, Jesus said, 'This sickness will not end in death.
No, it is for God's glory so that God's Son may be glorified through it.'
John 11:4

When Martha and Mary sent word to Jesus asking him to come to Bethany because their brother Lazarus was seriously ill, Jesus did something strange. He delayed until it was too late to heal Lazarus. Jesus' action must have been incomprehensible to Martha and Mary, because they knew that he had loved their brother, and that he could have healed him. Jesus did not heal Lazarus, but he did something far greater: he raised him from the dead. As Jesus had in fact told his disciples, Lazarus' illness did not end in death, but revealed the power of God and God was glorified through it.

Sometimes God uses your illness to reveal his power and glory. When you pray for healing without being healed, the Lord may have something better in mind for you personally. Be prepared to wait upon the Lord when you are ill. Be a witness for him on your sickbed. Perhaps God wants to give you an even greater revelation of his power through his silence.

Heavenly Father, help me to be a witness for you when I am ill.
Please make me willing to wait upon you so that my illness
will also become a revelation of your power. Amen.

11 May
God listens to your cry for help
Read: Psalm 40:1–7

I waited patiently for the Lord; he turned to me and heard my cry.
He lifted me out of the slimy pit ... he set my feet on a rock.
Psalm 40:1, 2

Psalm 40 is a prayer for help in a time of crisis. The psalmist confessed that he had already experienced God's saving power before, and asked him to do it again so that he could sing him a hymn of praise again.

In times of crises, it is very difficult to wait patiently. You want the Lord to listen to you immediately and to respond to your prayers. Although God sometimes lets us wait for his answer, he always hears when his children pray.

When in trouble, you may call to God with confidence. He hears your cries for help, and he will always lift you out of 'the slimy pit' David refers to and set your feet on a rock. When this happens, you should praise God as the psalmist did in verse 5: 'Many, O Lord my God, are the wonders you have done. The things you planned for us no-one can recount to you.'

Heavenly Father, thank you for helping me in the past.
I now pray that you will hear my cry for help again, and that
you will make me willing to wait for your answer. Amen.

12 May
When your feet are slipping …
Read: Psalm 94:12–22

When I said, 'My foot is slipping,' your love, O Lord, supported me. When anxiety was great within me, your consolation brought joy to my soul.
Psalm 94:18–19

In this psalm the psalmist witnessed to his personal experience that the Lord had always assisted him in crisis situations in the past. Even when his feet started slipping, God's love supported him, when he was anxious, God comforted him.

Children of God also experience times of doubt, even when they know from past experience that God has always helped them. Sometimes you pray fervently for months on end without receiving the things you ask (which you have sincerely regarded as the will of the Lord). At such times it is perfectly natural for Christians, even those close to God, to be filled with fear and anxiety, doubt and discouragement.

Should you experience another crisis which makes your feet slip, hold God's hand tightly, even if you do not receive answers to all your questions. He wants to be your fortress as he was to the psalmist; he is the rock where you may always take refuge, regardless of the circumstances (verse 22).

Heavenly Father, at the moment I really cannot understand why you are not answering my prayers. You know my feet are slipping, Lord. Please support me by your love. Amen.

13 May
Believe like a child
Read: Matthew 18:1–15

> *He called a little child and had him stand among them. And he said: 'I tell you the truth, unless you change and become like little children, you will never enter the kingdom of heaven.'*
> Matthew 18:2–3

Humility and unwavering faith are two of the most characteristic qualities of children. They believe implicitly that the Lord will give them the things they ask of him.

Years ago our beach cottage at Struisbaai was nearly burnt down. The flames came so close that we had to evacuate the house. Our nine-year-old son assured us that he had prayed and that the house would not be burnt down. When the flames were practically on top of our house, the wind suddenly veered at an angle of 90 degrees and the house remained untouched. That evening as we were replacing everything, the lad said, 'Now why wouldn't you believe me when I said the house would not burn down?' I am still convinced that our house was saved because our eldest son had believed that the Lord would answer his prayer.

If you can pray in faith like a child, the Lord will also answer your prayer requests and, what is more, you will also enter the kingdom of heaven!

Heavenly Father, please forgive me for sometimes praying without faith. Give me the pure faith of a child so that I will enter your kingdom. Amen.

14 May
When you cannot fall asleep
Read: Job 7:10–11

When I lie down I think, 'How long before I get up?'
The night drags on, and I toss till dawn.
Job 7:4

When you are anxious, you sometimes battle to fall asleep. During Job's time of trouble, he confessed: 'When I lie down, I think, "How long before I get up? The night drags on, and I toss till dawn."' As I tend to wake up at about three in the morning and then lie awake for a couple of hours before I drop off again, I have sympathy with Job! While David fled before his son Absalom, he also battled to fall asleep.

However, something can be done about sleeplessness. If you wake up at night and you cannot fall asleep again, talk to God. Pray for your loved ones and for people in crisis situations. Then ask God to give you peace of mind and count your blessings instead of sheep! Think about God's loving care in the past – you will then find that you will soon fall asleep again. You could even say with David: 'I lie down and sleep; I wake again, because the Lord sustains me. From the Lord comes deliverance' (Psalm 3:5, 8).

Heavenly Father, thank you that I may talk to you when I lie awake at night. Give me peace and please put an end to the sleeplessness. Amen.

15 May
Weep no more!
Read: Isaiah 30:18–21

*O people of Zion, who live in Jerusalem, you will weep no more.
How gracious he will be when you cry for help!
As soon as he hears, he will answer you.*
Isaiah 30:19

God's people were in such a desperate situation that they could not stop weeping. However, they did have a choice: God promised to have mercy upon them if they would cry to him for help. God still wants to help his children in times of crisis. He wants to have mercy upon us and answer our prayers.

During a time of crisis in our family, this verse became very precious to me. Ironically, the Lord did not answer my prayers, but he nevertheless gave me the grace to work through the painful situation.

You also have the assurance that God wants to help you, that he will hear your prayers when you cry out to him.

Sometimes he wants to teach you very precious lessons for life by bringing extremely difficult circumstances into your life. 'Although the Lord gives you the bread of adversity and the water of affliction, your teachers will be hidden no more,' Isaiah writes (Isaiah 30:20). If you experience difficult times again – weep no more. Trust the Lord to answer your prayers. He promises that he will do so as soon as he hears them. Take the beautiful promise in Revelation 21:3 to heart: one day in heaven he will wipe every tear from your eyes!

Lord, I find it difficult to understand why I am suffering so much right now. I pray that you will help me to stop weeping. Thank you for your promise that you will wipe away all my tears one day. Amen.

16 May
The suffering has become too much
Read: Psalm 88:1–3, 9 and 13–14

O Lord, the God who saves me, day and night I cry out before you.
May my prayer come before you; turn your ear to my cry.
For my soul is full of trouble and my life draws near the grave.
Psalm 88:1–3

Psalm 88 is regarded as the most melancholic prayer in the Bible. It sounds as if the psalmist was suffering from severe depression! He prayed repeatedly: 'day and night I cry out before you' (verse 2) because his troubles were just too much to bear. He felt as if he were dying, he had no energy, he was trapped in a deep pit. In brief, he felt God had deserted him, and wanted to know why God had rejected him and withdrawn from him (verse 14). Unlike the other psalms which also start on a melancholic note, this psalm does not even end with hope.

The feeling that God is far away in times of crisis is not new. All of us experience times in our lives when we really feel that the suffering has become too much to bear. Times when God feels like a stranger, far away. When you feel like that, all you can do is ask the Lord's help. Ultimately he will hear and answer your prayers because he is the God 'who saves' (verse 1).

Lord, the suffering has become too much to bear; I cannot continue.
It also feels as if you have rejected me. Thank you for being the God
who always saves me – please save me now!

17 May
Pray in your day of trouble
Read: Psalm 86:1–13

In the day of my trouble I will call to you, for you will answer me.
For you are great and do marvellous deeds.
Psalm 86:7, 10

Like Psalm 88, Psalm 86 is also a lamentation in which the psalmist beseeches God to help him. We may also go to the Lord with confidence to ask for help in times of crisis, provided we never lose sight of the fact that the promises in the Bible are intended for God's children only.

It is all very well to ask the Lord's help in your personal emergency situations, but you should not keep him around for emergency situations only. It has been said that prayer should be the steering wheel of our lives and not the spare wheel. If you only pray when you experience crises, it is most unlikely that the Lord will answer your prayers. You should therefore be faithful in prayer even when all is well. Build a relationship with the Lord, then he will hear when you call out to him in times of trouble. After he has delivered you, you will also be able to praise him like the psalmist in verses 12 and 13: 'I will praise you, O Lord my God, with all my heart; I will glorify your name for ever. For great is your love towards me; you have delivered me from the depths of the grave.'

Heavenly Father, forgive me for praying so much more in bad times than in good times. Thank you for always hearing me when I cry, and for always delivering me. Amen.

18 May
God is your hiding-place
Read: Psalm 32

---

*Therefore let everyone who is godly pray to you while you may be found ...
you are my hiding-place.*
Psalm 32:6–7

God is called the hiding-place or refuge of his children in various passages in the Bible. 'The eternal God is your refuge, and underneath are the everlasting arms,' Moses said (Deuteronomy 33:27). The psalmist also called God a 'hiding-place' or 'refuge' in several psalms. 'The Lord is my rock, my fortress and my deliverer; my God is my rock, in whom I take refuge,' David wrote in Psalm 18:2. 'He will cover you with his feathers, and under his wings you will find refuge; his faithfulness will be your shield and rampart,' he promised in Psalm 91:4. All his life, Israel's poet-king also relied on the protection of this God who was his refuge.

God still undertakes to protect his children, to be their refuge in times of trouble and danger. And all of us need a refuge – a place of safety where we can always find help. God wants to be your refuge, a rock where you can hide. He sends his angels to protect you in times of danger. You may therefore underline the wonderful promise in Psalm 32:10 in your Bible: 'The Lord's unfailing love surrounds the man who trusts in him.'

Heavenly Father, I praise you for being my refuge, for protecting me in danger. Thank you for also delivering me from evil. Amen.

19 May
Call when you are in trouble
Read: Psalm 10:1–12

Why, O Lord, do you stand far off? Why do you hide yourself in times of trouble? Lift up your hand, O God. Do not forget the helpless.
Psalm 10:1, 12

When the psalmist wrote this psalm, he was in such a desperate situation that he felt as if God was standing far off, as if the God who had always helped him in the past had now withdrawn from him, as if God had forgotten him.

The psalmists often called to God in times of trouble, and they invariably found that God was always there, that he was aware of all their pain and suffering. In the psalm for today, David therefore also pleaded that God should come as in the past and demonstrate his power, that he should not forget the helpless.

You may also call to God when you are in trouble. When you discover that you cannot do anything about your negative circumstances, those times when you realise your own helplessness, God is still there for you. He is perfectly willing to help, as he has always been willing to do in the past. Like the psalmist, you should know that your help can only come from the Lord. God is tuned in to you and aware of your troubles, particularly in times of discouragement. He wants to answer your prayers and give you peace.

Heavenly Father, thank you that I may call to you when I am really in trouble with the assurance that you will listen to me, that you will answer my prayer and end my sadness. Amen.

20 MAY
Your Father knows
Read: Psalm 10:13–18

But you, O God, do see trouble and grief; you consider it to take it in hand. You hear, O Lord, the desire of the afflicted; you encourage them, and you listen to their cry.
Psalm 10:14, 17

Here the psalmist was really in a crisis situation – he felt God was not even listening to him, God had withdrawn from him. 'Why, O Lord, do you stand far off? Why do you hide yourself in times of trouble?' he asked in verse 1. Then he compared the prosperity of the wicked with his own suffering and found it even more difficult to understand why he had to suffer so much. He nevertheless eventually realised that God never deserts his children – that he is aware of all our problems, every detail of our suffering – that he holds us in his arms when we suffer. Then he said in verse 14: 'But you, O God, do see trouble and grief; you consider it to take it in hand.'

Your Father knows every detail of your circumstances, even before you start praying. If you are suffering at the moment, you should know that God is aware of you. He knows your sadness and your problems. He is with you when you suffer, even if you sometimes feel he is far off. He also promises to take your suffering in hand in his own time and in his own way. Trust him to do so!

Heavenly Father, thank you that you know everything about me, that you also know the problems I am battling with at present. Please help me to resolve each of them. Amen.

21 May
When God withdraws
Read: Psalm 30

*When you hid your face, I was dismayed.
To you, O Lord, I called; to the Lord I cried for mercy.*
Psalm 30:7–8

In times of extraordinary affliction – if you lose a loved one or your job, or if you yourself are seriously ill – when circumstances are really desperate, even believers feel as if God no longer listens to their prayers, as if he has withdrawn from them, as if he no longer loves or cares about them as in the past.

In Psalm 30 David experienced similar emotions. He felt as if God had withdrawn from him. Perhaps you have also felt like this at times. You should then know that this can never be true. God is always there for you. He loves you, particularly in times of crises, he wants to help and assist you, even when you feel he is far off. God himself lives in you by his Holy Spirit – he is therefore never far away or deaf to your prayers.

A time of crisis is the very time to pray and to know – even when you feel God is not listening – that you never have to rely on your feelings but that you have to rely on God's promises. Rely on those promises in bad times – crises always end on a positive note for God's children. God will never withdraw from you.

David had the same experience: 'You turned my wailing into dancing; you removed my sackcloth and clothed me with joy,' he said in verse 11. Trust God in times of crises, pray to him, and he will fulfil this promise in your own life, too.

Heavenly Father, thank you that you are there for me in crisis situations, that you always listen to me and help me. I pray that you will remove my sackcloth once again and clothe me with joy. Amen.

22 May
God carries you
Read: Deuteronomy 1:19–32

Do not be terrified; do not be afraid of them ... in the desert ... you saw how the Lord your God carried you, as a father carries his son, all the way ...
Deuteronomy 1:29, 31

While they were wandering in the desert for forty years, God's people experienced daily that the Lord was carrying them. By day he was visibly present in their midst by means of a cloud and by night by means of a column of fire. He provided enough food and water for them, he protected them against their enemies and even saw to it that their clothes and shoes did not wear out (Nehemiah 9:21). He also provided laws which they had to obey. He provided for them in detail.

If you belong to God, you share in God's promises to his people. He promises to be present in your life every day and to provide for you, help you and protect you. God then also repeats this promise, in the words of the prophet Isaiah, that he will always carry them: 'Even to your old age and grey hairs I am he, I am he who will sustain you. I have made you and I will carry you; I will sustain you and I will rescue you' (Isaiah 46:4).

God wants to carry you from today if you run into troubles – but then you have to ask him and permit him to do so.

Heavenly Father, I pray that you will carry me when the path of life becomes too steep and too dangerous for me. Thank you for knowing that you are always with me. Amen.

23 May
When the spirit grows faint ...
Read: Psalm 142

*I cry aloud to the Lord; I lift up my voice to the Lord for mercy.
I pour out my complaint before him; before him I tell my trouble.
When my spirit grows faint within me ...*
Psalm 142:1–3

David was in a desperate situation when he wrote this psalm – he had to flee for his life and was hiding in a cave from King Saul. The discouraged David nevertheless knew what to do in his crisis – he took it to God in prayer. When he submitted his case to the Lord, he knew that the Lord would help him once again as he had always helped him in the past.

When things go wrong in your life, it is easy to become discouraged like the psalmist. If you are also experiencing a time of major crisis at present, you could follow David's recipe to your advantage. Tell the Lord about your anxiety – he wants to be your refuge and be good to you, as he was to his servant David. He promises to renew your courage if you are discouraged: 'Say to those with fearful hearts, "Be strong, do not fear; your God will come ... he will come to save you"', the prophet Isaiah wrote (Isaiah 35:4). Claim this promise for yourself today!

*Heavenly Father, you know I am really discouraged today.
Please strengthen and help me. Thank you for the promise
that you will renew my courage. Amen.*

24 May
Pray when your spirit fails
Read: Psalm 143

---

*I spread out my hands to you; my soul thirsts for you like a parched land.
Answer me quickly, O Lord; my spirit fails.*
Psalm 143:6–7

David was once again in a desperate situation while he was writing this psalm. He told the Lord that his spirit was failing and asked that God should answer him quickly. He realised that he was not completely innocent. In verse 2 he asked that God should not institute a court case against him, because he was not innocent. Yet he appealed to God's mercy. He believed that God would help him again as in the past (verses 3–6). He once again put his trust in the Lord.

Sometimes you also experience situations which ruin your positive attitude, which exhaust you completely. At other times you are merely tired and discouraged as a result of everything your family and your work demand of you. When this happens, you may, like the psalmist, ask the Lord to make his wonderworking power available to you to show you the right way, to help you as before, to let you experience his love every day. You may hope with confidence that God will deliver you. Those who trust in the Lord will not hope in vain.

*Heavenly Father, you know that I am totally exhausted at the moment.
Please help me, give me the necessary energy so that I can continue,
let me experience your love again so that I can continue hoping
for your deliverance. Amen.*

25 May
Cry out to the Lord
Read: Exodus 14:10–30

Then the Lord said to Moses, 'Why are you crying out to me?
Tell the Israelites to move on.'
Exodus 14:15

In this chapter the Israelites were really caught between a rock and a hard place. Pharaoh's army was pursuing them and the Sea of Reeds was lying before them. They obviously had cause for concern. However, the Lord did not think so – he asked Moses why the people were crying out to him in desperation. Moses himself trusted God. 'Do not be afraid,' he encouraged the people in verses 13 and 14. 'Stand firm and you will see the deliverance the Lord will bring you today … The Lord will fight for you; you need only to be still.'

We all know the result of the Israelites' cry to God – God did a miracle so that his people were able to pass through the sea on dry ground while all the Egyptians were destroyed when they tried to do the same.

If you belong to the Lord, you may know without a shadow of doubt that it does not matter how desperate your present situation is, you do not have to cry out to God in terror. It is right to pray, but pray in faith. God can still work miracles. He is on your side, and he is able to deliver you from every desperate situation that could overtake you.

Heavenly Father, thank you that I may pray when I feel desperate, knowing that you are with me, and knowing that you can and will save me from any crisis situation. Amen.

26 MAY
Out of the depths
Read: Psalm 130

Out of the depths I cry to you, O Lord; O Lord, hear my voice.
Psalm 130:1

David was once again in the depths of despair! However, as always, he called to the Lord from the depths. And the Lord gave him the answer which he wrote down in verse 5: 'In his word I put my trust'. Praying is not enough, praying without absolute trust in God cannot succeed. David therefore verbalises his trust: he puts his trust in the Lord, he is willing (even in the depths of despair!) to wait for the Lord to keep his word.

If you are in the depths of despair or depression, call out to God and trust him like David did. However, trusting him will require that you also hold on to God's promises even if not a single promise has been fulfilled for you yet. You will also have to believe that God will answer all your prayers, that you will know that God will ultimately make all things work together for your good – even these crises and problems you are struggling with. You will also have to be willing to wait for the fulfilment of God's promises in your life.

If you do this, you will be able to say with David: 'Even though I walk through the valley of the shadow of death, I will fear no evil, for you are with me; your rod and your staff, they comfort me' (Psalm 23:4).

Heavenly Father, thank you that I may call to you for help out of the depths. Please make me willing to trust you and to hold on to your promises. Amen.

27 May
Trust in God's love
Read: Psalm 13

How long, O Lord? Will you forget me for ever? How long will you hide your face from me? But I trust in your unfailing love; my heart rejoices in your salvation.
Psalm 13:1, 5

The psalmist felt as if the Lord was aloof, as if the Lord had forgotten him. He nevertheless refused to lose courage. He held on to God's love tenaciously and trusted him to deliver him – although this deliverance had not yet come to pass.

Although this psalm at first had a ring of despondency, the conclusion proved the expectation of a believer. While the psalmist saw only his own difficult circumstances, it seemed as if the Lord no longer cared, but as soon as he looked away from his own misery and looked to God, he once again became aware of God's love and mercy.

God loves you far too much to forget or ignore you. If negative circumstances make you doubt God's love, you should know that God is aware of you. 'For the eyes of the Lord range throughout the earth to strengthen those whose hearts are fully committed to him,' it says in 2 Chronicles 16:9. Look away from your hopeless circumstances and focus on God. His eyes are on you – he is looking to see where he can help you right now. He will give you the help you desire at the right time.

Heavenly Father, thank you that you never ignore me, but that you are always watching me to see where I need help. I praise you for always delivering me. Amen.

28 May
A compassionate heart
Read: 2 Corinthians 1:3–11

[He] comforts us in all our troubles, so that we can comfort those in any trouble with the comfort we ourselves have received from God.
2 Corinthians 1:4

When you have experienced a disaster yourself, others have more confidence to share their problems with you. Some time ago our family had to work through the pain of a divorce. We prayed together for months, but received no answers to our prayers. This was really confusing, particularly since we were convinced that the things we were asking God were in accordance with his will. However, eventually we had to discover that this painful experience had taught us a new compassion for others. Practically every family experiences a similar crisis when one bears in mind that one in three marriages in South Africa ends in a divorce court and there are about three children per family.

After our own painful experience, we were able to reach out to people who had had the same experience. 'Many blessings flow from the trials of life to those who have been through the mill. One of the most important is probably a compassionate heart,' Esperance Kelber writes.

If you have therefore been hurt, use that experience to help others and reach out to them.

Heavenly Father, thank you that you comfort me in times of suffering, and that you want to use me to comfort others by means of the lessons which I have learnt in my pain. Amen.

29 May
Wisdom in times of trial
Read: James 1:2–8

If any of you lacks wisdom, he should ask God, who gives generously to all without finding fault, and it will be given to him.
James 1:5

When you need wisdom, you may ask God to give it to you, James wrote, and he will give it to you. However, there is a condition: you have to pray in faith.

In times of trouble you often do not know how to handle the problem which confronts you. The solution to this problem is that you should always ask God for the necessary wisdom. Biblical wisdom is not the same as a high IQ – it will not make you more clever physically. Biblical wisdom means that God will help you to discern between right and wrong so that you will be able to make the right decisions. This wisdom will improve your quality of life dramatically.

Godly wisdom requires that you pray before you act and only the Lord can give you this kind of wisdom. Are you in a crisis situation today? Then ask the Lord to give you insight as to how you should act. Then believe that he will enable you to handle your difficult circumstances correctly.

Heavenly Father, I pray that you will give me the right insight so that I will know how to handle this crisis situation correctly. Thank you for the assurance that you give wisdom 'generously to all without finding fault'. Amen.

30 May
Do not doubt
Read: James 1:2–6

---

*If any of you lacks wisdom, he should ask God, who gives
generously to all without finding fault, and it will be given to him.
But when he asks, he must believe and not doubt ...*
James 1:5–6

Prayer should always be rooted in faith. According to James, faith always goes hand in hand with works. For example, if you are praying to pass your exam and you are studying as little as possible, God will not give you what you are asking. You must indeed pray and believe, but do your share as well!

God wants you to be happy, therefore he will not refuse you his wisdom when you ask him. Do you believe that God will answer your prayers? Are your prayers self-centred or do they concern God's honour? The main motive of your prayers should always be God's glory and not the fulfilment of your own selfish desires. God's answer to your prayers may be delayed if your motives are not right.

Before you pray, you should therefore check whether you are praying with the right motives as well as in faith.

If so, I should like to pray for you with Paul 'that the glorious Father may give you the Spirit of wisdom and revelation, so that you may know him better' (Ephesians 1:17).

*Heavenly Father, please purify my motives when I pray so that my
prayers will not be selfish, but will always be to your honour and glory.
Help me to overcome my unbelief. Amen.*

31 May
When God fails to answer
Read: Job 30:20–31

I cry out to you, O God, but you do not answer;
I stand up, but you merely look at me.
Job 30:20

In his desperation with regard to all the disasters which had struck him, Job tried in vain to communicate with God. He found time and again that God was not listening to him or answering him. When disasters strike, you could experience the same feelings as Job did in the above passage.

However, the reality of God's absence was experienced only once in history, and that happened on the cross when God turned his back on Jesus. Jesus is the only Person who has ever been forsaken by God, and he experienced this terrible absence of God so that you and I never have to be without God again.

When you therefore feel as if God is not answering your prayers, as if he is not there for you, you are wrong. Continue praying – God will answer your prayers in his own time and answer you the way he answered Job in the last chapter of the book of Job.

Job learnt that his suffering was the very means God was using to teach him to see God. This may also be true in your case.

Heavenly Father, forgive me if crises sometimes make me doubt your presence. Thank you for the assurance that you will never forsake me, but that you will always help me. Amen.

June

Jesus and prayer

Jesus is the greatest authority on prayer. While he was on earth, he regularly set aside time for prayer. 'But Jesus often withdrew to lonely places and prayed,' Luke said (Luke 5:16). He is our High Priest who intercedes for us before God. At their request, Jesus also taught his disciples to pray correctly. He was the one who, by his death on the cross, made it possible for sinners to communicate with a holy God. Each of us could learn a great deal about prayer if we were to model our own prayers on the prayers of Jesus, as recorded in the Bible.

This month we will focus on Jesus' prayers. He understood the real purpose of prayer. He asked very little for himself – his main objective was always that the Name of the Father should be glorified and that the will of his Father be done.

Once you have learnt to pray in this way, God will also answer your prayers as faithfully as he had answered the prayers of his Son.

1 June
When the Son asks …
Read: Psalm 2

> *You are my Son; today I have become your Father.*
> *Ask of me, and I will make the nations your inheritance.*
> Psalm 2:7–8

Psalm 2 is one of the royal psalms in which some aspect of the ancient kings of Israel is always highlighted. After the royal period these psalms were used to describe the reign of the Messiah. In Psalm 2 the kingship of Jesus is confirmed. He is the Son of God, and God would therefore give him the whole earth as possession should he ask this of God.

Jesus was involved in the creation right from the start. 'In these last days he has spoken to us by his Son, whom he appointed heir of all things, and through whom he made the universe,' reports the writer of Hebrews (Hebrews 1:2). By his death on the cross, he makes it possible for all who believe in him to be children of God – and, what is more, we are now heirs, co-heirs, with Jesus. Through Jesus, God becomes our Father, a Father who meets all the needs of his children. A Father we may approach with confidence to ask everything we need.

As God answered his Son's prayers, he will also answer your prayer requests because Jesus has made it possible for you to pray.

Lord Jesus, thank you that you have made it possible for me to be God's child, and that, with you, I may be an heir of God's abundance. Amen.

2 June
A sacrifice of atonement
Read: Romans 3:21–31

For all have sinned and fall short of the glory of God, and are justified freely by his grace through the redemption that came by Christ Jesus. God presented him as a sacrifice of atonement, through faith in his blood.
Romans 3:23–25

Jesus makes answer to prayer possible for us. God is perfectly holy – as sinners we can never reach him except through Jesus. On the cross, Jesus became a sacrifice of atonement for everybody who believes in him – he died so that we may have life, life eternal. He paid the price for our sin once and for all, therefore we are free, because God was prepared to forgive our sin on account of his Son's death of atonement.

'Therefore he is able to save completely those who come to God through him, because he always lives to intercede for them,' the writer of Hebrews says (Hebrews 7:25).

Jesus therefore not only makes it possible for you to pray to God because he has paid for your sin, he himself also prays for you. He intercedes for you before God, so that God will be sympathetic to you and listen to your stammering prayers.

Lord Jesus, how can I thank you for having made it possible for me to pray to God because you paid the penalty for my sin on the cross? I praise you that you are also praying for me. Amen.

3 June
Jesus, our High Priest
Read: Hebrews 4:14–5:3

> *For we do not have a high priest who is unable to sympathise with our weaknesses ... Let us then approach the throne of grace with confidence, so that we may receive mercy and find grace to help us in our time of need.*
> Hebrews 4:15–16

In Old Testament times the high priest had to act as mediator between the people and God. As God was holy, the Israelites could not speak to him themselves, and the priest offered a sacrifice to God on their and his behalf to obtain forgiveness of their sin.

God himself appointed Jesus High Priest. However, Jesus is a High Priest without sin. By his death on the cross he makes it possible for you and me to communicate with God directly, without a mediator. Since he has obtained this blessing for you, you may now approach God's throne of grace with confidence with the assurance that you will be helped on account of Jesus' sacrifice on the cross. Through Jesus, God is now your Father, too, and you are an heir of his glory. And since Jesus was human like you, he also knows your human weaknesses, and he sympathises with us. When you pray, you may therefore be assured that God will answer your prayers, just as an earthly father would grant the requests of his child.

> *Lord Jesus, thank you that I may approach God's throne of grace with confidence because you have obtained this privilege for me by your death on the cross. Amen.*

4 JUNE
Free access to God
Read: Hebrews 10:19–25

Therefore, brothers, since we have confidence to enter the Most Holy Place by the blood of Jesus, by a new and living way opened for us through the curtain, that is, his body ...
Hebrews 10:19–20

By his death on the cross, Jesus opened a new way for us to God. This way is Jesus' body broken for us on the cross. This way is new and leads to eternal life, and it passes through the curtain.

A heavy curtain always separated the Holy Place from the Most Holy Place of the temple. God set apart the Most Holy Place of the temple for himself, and only the high priest was permitted to enter this place once a year to offer a sacrifice to atone for the sin of the people. When Jesus died on the cross, the curtain was torn as proof that the distance between God and man had been bridged by Jesus' death on the cross (Mark 15:38). He himself is the propitiation of our sin, therefore we may now approach God directly, without the mediation of the high priest.

As by his death Jesus has removed the distance between you and God, you have free access to God and you may now talk to God directly when you pray, and he forgives your sin on account of his Son's death on the cross.

Lord Jesus, thank you that I may now talk to God directly because, by your body, you have opened a new way for me to God and broken down the barrier between us for ever. Amen.

5 June
Draw near to God ...
Read: Hebrews 10:19–25

Let us draw near to God with a sincere heart in full assurance of faith, having our hearts sprinkled to cleanse us from a guilty conscience and having our bodies washed with pure water.
Hebrews 10:22

In view of everything Jesus has done for you as High Priest and Mediator, you may now draw near to God with confidence when you pray. Sinners can still reach God in one way only, that is, by Jesus, the Mediator. He himself says in John 14:6, 'I am the way and the truth and the life. No-one comes to the Father except through me.' Jesus is still the only way to heaven.

The writer to the Hebrews mentions four reasons why you are permitted to pray:

- you have free access to the sanctuary through Jesus' blood;
- you have Jesus as great High Priest over the house of God;
- your heart has been cleansed from a guilty conscience; and
- your body has been washed with pure water (verses 19–22).

You should not, therefore, postpone the experience of drawing near to God by making contact with him personally through prayer. Draw near to him with a sincere heart and with full assurance of faith. He is already waiting impatiently to have mercy upon you!

Heavenly Father, thank you that I may make contact with you personally, because Jesus' blood has made that access available to me. Please forgive me all my sin, so that I may stand before you with a pure conscience. I pray this in the Name of your Son. Amen.

6 June
Through faith in him ...
Ephesians 3:6–13

In him and through faith in him we may approach God with freedom and confidence.
Ephesians 3:12

God gave Paul the ability to take his gospel to people who had never heard of him before. Without the power of God he would not have been able to accomplish anything, Paul admitted. However, thanks to Jesus, he could now approach God with confidence.

God wants to use you in his kingdom like he used Paul. If you are willing, he will equip you with his power to be his witness. It is a wonderful privilege to have an intimate relationship with God the Creator and to be able to approach him in prayer because you know he loves you and listens to you. 'You therefore do not have to be afraid of the Lord, or feel ill at ease about the privilege of approaching him directly,' writes *Die Bybel in praktyk*. 'Christ gave his life to prepare the way for you. Use it fully!' (p. 1828).

However, two things are required to be able to pray: you have to be committed to Jesus, have an intimate relationship with him, and really believe he is the Son of God. Only then may you kneel to pray, only then may you talk to God with freedom and in confidence.

Lord Jesus, please help me to work on my relationship with you daily, and strengthen my weak faith so that I may approach God with freedom and confidence when I pray. Amen.

7 June
Jesus made time to pray alone
Read: Matthew 14:22–23

After he had dismissed them, he went up on a mountainside by himself to pray. When evening came, he was there alone.
Matthew 14:23

Prayer always involves two people: God and the person who is praying. Prayer is a personal encounter between two people who love each other and you should draw aside to meet God in prayer. Jesus often did that – he sent the people away and sought solitude when he wanted to talk to his Father. 'But Jesus often withdrew to lonely places and prayed,' Luke wrote (Luke 5:16).

It must have been difficult for Jesus to find time to be alone in the midst of the crowds of people – yet he always made an effort to spend time alone with his Father.

You may not permit your overloaded programme to result in a diluted prayer life. You will need to discipline yourself to make time for God in your busy day. However, it is vital that you sometimes send away other people in order to be alone with God. To be able to listen to his voice in silence, to have fellowship with him. When you do this, you have the assurance that God himself will meet you and refresh you.

Heavenly Father, you know that I sometimes find it difficult to make time for you alone. Thank you for refreshing me spiritually during my time of prayer. Amen.

8 June
Jesus' prayers are answered
Read: Hebrews 5:6–10

During the days of Jesus' life on earth, he offered up prayers and petitions with loud cries and tears to the one who could save him from death, and he was heard because of his reverent submission.
Hebrews 5:7

While Jesus was on earth, he was always in touch with his Father. And his Father heard the prayer requests of his Son because Jesus obeyed him in everything, and always submitted his requests to the will of the Father. Jesus' prayers to his Father are heard because of his reverent submission to God. Jesus learned obedience from what he suffered, 'the way a father teaches his son obedience through discipline,' writes *Die Bybellennium* (p. 1685). By his implicit obedience he earns his Father's answer to his prayers.

In this way Jesus becomes our source of salvation, yours and mine – by believing in him we may approach God and also have eternal life one day.

Since Jesus is our High Priest who makes intercession before God on our behalf, who 'offers up prayers and petitions with tears', he makes it possible for the heavenly Father to hear our prayers. On account of his sacrifice we may now approach God and experience his grace and mercy first-hand in our lives.

Lord Jesus, teach me to be as obedient as you were.
Thank you that by your obedience to the Father,
you have earned me the right to pray. Amen.

9 June
Jesus chooses his disciples
Read: Luke 6:12–16

One of those days Jesus went out to a mountainside to pray, and spent the night praying to God. When morning came, he called his disciples to him and chose twelve of them, whom he also designated apostles.
Luke 6:12–13

Before Jesus had to make important decisions, he always discussed them with his Father. Prayer was the way Jesus prepared for what was to happen. Before he chose his disciples, he spent a whole night in prayer with God, said Luke. He acknowledged God in every decision he had to make – and he himself also said: 'The Son can do nothing by himself' (John 5:19). Since Jesus always consulted his Father, everything he did on earth was in line with the will of the Father, and also blessed by the Father.

What is your position? Do you pray before you make important decisions, or do you first decide what is most convenient or best for you before you consult God? 'We may rest assured that the secret of all failure is an unsuccessful prayer-life,' writes the Onbekende Christen *(Die Christen en gebed,* p. 10). If you can learn to pray first and then act, you will find that your work will be blessed much more and that you will make considerably fewer mistakes.

Heavenly Father, forgive me for so easily doing my own thing without consulting you. I pray that you will help me in future to pray before I act. Amen.

10 June
Whatever you ask
Read: John 11:17–26

But I know that even now God will give you whatever you ask.
John 11:22

Martha was sad that Jesus had not arrived in time to heal her brother. 'Lord, if you had been here, my brother would not have died,' she told him somewhat reproachfully (verse 21). And then she professed her faith in a remarkable way in our verse for today: 'But I know that even now God will give you whatever you ask.' Although Jesus was not there when she needed him, she believed that he would nevertheless be able to do something about the matter because God gave his Son whatever he asked. And Martha's faith in Jesus was confirmed in a way she could never have dreamt.

While Jesus was on earth, God indeed answered all his prayers. When Jesus prayed, miracles were performed: the blind regained their sight, the deaf their hearing, the lame walked. Shortly after Martha's confession of her faith, she saw Jesus raising her brother from the dead.

However, one of Jesus' prayers was not granted by his Father – the prayer which he prayed in Gethsemane. When Jesus pleaded with his Father to spare him the suffering on the cross, God remained silent. Jesus had to drink this cup of suffering to the last drop, so that you and I could one day have eternal life.

Lord Jesus, thank you that you were prepared to die the cruellest death imaginable so that I may have eternal life. Please make me willing to submit my will to God like you did. Amen.

11 June
Jesus and Lazarus
Read: John 11:33–44

Then Jesus looked up and said, 'Father, I thank you that you have heard me. I knew that you always hear me, but I said this for the benefit of the people standing here, that they may believe that you sent me.'
John 11:41–42

Raising Lazarus from the dead was probably the miracle performed by Jesus in which the role of prayer was underlined most clearly. Jesus said from the start that Lazarus' illness would not end in death (John 11:4). He never doubted that God would answer his prayer to raise Lazarus from the dead. He therefore thanked his Father for hearing his prayer even before Lazarus was raised from the dead.

Jesus still performs miracles when his children pray. Remember that Jesus is God himself and that the power of God works through him. It is therefore perfectly all right to expect the impossible from him! If your relationship with your heavenly Father is as intimate as the relationship of Jesus, you may do the same: you may thank God for hearing your prayers even before you see the manifestation. 'Whatever you ask for in prayer, believe that you have received it, and it will be yours,' Jesus once said (Mark 11:24).

Lord Jesus, I find it difficult to believe like you that I have already received the things I ask in prayer. I pray that you will strengthen my faith and teach me to pray like you. Amen.

12 June
Pray for your enemies
Read: Matthew 5:43–48

But I tell you: Love your enemies and pray for those who persecute you …
Matthew 5:44

It is not easy to pray for those who hurt and affront you. Yet Jesus commanded you to do so. You have to love your neighbour as yourself, Jesus said, and pray for your enemies.

Henri Nouwen writes that this prayer for your enemy is the most difficult type of prayer to pray, but also the most powerful, because it goes directly against one's grain. When you pray for your enemies, something wonderful happens: you discover that you cannot continue hating them. 'It is impossible to lift our enemies up in the presence of God and at the same time continue to hate them,' Nouwen writes *(Circles of love,* p. 10).

Don't you feel like starting to pray for those you really cannot abide right away? For the political leader who frustrates you on account of his utterances, for the person who spreads rumours about you, for those people who go out of their way to make life difficult for you? If you want to obey Jesus' command to pray for your enemies, you will find that they will soon no longer be enemies – you might even learn to love them!

Heavenly Father, there are so many people I battle to love. Help me to start praying for them so that I can obey Jesus' command. Amen.

13 June
Be a peacemaker
Read: Matthew 5:3–12

Blessed are the peacemakers, for they will be called sons of God.
Matthew 5:9

'The kingdom of God is not for sissies. It requires courage to stand before God, hat in hand, to confess your pride and self-righteousness, take the yoke of the kingdom on your shoulders and follow Jesus,' *Die Bybellennium* writes about the beatitudes (p. 1123).

We not only have to pray for our enemies, Jesus also asks us to be peacemakers. If you discover that someone has something against you, he wants you to go to her to make peace. Before you continue praying, you should first resolve all misunderstandings. For sincere prayer, your relationships with God as well as with those around you should be right. You should therefore restore all broken relationships you are aware of before you kneel in prayer, even if you are not the cause of the problem.

This sounds even more difficult than praying for your enemies! However, you have heard that the kingdom of the Lord is not intended for sissies! By his Holy Spirit within you, the Lord will give you the necessary power to do so because it is in line with his will for you.

Heavenly Father, I pray that you will help me to restore my relationships with others even if the broken relationships are not my fault. Please make me willing to follow you regardless of the circumstances. Amen.

14 June
The love of Jesus
Read: John 15:9–17

---

*Then the Father will give you whatever you ask in my name.
This is my command: Love each other.*
John 15:16–17

Jesus said he loved his disciples the way the Father loved and supported him. He instructed them to remain in his love and love one another in the same way. 'They have to think, feel and act love. It has to become the norm which governs their conduct,' writes *Die Bybellennium* (p. 1357). Only then will they be able to pray and know that the Father will answer their prayer requests.

This command to love one another is addressed to every believer. It is also the very command of Jesus with which all of us battle. We know perfectly well that we will never be able to love, believe, forgive, serve and pray the way God requires of us. This fact makes us beggars before God – when we pray, we stretch out our hands to him and ask him the one thing we cannot do without him.

Jesus has come to show you what love should look like when it is a way of life. If you are willing to follow in his footsteps, God will give you the things you ask him.

*Heavenly Father, you know how I battle to love other people
with the love of Jesus. Please make this possible for me
by the power of the Holy Spirit in my life. Amen.*

15 June
Feeding a multitude
Read: Luke 9:10–17

Taking the five loaves and the two fish and looking up to heaven, he gave thanks and broke them. Then he gave them to the disciples ... They all ate and were satisfied.
Luke 9:16–17

While he was on earth, Jesus was always aware of the physical needs of the people. When a crowd followed him, he noticed that they were hungry and when his disciples sent them away, Jesus said: 'You give them something to eat' (Luke 9:13). This was an impossible assignment, because we read that the men alone numbered about five thousand. However, Jesus knew that his Father would meet his needs.

When the disciples thereupon brought him the five loaves and two fish which they had, he looked up to heaven and gave thanks. He then broke the fish and the loaves and gave them to his disciples to serve to the people who were sitting in groups of fifty each. Luke reported that everybody ate and were satisfied and that there were still twelve baskets of food left.

When Jesus prays, a miracle is performed. He also wants to meet your basic needs today. Pray and tell him about them.

Lord Jesus, thank you for being the One who meets my needs. Teach me to pray and to ask God for those things which I really need. I praise you for still being able to perform miracles in my life. Amen.

16 June
Praying and fasting
Read: Mark 9:14–29

And when he was come into the house, his disciples asked him privately,
'Why could not we cast him out?' And he said unto them,
'This kind can come forth by nothing, but by prayer and fasting.'
Mark 9:28–29 (Authorised King James version)

When Jesus' disciples asked him why they could not cast out the evil spirit from the boy, he said, without hesitation, that they had failed because they had not prayed. Prayer means to confess your inability before God and to rely on God's power. In the Authorised version Jesus said prayer as well as fasting was required.

In biblical times fasting was a common practice and it was always accompanied by prayer. People fasted voluntarily so that their prayers could be more powerful.

Fasting can still make a significant contribution to making your prayers more powerful and meaningful today. To fast does not mean to go without food for days on end, but to make more time for God. Fasting therefore actually means to set aside all other things which monopolise your time and attention in order to have more time for God (and prayer). Start by sacrificing something which monopolises a great deal of your time – try to watch less television instead of going without food.

Heavenly Father, you know that I also fail often because I do not pray enough. Make me willing to set aside those things which monopolise my time so that I will have more time for you. Amen.

17 June
Jesus our Advocate
Read: 1 John 2:1–6

But if anybody does sin, we have one who speaks to the Father in our defence – Jesus Christ, the Righteous One. He is the atoning sacrifice for our sins, and not only for ours but also for the sins of the whole world.
1 John 2:1–2

Every mother knows perfectly well what it means to be an advocate. One who always has to put in a good word with dad! Jesus is our Advocate with his Father – He puts in a good word for us with God. And God listens to him, because he is the one who obeys his word and commands. God's love has been perfected in him.

You can check whether you are really in Jesus. 'Whoever claims to live in him must walk as Jesus did,' John wrote (1 John 2:6). If you are able to live on earth the way Jesus did, God will listen to your prayers too. This implies that you should do those things which Jesus did, that you should be willing to live in absolute obedience to your heavenly Father and be humble by considering others as better than yourself. Read the four Gospels carefully once again and study the way Jesus lived – go then and do likewise!

Lord Jesus, thank you that you are my Advocate with the Father. Please help me to follow your example by living the way you did. Amen.

18 June
Jesus prays for Peter
Read: Luke 22:24–34

*Simon, Simon, Satan has asked to sift you as wheat.
But I have prayed for you, Simon, that your faith may not fail.
And when you have turned back, strengthen your brothers.*
Luke 22:31–32

At the last supper Jesus told his disciples that those who wanted to be leaders in God's kingdom, should be prepared to serve one another. When a dispute arose among his disciples about which of them was considered to be the greatest, Jesus recognised the hand of Satan. He therefore warned Peter that he was going to fail his loyalty test, although Peter vehemently denied this. Jesus then prayed that Peter's faith would not fail but that he (Peter) should strengthen his brothers when he had turned back again. He also prophesied that Peter would deny him three times before the cock would crow that night.

The very first human qualities Satan attacks are always those of pride and selfrighteousness. Fortunately Jesus is still stronger than the devil and he intercedes for us. The devil's fiery darts can still be warded off today by the shield of faith. Faith means that God's children will hold on to Jesus during attacks – and when you are close to him you can also be assured of victory over the devil.

Lord Jesus, thank you for the shield of faith by which you have made it possible for me to ward off the devil's fiery darts. Amen.

19 June
To the glory of God
Read: John 17:1–8

And I will do whatever you ask in my name,
so that the Son may bring glory to the Father.
John 14:13

The final objective of our prayers should always be God's glory. When we look at the prayers of Jesus, we see that each of them conforms to this objective. However, Jesus can only give us things to God's glory if we know how to ask such things. Our prayer requests should therefore be in line with God's will as Jesus' requests were.

Jesus' prayers always concerned the honour of his Father. Jesus had already glorified his Father here on earth by the things he did, and he was now praying to ascend into heaven in order to glorify his Father there as well: 'I have brought you glory on earth by completing the work you gave me to do. And now, Father, glorify me in your presence with the glory I had with you before the world began' (John 17:4).

This prayer is answered when Jesus rose from the dead. His rising from the dead indeed shows that he is the Son of God.

By the things you do, you can also continue the work of Jesus here on earth so that people who look at you will glorify your Father because of them.

Lord Jesus, help me to glorify the Father, like you did,
by what I do for you here on earth. Teach me to pray
according to the will of God. Amen.

20 June
Jesus prays for his disciples
Read: John 17:6–12

They were yours; you gave them to me and they have obeyed your word ... I pray for them ... for they are yours.
John 17: 6, 9

Jesus knew his time on earth was drawing to a close. For this reason he then introduced his beautiful High-priestly prayer for his disciples in John 17 with the words: 'Father, the time has come ... ' He said that he had completed his work on earth, and that he was ready to return to his Father. Jesus loved his disciples sincerely and therefore prayed for them. In his moving prayer he brought his disciples before God – he also prayed that they would be protected (John 17:15) and sanctified (John 17:21) and that they would love one another in a world where hatred and strife abounded (John 17:26).

If you belong to Jesus, you have the assurance that he also intercedes for you before his Father. 'Between the Father and the Son, the child of God is held in two pairs of godly hands. There is no safer place. This is the glorious meaning of Christ's intercession for his disciples,' writes Dr Hennie Conradie in *ABC van die gebed* (p. 23).

Lord Jesus, thank you that you are still interceding for me before the Father, as you did for your disciples. Teach me in turn to intercede for others before God. Amen.

21 June
Protection from the evil one
Read: John 17:10–13

My prayer is not that you take them out of the world but that you protect them from the evil one.
John 17:15

The devil is real and he will never leave God's children in peace. Jesus knew that very well, and therefore prayed that his Father should protect his disciples from the evil one. We will never be able to resist the devil in our own power, but fortunately in God's power this is a different matter altogether.

Christians tend to become complacent and no longer pay much attention to the devil. The world in which we live has become increasingly tolerant of sin. In fact, very few things are still really wrong in the eyes of the world. However, we are playing a dangerous game. The devil is alive and well and he is continuously encouraging us to commit wrong deeds.

We should therefore always remember: God is holy and he hates sin. He always punishes by death. In this world you should live like God's child by hating the things of the world. Check yourself against John's warning: 'Do not love the world or anything in the world. If anyone loves the world, the love of the Father is not in him' (1 John 2:15).

Heavenly Father, forgive me for having such a soft spot in my heart for the world. I pray that you will keep me from the evil one every day. Amen.

22 June
Consecrated to God
Read: John 17:13–17

Sanctify them by the truth; your word is truth.
John 17:17

Jesus prayed that his disciples would be consecrated to his Father. The Greek word used here means that the believers would be set aside for God, that they would serve him only. Few people know the secret of true consecration. To be consecrated to God means to be totally committed to God, totally focused on God, to do something about your relationship with the Lord. People who live in this way, have learnt to place their own interests second.

Commitment to God implies that you will make time for him, time to pray, time to listen closely to what he is saying in his word, but it also means that you should live a committed life. In Romans 12:9–21 Paul sketched a picture of what a life committed to God should look like: your love for others will be sincere, you will be prepared to help others, you will be humble and forgiving, and always prepared to serve God as well as your neighbour. Read the passage of Scripture on commitment in Romans carefully and decide whether you are living a life of commitment or whether you should commit yourself to God anew.

Heavenly Father, I pray that you will help me to be fully committed to you, to place my own interests second so that I will be able to serve you and my neighbour better. Please help me to do this. Amen.

23 June
Sent into the world
Read: John 17:13–18

As you sent me into the world, I have sent them into the world. For them I sanctify myself, that they too may truly be sanctified.
John 17:18, 19

As his Father had sent him, Jesus sent his disciples out into the world to continue his work here on earth. It implied that they would live in such a way in the world that their way of life would be the mirror in which the world would be able to see God.

In Matthew 28:19 he said: 'Therefore go and make disciples of all nations, baptising them in the name of the Father and of the Son and of the Holy Spirit, and teaching them to obey everything I have commanded you.' Jesus not only sent them out, he also equipped them. He promised to be with them to the very end of the age (Matthew 28:20).

Every child of God is a 'sent one' – like Jesus you should also be prepared to make disciples and continue God's work on earth. Fortunately you do not have to carry out this important command in your own power. If you are prepared to be sent by God, he himself equips you by his Holy Spirit. Be a mirror in which others will be able to see Jesus every day.

Heavenly Father, I should like to continue your work and tell others about you so that your kingdom can be proclaimed. Thank you for equipping me with your Holy Spirit. Amen.

24 June
Prayer for unity
Read: John 17:17–21

I pray ... that all of them may be one, Father, just as you are in me and I am in you. May they also be in us so that the world may believe that you have sent me.
John 17:21

If the disciples of Jesus were to be obedient to this command and proclaim his gospel in all the world, people all over the world would hear about Jesus and believe in him. Jesus also prayed that God would protect these new believers. He asked that his disciples should be one in the world just as he and his Father were one. This unity means that the disciples should act as 'one man', *Die Bybellennium* writes (p. 1361). 'This unity is a unity of thought, will and deed.' The unity among God's children must therefore be visible in their action.

The unity between Jesus and his Father comes to the fore in a relationship of mutual love and obedience. When we look at Jesus, we also see his Father. Jesus prays here that his disciples should be one and love one another because they love God. Apparently Christians can never be one outwardly, because their churches inevitably differ from one another. However, in Jesus we are nevertheless one because our love for God bridges our differences and is anchored in his love.

Heavenly Father, I pray that you will unite all your children in the world, and that we will love one another sincerely because we love you. Amen.

25 June
May this cup be taken from me ...
Matthew 26:36–46

My Father, if it is possible, may this cup be taken from me.
Yet not as I will, but as you will.
Matthew 26:39

Although Jesus was God's Son, he was also very human. He knew from the beginning that he would have to suffer and die, but in the flesh the mere thought of the inhumane suffering that was waiting became too much for him. Luke wrote that Jesus experienced a fear unto death and that he prayed so fervently that his sweat was like drops of blood falling to the ground (Luke 22:44). Jesus discussed his fear with his Father and beseeched him to take the cup from him.

There has probably never been a prayer request which God wanted to grant as badly as this particular request by his Son. Yet God refused. He did not grant Jesus' request because he loves you and me so much. God said no to his Son because he knew that Jesus had to suffer and die so that we could one day have eternal life.

Perhaps God also sometimes says 'no' to your most fervent prayer requests. If you do not understand why God refuses to take away your suffering, remember Jesus in Gethsemane and know that God is saying 'no' because he has a greater purpose for your life.

Heavenly Father, thank you for the assurance that when you do not grant my prayer requests, you have a greater purpose for my life. Help me to hold on to this promise. Amen.

26 June
Your will be done ...
Read: Luke 22:39–46

Father, if you are willing, take this cup from me;
yet not my will, but yours be done.
Luke 22:42

Jesus was praying in Gethsemane – his time of suffering was drawing near. He realised very well what he had consented to, and because he was human like us, he no longer felt he could do it. He pleaded with his Father to take the cup away from him, but God refused. If he had granted Jesus' request, the history of the world would have been very different! It would have meant that you and I would never have had the opportunity to reach God.

However, Jesus always put his Father's will first. Although he badly wanted to avoid the inhumane suffering, he submitted himself to God's will. 'His prayer is nevertheless answered in a surprising way,' Dr Hennie Conradie writes. 'The cup remained but the fear and the cross were conquered' (*ABC van die gebed*, p. 98).

During your own difficult times, you may ask your heavenly Father to take the suffering away with confidence, provided you remember that you have no guarantee that he will do so. Always be prepared to submit your will to his like Jesus did. If you badly want something, you should always first of all determine whether it is in line with God's will for your life.

Heavenly Father, I pray that you will focus me on your will with such precision that I will always put your will first, like Jesus did, whenever I submit my prayer requests to you. Amen.

27 June
Pray that you will not fall into temptation
Read: Luke 22:39–46

*On reaching the place, he said to them,
'Pray that you will not fall into temptation.'*
Luke 22:40

The weapon which Jesus held up here to his disciples as protection against Satan was prayer and not the sword as they had misunderstood in Luke 22:35–38. Persevering prayer was the only way in which they would be able to remain faithful to him in the difficult time which lay ahead. Jesus' request that they should pray was supported by the fact that he put his own words into action. He also needed power to resist the temptation of the devil – that he should refuse to be crucified.

Jesus must have been very disappointed when the three disciples whom he had chosen to support him in his hour of suffering were not even able to keep watch with him for one hour. 'Why are you sleeping?' he asked them. And he then repeated the instruction in verse 40: 'Get up and pray so that you will not fall into temptation' (Luke 22:46).

Jesus is the perfect example to all of us as to what we should do in times of temptation. To this day prayer is still the most important weapon to use to remain standing against the temptations of the devil. In times of crisis, prayer might also be the only way in which you will find the power to remain faithful to God.

Lord Jesus, I pray that you will give me the power to remain standing against the temptation of the devil. Teach me to pray in times of crisis so that I will be able to remain faithful to you. Amen.

28 June
Father, forgive them ...
Read: Luke 23:27–34

Jesus said, 'Father, forgive them, for they do not know what they are doing.'
Luke 23:34

The road to Golgotha made superhuman demands on Jesus. His spiritual suffering was even worse than his physical suffering. His Father had not responded to his supplication to save him from the suffering – he had to walk the way of the cross alone, because God had forsaken him when he became sin for the whole world.

Jesus nevertheless still interceded before God for his persecutors. On the cross he prayed that God should forgive those who were responsible for his suffering because they did not know what they were doing. The saddest part of the crucifixion is that the religious people of his day were responsible for having him crucified – the same people who had been looking forward to the coming of the Messiah.

Johan Smit writes, 'This prayer for forgiveness is the first indication of the miracle of the cross, because if those people who were crucifying the Son of God are included in the mercy of God, everybody who asks for mercy will receive it' *(Trefferwoorde van Jesus,* p. 254).

Jesus also purchased God's mercy for you on the cross. If you believe in him, he enables you to be God's child, and one day have eternal life.

Lord Jesus, thank you for having purchased God's mercy for me on the cross. Make me willing to forgive others like you did. Amen.

29 June
Forsaken by God ...
Read: Matthew 27:45–54

About the ninth hour Jesus cried out in a loud voice, 'Eloi, Eloi, lama sabachthani?' – which means, 'My God, my God, why have you forsaken me?'
Matthew 27:46

This cry of Jesus is one of the most moving prayers in the Bible and the clearest expression of the intensity of his suffering on earth. Jesus' suffering started at his birth. All of us empathise with Jesus' physical suffering during the crucifixion: the flogging, the crown of thorns, the carrying of the cross, the nails though his hands and feet. However, we often lose sight of the fact that while Jesus hung on the cross, he endured the climax of his suffering because he had been forsaken by God.

You and I will experience difficult times during our lives on earth – no-one will escape such times – but even in our greatest need and suffering we still have the assurance that God's arms are around us, that he will help us in our crises and carry us when we cannot continue.

On the cross Jesus for the first time had the experience that God was not hearing his prayers. On the cross Jesus had to bear God's wrath aimed at sin alone so that we would never have to be without God again. In times of crisis you may therefore go to God with confidence to ask for help and because Jesus prayed the above prayer on the cross, you never have to be without God again.

Lord Jesus, I praise you for having been willing to be forsaken by God on the cross so that I will never have to experience a crisis alone and without him. Amen.

30 June
Jesus is praying for you
Read: Romans 8:31–37

Christ Jesus, who died – more than that, who was raised to life – is at the right hand of God and is also interceding for us.
Romans 8:34

Jesus had continuous communication with his Father while he was on earth. He prayed for his disciples regularly. He also prayed before he had to make important decisions. In Romans 8 Paul summarised Jesus' death on the cross and the consequences of his death for the church in Rome: Jesus died, Jesus was risen from the dead, he is sitting on the right hand of God and he is interceding for us! Jesus is continuing his phenomenal prayer ministry where he is sitting on his Father's right hand, but now he is praying for you and me. This is an incredible thought – because Jesus is interceding for us, we can live victoriously every day because nothing in the world can separate us from the love of Jesus. 'He is able to save completely those who come to God through him, because he always lives to intercede for them', the writer to the Hebrews wrote (Hebrews 7:25).

Because Jesus is at this very moment interceding for you personally before your heavenly Father, you may claim the wonderful promise in 1 John 2:1 for yourself: 'But if anybody does sin, we have one who speaks to the Father in our defence – Jesus Christ, the Righteous One.' Should you therefore become discouraged again because you just cannot succeed in shaking off your sin – remember that Jesus is praying for you!

Lord Jesus, I praise you for still praying for me in heaven.
Thank you for the assurance that when I sin, you are
interceding for me before God. Amen.

July

Obstacles to prayer

Many things prevent Christians from experiencing a dynamic prayer life. Unfortunately most of these obstacles to prayer are self-inflicted. We often occupy ourselves with the 'obstacles' which make our prayer life weak and watered-down while we ourselves are actually the problem. 'Prayer has no problem. The problem is in the heart which is not focused on Christ,' writes Onbekende Christen (*Die Christen en gebed*, p. 104). God wants his children to talk to him, while the devil in turn is doing his level best to sink our prayer life.

If your personal prayer life is not as it should be at present, it has perhaps become time to look for the problem in yourself! 'God answers our prayers if his honour is our highest objective. We should therefore primarily look for the Giver and not merely for his gifts,' is the advice given by Onbekende Christen (p. 107).

This month we will focus on the things which prevent us from praying.

1 July
Pray without obstacles
Read: 1 Peter 3:1–7

So that nothing will hinder your prayers.
1 Peter 3:7

In his letter Peter warned married couples that certain things in their lives could hinder their prayers. He also asked them to get rid of such things.

When you do things which God does not approve of, they could sink your prayer life. The hot line between you and God is subjected to much static. You can also be assured of one thing in particular: the devil is a master at erecting jamming stations when you want to communicate with God in prayer. See how often your thoughts wander, your telephone or doorbell rings or someone disturbs you when you want to make time to be alone with God.

However, there are also other things in your own life which you could in fact change – things by which God is prevented from listening to your prayers. Things such as sin, broken relationships, exhaustion, unfaithfulness in marriage and anger can weaken or sever the relationship of trust between you and God which is so vital to prayer.

If you therefore again feel God is not listening to your prayers, first check whether any of the obstacles to prayer we are going to discuss this month are lurking in your life.

Heavenly Father, I confess that I often battle to pray because there are still so many things in my life which sink my fellowship with you. Please point them out to me and help me to get rid of them. Amen.

2 July
Draw near to God with a sincere heart
Read: Hebrews 10:19–25

Let us draw near to God with a sincere heart in full assurance of faith, having our hearts sprinkled to cleanse us from a guilty conscience and having our bodies washed with pure water.
Hebrews 10:22

People often evaluate certain sins, but God never draws comparisons – he regards sin as sin, and he hates all sin because he is holy. Sin is always rebellion against God himself. 'Against you, you only, have I sinned and done what is evil in your sight,' David called out in Psalm 51:4 after the prophet Nathan had confronted him about his sin.

If you want to draw near to God in prayer, it should always be with 'a sincere heart in full assurance of faith' because the God to whom you are praying has purified your heart and washed you with the blood of his Son.

When you therefore pray again and find that God is not listening, consider whether the sin in your life is perhaps building a wall between you and God. Then ask the Holy Spirit to point out your specific sin to you, confess and renounce it. You will soon discover that God will listen to you again and answer your prayers as in the past.

Heavenly Father, I pray that you will make me aware of the sin in my life which is still between you and me, and also that you will make me willing to renounce it. Amen.

3 July
Do not sin deliberately
Read: Hebrews 10:26–31

If we deliberately keep on sinning after we have received the knowledge of the truth, no sacrifice for sins is left.
Hebrews 10:26

The writer of the letter to the Hebrews puts it unequivocally that there is no sacrifice for deliberate sins. All of us sometimes sin while we know perfectly well what we are doing. If you know the right way and deliberately continue doing the wrong things (which you like and find satisfactory), you are playing with fire. In that case there is no longer any sacrifice you can bring that could make God look past your sin. When you think about this, it would almost seem as if God would never be able to forgive you.

Fortunately it is not as bad as it sounds! The readers of the letter to the Hebrews are warned here against apostasy. People who have fallen away from the church have actually sided against God. They have not accepted the grace of God. According to *Die Bybellennium*, they have 'despised the Son of God and the blood of the covenant which has sanctified them' (p. 1695). God has no mercy on such people. However, he is still prepared to forgive the sin of his children, provided they do not deliberately persist in doing the things his word warns against – and reject his mercy in the process.

Heavenly Father, forgive me for so often still doing things which I know are wrong. Please help me never to reject your mercy in this way. Amen.

4 July
The consequences of sin
Read: James 1:12–18

Then, after desire has conceived, it gives birth to sin;
and sin, when it is full-grown, gives birth to death.
James 1:15

In this letter, James stressed that God cannot tempt anybody. If sin gets the upper hand in your life, your own desires are tempting you. *Die Boodskap* uses a beautiful picture here: sin tempts you deeper into problems like a child chasing a butterfly (p. 751). If you side against your Christianity time and again, you will permit increasingly more sin into your life.

If the things which your heart desires therefore come in contact with what your eyes see, the obvious next step is often doing that which desire tempts you to do. However, be careful! The Bible teaches that the consequences of sin invariably lead to death.

You will have to get used to being on your guard against any kind of sin, and furthermore come to terms with the fact that you will be locked in a struggle against that sin for the rest of your life!

Lord, I just don't seem to be able to live the way you want me to live.
Please forgive me once again for the wrong things in my life, and help
me not to be dragged along by the sin within me. Amen.

5 July
Sin starts in the mind
Read: Proverbs 27:17–21

As water reflects a face, so a man's heart reflects the man.
Proverbs 27:19

Nobody does wrong things unless he has thought about them a couple of times. You sometimes really shudder at the sinful thoughts you harbour. I too have often been grateful that others could not read my thoughts! However, God is not satisfied with a good life and sinful thoughts. He expects the things his children are thinking to match their confession. Children of God should therefore start with their thoughts and discipline themselves to think right and concentrate on the good and lovely things.

If you continue battling with this, ask the Lord to change you by renewing your mind so that you will discern his perfect will for your life (Romans 12:2). Then follow Paul's good advice in Colossians 3:2 and set your mind on the things above, and not on earthly things. God has made you a new creation – he will also give you the power to say no to sin and teach you to think in a new way so that in future he will be able to approve of the things which live in your mind.

Heavenly Father, I pray that you will remove all unworthy and sinful thoughts and that you will teach me to think in a new way and sense where you are. Amen.

6 July
Do some spring-cleaning!
Read: James 1:19–27

Therefore, get rid of all moral filth and the evil that is so prevalent, and humbly accept the word planted in you, which can save you.
James 1:21

At the end of winter our ancestors used to clean their homes from floor to ceiling. It might be a good idea if Christians were to take over this 'spring-cleaning'. *Die Boodskap* version of our verse for today reads: 'Get rid of even the minutest piece of rubbish or dirt which could tarnish or spoil your spiritual life.'

If you like gardening, you will know that keeping a garden weed free requires effort, time and the sweat of your brow, because you have to weed regularly – weeds always grow again. A gardener therefore has to keep at it if she wants to take pride in a weed-free garden.

The same is true in the case of the Christian who wants to keep her life pure and sinless. Time, effort and care will definitely be required of you! God's law is the road map keeping you on the right track which will eventually take you, washed clean, to God. Therefore, be obedient to God – do what the Bible tells you to do, and 'spring-clean' regularly by confessing your sin.

Heavenly Father, I pray that you will help me to get rid of the wrong things which are still in my life so that, with your help, I will be able to keep my life pure in future. Amen.

7 July
Confess your sin!
Read: Proverbs 28:13

*He who conceals his sins does not prosper,
but whoever confesses and renounces them finds mercy.*
Proverbs 28:13

The Bible is consistent about the following: it is useless to try to hide your sin from God. It only results in unhappiness. Four things are required to obtain forgiveness of sin: you have to admit your sins, confess them before God one by one (by name and not merely in general) and also be willing to renounce the sin and in future bear fruit in keeping with your confession. If you are prepared to do this, you will receive the mercy our verse promises.

Although it sounds very simple, it is nevertheless not so easy to renounce sin once and for all. We all fall into the trap of repeatedly doing the wrong things we have just confessed. Fortunately God is 'faithful and just', John wrote, 'He will forgive us our sins and purify us from all unrighteousness' (1 John 1:9). And God's forgiveness differs vastly from ours – when he has forgiven your sin, he never remembers that sin again. Unlike us, he does not keep a record of wrongs.

*Heavenly Father, I now want to confess my sins to you one by one.
Thank you that you are willing to forgive my sin again and again
and to wash me with the blood of your Son. Amen.*

8 July
God forgives sin
Read: Malachi 3:6–8

> *'Ever since the time of your forefathers you have turned away from my decrees and have not kept them. Return to me, and I will return to you,' says the Lord Almighty.*
> Malachi 3:7

Speaking through the prophet Malachi, God promised that he would forgive his unfaithful people their sins if they would, in turn, return to him. Sin is inherent in human nature. Fortunately God never changes and is forgiving. If we return to him, he will forgive our sins and return to us.

Sin has become dirt cheap in our modern world. We hear daily how people take the Name of the Lord in vain, tell lies, commit fraud, violence and white-collar crime. Things such as premarital sex, euthanasia and abortion have become habitual practices – all the sins the Bible warns us against have become common-place. The modern Christian has consequently become insensitive to sin. Sin no longer really upsets us. We sometimes even join in and in this way move further and further away from God.

God's promise to Malachi still applies to you even today. If you are prepared to confess your sin and renounce it, if you undertake to return to the Lord, he will forgive you and return to you.

> *Heavenly Father, I confess that sin has become cheap to me. Please make me sensitive to it again, help me to return to you so that I can be forgiven by you. Amen.*

9 July
On your way to the altar
Read: Matthew 5:23–24

Therefore, if you are offering your gift at the altar and there remember that your brother has something against you, leave your gift there in front of the altar. First go and be reconciled to your brother; then come and offer your gift.
Matthew 5:23–24

In Old Testament times the altar was the place where the priests had to offer the sacrifice for the sin of the people, and also the place where forgiveness was received. Relationships always play an important role in the forgiveness of sin. If someone was therefore on his way to the altar and he remembered that his brother had something against him, he had to leave his gift at the altar and first be reconciled with his brother, Jesus said.

Jesus is the Great Reconciler. He came to the world specifically to reconcile people with one another and with God. Reconciliation and forgiveness are extremely important to Jesus. An unforgiving spirit is frequently mentioned in the Bible as a reason why God does not answer our prayers. Sometimes we are slow to admit that our unforgiving way of life could be an obstacle in our prayer life. If you know of someone who needs your forgiveness, give it to them. If you yourself should ask forgiveness, do so! If you are willing to do this, God will answer your prayers and forgive your sin.

Heavenly Father, please make me willing to restore my relationships with everybody in my life, to set right the wrongs, to forgive them wholeheartedly as you forgive me. Amen.

10 July
Do not wrong others
Read: Numbers 5:5–10

When a man or woman wrongs another in any way and so is unfaithful to the Lord, that person is guilty and must confess the sin he has committed. He must make full restitution for his wrong, add one fifth to it and give it all to the person he has wronged.
Numbers 5:6–7

In Old Testament times, people were held responsible for their wrongs – and they were expected to make full restitution.

All of us want to do those things which are right in the eyes of God. Before you pray, says the Bible, you should think carefully whether there is someone you might have wronged. You can so easily hurt others by the things you do, the things you say, even the things you think! Peace and harmony are extremely important to Christians who are serious about praying. You merely waste your breath if you try to pray while you are at the same time harbouring feelings of bitterness and rebellion towards other people.

Although God no longer makes us accountable for our sin because Jesus has bought us forgiveness for that sin on the cross, we are still held responsible for those people we have wronged or hurt by our insensitive action. First make restitution for the wrongs before you kneel to pray.

*Lord, I sin against others so often. Please forgive me
and help me to restore my relationships with those people
I have hurt before I pray. Amen.*

11 July
Be slow to speak
Read: James 1:17–21

My dear brothers, take note of this: Everyone should be quick to listen, slow to speak and slow to become angry.
James 1:19

Listening is much better than speaking, James wrote. If only we would learn the costly lesson of listening rather than speaking we would be able to avoid many sins in our lives! In James 3 he elaborated on the dangers of our tongues. Anyone who is never at fault in what he says, is able to keep his whole body in check, he said. The tongue is a small part of the body which could corrupt the whole body. 'No man can tame the tongue. It is a restless evil, full of deadly poison!' (James 3:2, 5, 6 and 8).

The things you say, immediately tell those who are listening who you are. Just as an orange tree can only bear oranges, you are known by the things you say. 'For out of the overflow of your heart the mouth speaks,' Jesus himself once said (Matthew 12:34). You should therefore be careful with regard to the things you say and follow James' good advice: always be willing to listen and do not be quick to answer!

Heavenly Father, you know how often my tongue has got me into trouble. I pray that you will set a guard over my mouth and make me listen rather than speak. Amen.

12 July
Do what God says
Read: James 1:19–27

Do not merely listen to the word, and so deceive yourselves. Do what it says.
James 1:22

It is not enough that we read our Bibles, we also have to be willing to do what the word says, or we are merely bluffing ourselves, James warned. Look at yourself in the mirror of the word. Here you can see clearly what God wants your life to look like.

When you read the Bible, it points out your sin to you. However, once you have closed your Bible, there are so many other things you have to pay attention to that you often forget the distorted image of yourself you have just seen in the mirror of your Bible.

Are you prepared to do what has been written in the Bible yet? If you are prepared to do this, you may claim the promise in verse 25 for yourself: 'He will be blessed in what he does.'

Always remember: you cannot deceive God – he is aware of every one of your sins. Nothing in all creation is hidden from God's sight. Everything is uncovered and laid bare before the eyes of him to whom we must give account, Hebrews 4:13 reads. Do something about the remaining sins in your life and get rid of them as it says in the word.

Heavenly Father, please forgive me for tending to read the Bible without being a 'doer' of the word. Help me to obey each guideline in your word in future. Amen.

13 July
Pray in faith
Read: James 1:6–8

But when he asks, he must believe and not doubt, because he who doubts is like a wave of the sea. That man should not think he will receive anything from the Lord.
James 1:6–8

Answer to prayer has a condition: faith. According to James, faith and deeds cannot be separated. You will not benefit from asking things of the Lord if you do not believe that your prayers will be answered. Your way of life should underline your faith. For example, you cannot pray to pass your exams with flying colours unless you study earnestly.

Prayer and faith therefore go hand in hand. James writes unequivocally that someone who is always doubting should not even think he will receive anything from the Lord. Lack of faith is one of the major obstacles to answer to prayer.

'Those with hope do not get tangled up with concerns of how their wishes will be fulfilled. So, too, their prayers are not directed toward the gift, but toward the one who gives. Their prayers might still contain just as many desires, but ultimately it is not a question of having a wish come true but of expressing an unlimited faith … ,' Henri Nouwen writes (*Circles*, p. 33).

Pray so that your prayers will strengthen your faith in future.

Heavenly Father, I pray that you will give me more faith, so that, when I pray, I will truly believe that you will answer my prayers. Amen.

14 July
Obey the law!
Read: Proverbs 28:9–13

If anyone turns a deaf ear to the law, even his prayers are detestable.
Proverbs 28:9

Disobedience to God's law and word is another obstacle to prayer. God sets a very high premium on obedience. 'Sacrifice and offerings you did not desire, but my ears you have pierced; burnt offerings and sin offerings you did not require,' the psalmist wrote (Psalm 40:6). Deliberate disobedience with regard to those things which God instructs in his word, could therefore prevent God from hearing your prayers. The opposite is fortunately also true: 'And [we] receive from him anything we ask, because we obey his commands and do what pleases him. Those who obey his commands live in him, and he in them,' John writes (1 John 3:22, 24).

The ten commandments have become so routine to us that we run the risk of no longer hearing when they are read in church on Sundays. Take time to read exactly what God's law says. This is how God wants you to live. However, remember Jesus' summary of the law in Luke 10:27: 'Love the Lord your God with all your heart and with all your soul and with all your strength and with all your mind'; and 'Love your neighbour as yourself.'

Lord, I want to obey your word and your law. Please enable me to love you above all else in future and love my neighbour as myself. Amen.

15 July
Make God's desires yours
Read: Psalm 37:1–8

> *Trust in the Lord and do good; dwell in the land and enjoy safe pasture. Delight yourself in the Lord and he will give you the desires of your heart.*
> Psalm 37:3–4

You have most probably already underlined this verse in your Bible because it sounds so simple – and all of us want our hearts' desires to be fulfilled. Unfortunately we all know that this does not always happen. We simply do not receive everything we ask in prayer. The secret is to learn to align your desires with the desires God has for you. If you can do this, you will receive the things you ask in prayer, because they are God's will for you.

For example, should you pray that your relationship with a married man should succeed, it will not happen – an extramarital affair is against God's will. However, should you pray that the Lord make your unhappy marriage happy, it will probably happen, because it is God's will that people he has joined together should be happy.

You should also be willing to wait until God has fulfilled your desires, provided you have checked whether those desires are in line with his will for your life.

Lord Jesus, I want to remain in you – as close as the branch to the vine – help me not to ask things of you which are not part of your will for me. Amen.

16 July
Fear can wreck prayer
Read: Psalm 55:1–9

My heart is in anguish within me; the terrors of death assail me.
Fear and trembling have beset me; horror has overwhelmed me.
Psalm 55:4–5

Sometimes things happen to you which terrify you, which make you too scared to pray. If your child is terminally ill, you may be afraid to pray, because you are afraid that it might not be God's will that your child should be healed. If your children's marriage is in the balance and you pray for months on end without seeing any change, you fear that God is probably never going to answer your prayer – or that his answer will not be what you really want. Catherine Marshall once wrote: 'We know that fear obstructs prayer. Fear is a barrier erected between God and us so that his power cannot reach us.' If you are at present afraid to pray, you have two options:

- Go to God and share your fears with him – 'Cast all your anxiety on him because he cares for you,' Peter wrote (1 Peter 5:7).
- Trust the Lord to fulfil his promises in his word for you personally:

'Do not fear; I will help you,' he promised in Isaiah 41:13.
He wants to do this for you, too.

Lord, I am so scared to tell you about my fears. I am afraid to pray because you might not grant my urgent prayer request. Give me your peace in my life, regardless of your answer to my prayers. Amen.

17 July
Pray when you are ill
Read: James 5:13–20

Confess your sins to each other and pray for each other so that you may be healed.
James 5:16

Illness must never be regarded as punishment for sin. However, the Lord is able to heal our illness when we pray. God also promised in Exodus 15:26 that he would keep his people well: 'I will not bring on you any of the diseases I brought on the Egyptians, for I am the Lord, who heals you.' According to James, when someone was ill, he should call the elders of the church to pray for him and anoint him with oil and if they prayed fervently, the sick person would be healed. 'The prayer of a righteous man is powerful and effective,' James wrote (James 5:16).

In the time of James, oil was used as a symbol of God's Spirit as well as for medicinal purposes. Some faiths see this verse as proof that they should not consult doctors when they are ill, because the Lord will heal them. However, the Lord does in fact use doctors and medicine to heal us and although he is perfectly able to heal us of our illnesses, he does not always do so. I believe the right recipe is to go to a doctor but to pray as well!

Heavenly Father, thank you that you can heal me of every disease, but that you also make use of medical science to heal people. Amen.

18 July
Anger as obstacle
Read: Galatians 5:19–25

The acts of the sinful nature are obvious: sexual immorality, impurity and debauchery; idolatry and witchcraft; hatred, discord, jealousy, fits of rage …
Galatians 5:19–20

Perhaps you have already discovered that when someone upsets you, or when others are insensitive and egocentric towards you, your prayer life is affected. Anger is one of the main obstacles to prayer.

While Henri Nouwen lived in a monastery, he discovered that the feelings of anger in his heart were actually from within himself, because, he says, everyone here in the monastery is so good that one cannot be angry with them! The longer he remained in the monastery, the more Nouwen discovered that anger was obstructing his way to God. In the monastery he actually had no reason to be angry, and when he therefore found himself to be angry or morose, he could trace the roots of these feelings to himself.

Evragrius wrote: 'The state of prayer can be aptly described as a habitual state of imperturbable calm' (both quotations: *Circles of love,* p. 17).

If you are therefore still cherishing feelings of anger about something or someone, ask God to forgive you, get rid of those angry feelings, and your channel to God will be open again.

Lord, I am sorry that I allow myself to be angered by others so easily. Forgive me my anger – and help me to get rid of it for ever by the work of your Spirit in my life. Amen.

19 July
Too wealthy to pray?
Read: Luke 18:18–27

It is easier for a camel to go through the eye of a needle than for a rich man to enter the kingdom of God.
Luke 18:25

Your possessions could become an obstacle to prayer. Wealthy people never have enough – they always want more. The more possessions you have, the more important they become to you. It could, however, be dangerous to have too much – you cannot serve God and Mammon, because you will hate the one and love the other, Jesus warned in his sermon on the mount (Matthew 6:24).

How attached are you to your possessions and money? Are you so attached that they at times come between you and God? In that case you may be too wealthy to be able to pray!

The rich young man wanted to follow Jesus, but he could not manage to sacrifice all his many possessions. Fortunately God does not expect this of you. You do not have to sell everything you own before you may follow God. However, the more wealth and possessions you have, the more difficult it will be for you to surrender your purse to God. Guard against regarding your possessions and securities as more important than your faith.

Lord, I pray that you will forgive me for allowing my money and possessions to become so important. Make me willing to open my heart and my purse to you. Amen.

20 July
Promises when you pray
Read: Jeremiah 33:1–9

*Call to me and I will answer you and tell you great
and unsearchable things you do not know.*
Jeremiah 33:3

In verses 6–8, in the words of the prophet Jeremiah, the Lord promised his people a whole series of blessings should they call to him: he would heal them, be a strong fortress to them, change their fate, give them children and forgive them their sins.

The whole list of wonderful promises in these verses is subject to the prayers of God's people. Your prayers could open the storehouses of God's promises for you! And God is faithful, he always keeps all his promises. 'Let us hold unswervingly to the hope we profess, for he who promised is faithful,' the writer to the Hebrews wrote (Hebrews 10:23).

Do not hesitate to remind God of his promises when you pray. And do not fail to speak to him in prayer – he wants you to call to him so that he can answer you and fulfil each of the promises in his word for you personally.

*Heavenly Father, thank you for each of your promises which you have
recorded for me in your word. I now want to claim each of these
promises and remind you of them when I pray to you. Amen.*

21 July
Is God perhaps appalled that you are not praying?
Read: Isaiah 59:14–17

He saw that there was no-one, he was appalled that there was no-one to intervene; so his own arm worked salvation for him, and his own righteousness sustained him.
Isaiah 59:16

God was amazed that there was no-one to plead with him for his people, the prophet Isaiah wrote. He himself therefore intervened and offered his promises to his unfaithful people. The prophet stated the reason for this prayerlessness in Isaiah 59:2: 'Your iniquities have separated you from your God; your sins have hidden his face from you, so that he will not hear.'

Fortunately you are in a much better position than ancient Israel. Jesus is your Mediator, he pleads for you with God. His Holy Spirit who lives in you not only teaches you to pray, but also prays for you. He submits each of your prayer requests to God. He also teaches you to pray according to the will of God.

You should in turn be an intercessor for others. Do not pray only for yourself and your own needs, but plead with God for others as well. Pray also regularly that God's kingdom will come here on earth.

Heavenly Father, please teach me to pray – for your kingdom and for others – and show me when my sin becomes an obstacle to my prayers. Amen.

22 July
When you feel too secure!
Read: Psalm 30

When I felt secure, I said, 'I shall never be shaken.' O Lord, ... but when you hid your face, I was dismayed. To you, O Lord, I called ...
Psalm 30:6–8

It is ironical that prosperity and success can also be obstacles to prayer! When you are very prosperous, you sometimes become so complacent that you feel you will be able to handle everything yourself. You are positive that nothing in your life will ever shake you again. In these times of prosperity you therefore pray much less than usual – you spend less time with God because you do not need him as much as usual.

However, when crises occur in your life again, you soon discover that only God can help you now – and in such times you run back to God like the Israelites of old. Fortunately God is always willing to help you again. He is faithful, despite our faithlessness. He will also ultimately work all things together for your good again if you ask him to.

Heavenly Father, please forgive me for the many times in the past when I prayed less because I felt so secure. Help me not to pray to you only in times of crisis, but to live close to you every day. Amen.

23 July
What does God want?
Read: Matthew 16:23

Jesus turned and said to Peter, 'Get behind me, Satan! You are a stumbling-block to me; you do not have in mind the things of God, but the things of men.'
Matthew 16:23

Peter did not like what Jesus told his disciples regarding his impending suffering and death. He could not believe that it would be possible for Jesus to rise from the dead either. These things did not fit into the human expectations he had about Jesus. These were the reasons for his rebuking him: 'Never, Lord! This shall never happen to you!' (Matthew 16:22).

Hereupon Jesus rebuked him in no uncertain terms. Peter had become a stumbling-block to Jesus because he was thinking in human terms, he was focusing on human expectations and God's will was therefore of less importance to him.

We are also inclined to be people-pleasers. We like doing the things which make our loved ones happy. This is not wrong either, but if the wishes of people become more important than God's law, you have problems.

When you pray, God's will for you should be the most important criterion. When you pray again, forget about what people (or you yourself) want and focus on God's will. Then God will answer your prayers.

Heavenly Father, I am sorry that people's opinions are still so important to me. Please make me willing to set your will before my pleasing others. Amen.

24 July
Broken marital relationships
Read: 1 Peter 3:7

Wives have to be submissive to their own husbands and husbands you have to be considerate as you live with your wives ... so that nothing will hinder your prayers.
1 Peter 3:5, 7

Divorce has become common practice today. One in three marriages in South Africa ends in the divorce court. Happy marriages are the exception rather than the rule. If something is wrong in your own marriage, do not ignore it. Discuss the matter with your spouse or a marriage counsellor before these problems result in divorce. God instituted marriage himself and divorce is against his will. 'What God has joined together, let man not separate,' Jesus himself said in Mark 10:9.

Consider the possibility of your current marital problems as the reason for your personal prayer life being weak and unsatisfactory at the moment. You will only be able to talk spontaneously to God again without any hindrances once you have prayed about your marriage and worked on your marriage and matters between your spouse and yourself have been settled.

Your attitude in everyday life is extremely important to God. Think carefully: is your attitude towards your spouse such that it will never be an obstacle to your prayer life?

Lord, I'm sorry that my marriage is so often torn by strife and that these marital problems at times prevent me from praying with confidence. Help me to resolve the problems. Amen.

25 July
First pray and then act!
Read: 1 Kings 22:1–5, 27

> *[The king of Israel] then asked Jehoshaphat, 'Will you go with me to fight against Ramoth Gilead?' Jehoshaphat replied, 'I am as you are ... but ... first seek the counsel of the Lord.'*
> 1 Kings 22:4–5

In the Bible story, the king of Israel consulted God only after he had already worked out his own strategy for war. He was prepared to listen to the Lord, but only as long as God supported his plans.

Sometimes we work out our plans in detail, and then we consult God about them as King Ahab did in our passage of Scripture. Have you ever bought a house or accepted a job without consulting the Lord and only then prayed for his blessing? That is not what God wants. Children of God know the secret of first praying and then doing. The results of deciding first and then praying are invariably catastrophic, as Ahab discovered regarding his plans of war against Ramoth.

Consult God first next time – then you can claim his blessings and answers to your prayers – provided you are still willing to accept his answer even if it differs from that which you wanted.

Lord, please help me to consult you first in future before I make my own plan. Thank you that I may then ask your blessing and that you will answer my prayers. Amen.

26 July
Exhaustion could weaken your prayers
Read: Luke 22:39–46

*When he rose from prayer and went back to the disciples,
he found them asleep, exhausted from sorrow.*
Luke 22:45

While Jesus prayed in the garden of Gethsemane, his disciples could not even stay awake with him for one hour. In his hour of greatest need, his disciples fell asleep twice. Jesus must have been very disappointed in them.

Exhaustion can also weaken your prayer life. Most women work outside the home these days and attending to your occupation, your husband, your children as well as your home is very demanding. If you sometimes discover that your programme is so full that you go to bed very late at night, it is time to call halt or you will fall asleep on your knees during your quiet time.

Try to scale down your overloaded programme in future. Make more time for recreation and see to it that you choose a time for communicating with God when you are refreshed and wide awake and rested – then exhaustion will not be the cause of a weak prayer life.

*Lord, you know I am often so tired at night that I fall asleep
when I want to communicate with you, just like your disciples
in Gethsemane. Forgive me and help me to scale down
so that I will have enough time for you. Amen.*

27 July
Do not be impatient!
Read: Isaiah 28:14–22

---

*He who believes will not be ashamed or give way
or make haste in sudden panic.*
Isaiah 28:16 (Amplified Bible)

On the day when impatience was handed out, I was definitely right in front! I find it very difficult to be patient – and even more difficult to wait – regardless of whether it is in a queue at a shop, in a traffic jam or for the Lord to answer my prayers. For this reason I have a tremendous admiration for Abraham who waited so patiently and faithfully for the Lord to fulfil his promise for a son.

However, people who wait upon the Lord are never disappointed says the Bible. If you believe, you should not be impatient at the same time. You should not think that God is not hearing your prayers either if he is asking you to be patient for a while. Sometimes God is waiting with his answers to test your faith and patience. He often uses your time of waiting as an examination!

Be more patient in future; be prepared to wait for God's answers. Then you may claim the wonderful promise in Luke 18:7–8 for yourself: 'And will not God bring about justice for his chosen ones, who cry out to him day and night? Will he keep putting them off? I tell you, he will see that they get justice, and quickly.'

Heavenly Father, as I have done so many times before, I once again confess before you my inability to wait and my impatience. Forgive me, Lord, and make me patient and willing to wait. Amen.

28 July
Lovelessness
Read: 1 Corinthians 13

*If I speak in the tongues of men and of angels, but have not love,
I am only a resounding gong or a clanging cymbal. If I have the gift
of prophecy and can fathom all mysteries and all knowledge, and if I have
a faith that can move mountains, but have not love, I am nothing.*
1 Corinthians 13:1–2

A loveless heart is probably the greatest obstacle to prayer. A heart which reflects the unconditional love of God is vital to a fervent prayer life. All other commandments are summarised in the two which Jesus selected in Matthew 22:37–40 to describe the whole law: 'Love the Lord your God above all and your neighbour as yourself.'

'If I do not love, I cannot pray either, because to be able to pray I have to have a spirit of love in my heart,' writes Onbekende Christen *(Christen en gebed,* p. 108). For this reason we naturally pray for those we love and, for the same reason, we often forget to pray for those who do not have such an important place in our hearts.

In your own power it is impossible to love others the way God loves you. However, the Holy Spirit wants to enable you to do so and once you can do so, your prayer life will benefit from it tremendously.

*Heavenly Father, I pray that you will help me to channel
my love for others to them by praying for them.
Please enable me to love like you. Amen.*

29 July
Do not doubt!
Read: Mark 11:24

Whatever you ask for in prayer, believe that you have received it, and it will be yours.
Mark 11:24

Doubt is another obstacle to prayer. Once when Jesus' disciples were unable to cast out an evil spirit, they asked him the reason for their inability, and Jesus then replied: 'Because you have so little faith' (Matthew 17:20). The power which Jesus makes available to you can never be separated from prayer and faith. When you pray and firmly believe that God will give you the things you ask (obviously provided they are in line with his will), it will be done for you.

The secret of this kind of answer to prayer is that we should be so close to God that we will not ask things which are not in line with his will for our lives.

This was the way Jesus prayed. Read his prayer before he raised Lazarus from the dead (John 11:41–42).

Always remember that what God gives you is what is best for you. In Gethsemane Jesus prayed that the cup should be taken away from him, and God did not answer this prayer the way he had asked – but God's answer ensured that you and I were able to become his children.

Heavenly Father, thank you for the assurance that I may ask without doubting and for the assurance that your answer to my prayer will always be what is right for me. Amen.

30 July
Clean hands and pure hearts
Read: Psalm 24

Who may ascend the hill of the Lord? Who may stand in his holy place? He who has clean hands and a pure heart, who does not lift up his soul to an idol or swear by what is false. He will receive the blessing from the Lord and vindication from God his Saviour.
Psalm 24:3–5

When you pray to God and do not want any obstacles between you which would hinder your fellowship with God, you need clean hands and a pure heart. Unfortunately all of us are sinners from birth. However, the Holy Spirit enables you to approach God's throne of grace with clean hands and a pure heart.

When Jesus died on the cross, he paid for your burden of sin once and for all – for the sins of the past as well as the sins of the future which you have not yet even committed. All you have to do is to confess your sin when you pray. And God is always prepared to forgive your sin on account of his Son's sacrifice so that you, although you are a sinner, can approach a holy God with confidence.

For this reason he also answers your prayers – in the Name of his Son who has already bought God's forgiveness for you on the cross.

Heavenly Father, I pray for clean hands and a pure heart so that I can communicate with you without any obstacles between us. Thank you that Jesus has made it possible for me. Amen

31 July
Praise the Lord for his faithfulness!
Read: Psalm 66:13–20

Praise be to God, who has not rejected my prayer
or withheld his love from me!
Psalm 66:20

In this beautiful psalm of praise, the psalmist confessed that he had hardly called to God when there was a song of praise on his lips. If he had cherished sin in his heart, the Lord would not have listened, but God did indeed listen, he heard his prayer (verses 17–18).

If you pray asking God to remove the obstacles which prevent you from drawing near to God, you may know that God is absolutely faithful – that he will answer your prayers even when you are sometimes not faithful to him. 'If we are faithless, he will remain faithful, for he cannot disown himself,' Paul wrote to Timothy (2 Timothy 2:13).

Sometimes you do in fact receive answers to your prayers which differ from those you had asked. Even then you have to know that God's answer is the right one for you, although it might not be the one you had asked. Sometimes you are disappointed in God because you have been praying fervently for something which, to the best of your knowledge, is in fact in line with his will, yet you do not receive it. Even then God's 'no' is the answer of a Father who loves you and who is absolutely faithful to you.

Heavenly Father, I praise you for being absolutely faithful,
for always answering my prayers in the best possible way.
Make me willing to cling to you. Amen.

August

Praying for others

We have to pray for others regularly. We all pray for those close to us as a matter of course. However, it is the Lord's will that we also pray for people we do not know, for people who have never been confronted with the gospel, for people working in God's harvest fields and for people we read about in newspapers or whose names we hear on the news.

When you pray for someone else, a miracle almost always follows: you actually start becoming interested in those you are pleading for with God. A seed of sincere love and interest starts germinating with regard to the people whose names you bring before God. When you pray for people you do not get on with, you discover that you become much more tolerant towards them. Interceding for others changes yourself: it turns you into the person God has made you to be, a person who has empathy with others. However, intercession never comes naturally – it is a discipline which you have to practise with perseverance.

It is my prayer that you will be able to intercede for others before God more easily than before after you have studied the daily readings prepared for this month.

1 August
Pray for the workers in the harvest field
Read: Matthew 9:35–38

Then he said to his disciples, 'The harvest is plentiful but the workers are few. Ask the Lord of the harvest, therefore, to send out workers into his harvest field.'
Matthew 9:37–38

Jesus urges his disciples to pray that the Lord should send out workers into his harvest field. If there is no-one to proclaim Jesus' good news to those who have not yet heard the gospel, the harvest of the Lord cannot be gathered.

It is vital to pray for God's kingdom. At *Amsterdam 2000*, the largest mission conference ever held, one of the speakers, pastor Pilau, said, 'What a privilege it is that 50 per cent of the world has still not been converted to Christ!' He beseeched the conference-goers not to wait for the call to evangelise because we received the call 2000 years ago (quoted from an article in *Kerkbode*).

You can participate in this call to the mission field by undertaking right now to pray faithfully for workers to be sent into God's harvest field. Who knows, perhaps the Holy Spirit will convict you to become one of these workers yourself!

Heavenly Father, forgive me for not praying faithfully for workers to be sent out into your harvest field and for your kingdom to come in the world. Teach me to pray more and to be prepared to be a co-worker myself. Amen.

2 August
Pray for those who do not yet know God
Read: 2 Corinthians 5:16–20

We are therefore God's ambassadors, as though God were making his appeal through us. We implore you on Christ's behalf: Be reconciled to God.
2 Corinthians 5:20

Converting souls to Christ was a passion with Paul to which he dedicated his whole life. He told the heathen that God had brought about reconciliation for them by the death of his Son, and he also pleaded with them on every occasion to accept this reconciliation.

Evelyn Christenson writes in her book *A journey into prayer* that she cannot understand why Christians pray so regularly for the sick Christians who, if they die – and they will eventually – will go to heaven, but completely neglect praying for those who do not know God. Should they die, they will go to a Christless eternity (p. 49).

As in Paul's case, God is also sending you to make disciples of people. Make a point of praying for people whom you know do not yet know the Lord. Pray for people you know who have not yet invited God into their lives, but pray also for those in countries where the gospel is not readily available.

Heavenly Father, please give me a passion for converting souls so that I, like Paul, will dedicate my life to telling others about you. I pray for everybody who does not yet know you. Amen.

3 August
Pray that God's kingdom will spread
Read: Ephesians 6:18–20

Pray also for me, that whenever I open my mouth, words may be given me so that I will fearlessly make known the mystery of the gospel ... Pray that I may declare it fearlessly, as I should.
Ephesians 6:19, 20

Prayer was extremely important to Paul – for this reason he also repeatedly insisted that people and churches should pray for his ministry. 'I urge you ... to join me in my struggle by praying to God for me,' he asked the church in Rome (Romans 15:30). 'Pray for us that the message of the Lord may spread rapidly,' he requested in 2 Thessalonians 3:1. As far as he was concerned, the power and success of his ministry depended on the prayers of other believers.

On his part he undertook to pray faithfully for his converts. 'God ... is my witness how constantly I remember you in my prayers at all times,' he wrote in Romans 1:9, 10. 'In all my prayers for all of you, I always pray with joy,' he wrote in his letter to the church in Philippi (Philippians 1:4).

It is an impossible task to work for the Lord without others praying for you. God's kingdom cannot be spread either unless you pray faithfully that this should happen.

Heavenly Father, I pray that your kingdom will be spread. I also pray for everyone who is proclaiming your word in the world. Please confirm that word yourself. Amen.

4 August
Pray for your minister!
Read: Ephesians 6:18–20

Pray also for me, that whenever I open my mouth, words may be given me so that I will fearlessly make known the mystery of the gospel.
Ephesians 6:19

'Pray for me,' Paul asked the church in Ephesus. Then he also told them what they had to pray for: That God may give me the right words so that I will proclaim the mystery of the gospel fearlessly.

Few people realise how stressful the work of a minister can be. It is his responsibility to preach God's word from the pulpit every Sunday. He bears the burdens of his whole congregation on his shoulders, and he also has to be available to his congregation day and night. People criticise him very easily if he does not toe the line. He and his family live in the proverbial fish bowl, visible to all. It is therefore not at all strange that many ministers change jobs and others need psychological counselling.

Your minister really needs your prayers. Pray for him and his family regularly – and tell them that you are interceding for them before God (to do this you have to know their names!). Pray right now that God should give your minister the right words to proclaim the gospel to your congregation.

Heavenly Father, I want to pray for our minister and his family today. I pray that you will help him to proclaim your word, that you will give him wisdom and power to perform his duties in the congregation with your help. Amen.

5 August
Pray for those in authority
Read: 1 Timothy 2:1–7

I urge, then, first of all, that … prayers … be made for everyone – for kings and all those in authority, that we may live peaceful and quiet lives in all godliness and holiness.
1 Timothy 2:1–2

After Paul had told Timothy that everyone should be prayed for, he became more specific. We must pray for all in authority, he wrote in verse 2. Christians must pay attention to the attitude they should have towards those who govern their country. Everyone should submit himself to the governing authorities, Paul wrote to the church in Rome. In fact, all authority has been established by God. He who rebels against the authority is rebelling against what God has instituted (Romans 13:1–2).

However, since those in authority are only human, they easily make mistakes which could anger the rest of us. Perhaps you are dissatisfied with the specific governing authorities at present – then make a point of praying for them rather than criticising them. Always remember that God himself has given them the power to rule over you.

Heavenly Father, please forgive me for criticising the authorities of my country instead of praying for them. Please change my attitude so that I will pray for the authorities regularly in future. Amen.

6 August
Pray for the head of state
Read: Psalm 84

Hear my prayer, O Lord God Almighty; listen to me, O God of Jacob.
Look upon our shield [or sovereign], O God;
look with favour on your anointed one.
Psalm 84:8–9

In Psalm 84 the psalmist pleaded with God, particularly for the king. He pleaded that God himself should look after the king and help him. In the Old Testament times the king was anointed by God himself and the psalmists then also interceded for their kings.

Although South Africa has no 'king', we should pray much more for our head of state.

The opinions of many members of the 'governing authorities' appointed over us differ radically from ours. The actions of those who are not Christians are sometimes totally unacceptable to us and we battle to come to terms with the laws they make and the decisions they take. It is rather difficult to pray for these people – yet Paul says we should do so.

How often do you pray for our country and government, for our state president? The more criticism you have about modern leaders, the more you should intercede for them before God.

Heavenly Father, I confess that I tend to criticise our leaders rather than pray for them. Today I pray specially for our president. Please assist him and help him to take the right decisions every day. Amen.

7 AUGUST
Pray for all people
Read: 1 Timothy 1:19, 2:1

*I urge, then, first of all, that requests, prayers,
intercession and thanksgiving be made for everyone ...*
1 Timothy 2:1

On writing to Timothy, Paul impressed on him the importance of prayer: pray for everyone, he said.

When we pray, we should not only bring those we know and our loved ones before the throne of God's grace. Everyone we come into contact with deserves our prayers.

When you sometimes do not know who to pray for, you only have to open your newspapers or watch television news. You will find the names of dozens of people who need your prayer that particular day. On the day on which I was writing this daily reading, a well-known figure in show business, who was at school with me, died tragically in a car accident. So many things happen daily to people you know (or do not know), that you may as well make some time in your prayer to talk to the Lord about people who are battling, people who have met with disaster, people who have lost loved ones.

Make a point from today to pray for all people – those you know as well as those you do not know. That is what the Lord wants.

*Heavenly Father, today I not only want to bring those I know
and love before your throne of grace, but also those I read about
in the paper and those I saw in the news bulletin.
Please comfort those who need you specially today. Amen.*

8 August
How you should pray
Read: 1 Timothy 2:1–7

I urge, then, first of all, that requests, prayers, intercession and thanksgiving be made for everyone ... that we may live peaceful and quiet lives in all godliness and holiness.
1 Timothy 2:1–2

Paul not only told Timothy to pray, he also explained how to pray for these people: by requests, prayers and intercession. In *Die Boodskap* version the consequences of this type of prayer are set out clearly: You will gather the fruit of such prayer, because you will then be able to live in peace and live the way God wants you to live. This is how it should be and this is also the way God who saved us wants it to be (verses 3–4, p. 686).

If you comply with these instructions, you will also gather the positive fruit involved: the Lord assures you of a peaceful life and enables you to live peaceful and quiet lives in all godliness and holiness.

While you are praying for all people, always see to it that your prayers are sincere. Beseech the Lord to hear your prayers. Should someone you have been praying for specially be converted, remember to thank the Lord for having answered your prayers.

Lord Jesus, thank you for the privilege of being an intercessor. Teach me to intercede for others before you with requests, intercession and thanksgiving. Amen.

9 August
Pray for people who are struggling
Read: 2 Corinthians 1:3–11

As you help us by your prayers.
2 Corinthians 1:11

When Paul was writing this letter to the church in Corinth, his circumstances were quite desperate: 'We were under great pressure, far beyond our ability to endure, so that we despaired even of life,' he wrote in verse 8.

At the end of the chapter, Paul nevertheless expressed his hope on God: despite his negative circumstances he was still sure that the Lord would deliver him from his difficult circumstances.

In these dreadful circumstances only the prayers of believers were helping Paul to persevere and endure. 'You help us by your prayers. Then many will give thanks on our behalf for the gracious favour granted us in answer to the prayers of many,' he wrote in verse 11.

When you hear of or read about people who are experiencing difficulties (while I am writing this daily reading, our prayer chain is in fact praying for the Strydom couple who are held captive in the Philippines), you should pray regularly for people who are suffering. By means of your prayers the Lord will bless them and even change their circumstances.

Heavenly Father, today I want to pray for people who are going through deep waters at the moment. For those who are discouraged and mourning. For those in danger. Please help them, I pray. Amen.

10 August
Thank God for difficult times
Read: 2 Corinthians 4:10–17

All this is for your benefit, so that the grace that is reaching more and more people may cause thanksgiving to overflow to the glory of God.
2 Corinthians 4:15

People are fragile, like jars of clay, Paul wrote to the church in Corinth. And these jars of clay are subjected to dangers every day, but although such a jar is pressed hard, it is not crushed, because the power of God is in these jars.

In times of trouble – which every Christian has to endure – we should hold on to God. When you are suffering, Paul wrote, you are carrying the death of Jesus in your own body, you become part of it. When this happens, the way you respond reveals to others that he is the Lord of your life.

If you are at times experiencing very bad problems, you may be comforted knowing that the trouble is momentary and will last only for a while. Do underline verse 17 in your Bible – the trouble of today is light and momentary, but you may claim the promise in the same verse – you are assured of one day being raised from the dead with Jesus. For this reason you will also manage, by the power of God, to thank him while you are suffering so that he can be glorified.

Lord Jesus, thank you for the assurance that my trouble will not last for ever, but that it will eventually lead to eternal glory with you. Amen.

11 August
Pray for sinners
Read: 1 John 5:13–17

If anyone sees his brother commit a sin that does not lead to death, he should pray and God will give him life.
1 John 5:16

When a believer sees someone committing sin which does not lead to death, he should pray for such a person rather than judge him, John wrote. (The sin 'which leads to death' here merely means that such a person stubbornly refuses to accept Jesus as Saviour and denies that he is the Son of God.)

All the commands are summarised in one command, that is, that we should love one another. Love is the fulfilment of the law, reads Romans 13:10. If you really love others and care about them, you will also be prepared to pray for them when you see they are doing wrong.

What do you do if people you know sin? Do you gossip about the wrong things they are doing, or are you willing to pray for them sincerely and at the same time stretch out a helping hand to them? If you are willing to do this, God himself will intervene and bring them back on track.

Lord, I am sorry that I gossip about people rather than pray when they sin. Please give me your attitude of love in my heart so that I can reach out to them. Amen.

12 August
Pray for other Christians
Read: Ephesians 6:10–18

And pray in the Spirit on all occasions with all kinds of prayers and requests. With this in mind, be alert and always keep on praying for all the saints.
Ephesians 6:18

Here on earth every child of God is involved in warfare against the devil daily. When Paul explained to the church in Ephesus the armour the Christian could put on to withstand the attacks of the evil one, he ended his illustration with the instruction: And pray in the Spirit on all occasions and always keep on praying for the saints (verse 18).

Jesus prayed regularly and also pleaded with his Father for his disciples on a regular basis. We should also guard against the onslaughts of the devil and pray regularly for our brothers and sisters in Christ. No Christian can remain standing without prayer. If you want to live according to the will of God, you have to learn to live prayerfully.

Only when we really intercede for one another before God will believers be able to remain standing against the cunning onslaughts of the devil. Christians desperately need one another's prayers! Make praying for God's children one of your priorities in prayer from today – praying for those you know as well as for those you do not know.

Heavenly Father, I pray for all believers in the world. Please strengthen them by the power of your Holy Spirit so that they will be able to resist the devil by your power day by day. Amen.

13 August
Pray for your enemies
Read: Matthew 5:43–48

But I tell you: Love your enemies and pray for those who persecute you, that you may be sons of your Father in heaven.
Matthew 5:44–45

God pours out his unlimited mercy on everybody – the good as well as the bad. In the light of this love, Jesus commands us to be willing to love our enemies and pray for them.

It is practically impossible to pray for your enemies – you will definitely not be able to do this unless God himself helps you. However, when you pray for your enemy, a strange thing happens: you discover that the people you cannot abide are not really that bad – that it even becomes easy to like them once you start praying for them!

How about it: can you, with God's help, love your enemies yet – and pray for them? If not, read the warning in 1 John 4:20: 'If anyone says "I love God," yet hates his brother, he is a liar. For anyone who does not love his brother, whom he has seen, cannot love God, whom he has not seen.'

Heavenly Father, you know how I battle to love certain people, and you also know that I do not really feel like praying for them! Forgive me and help me to love my enemies and pray for them. Amen.

14 August
Pray for your friends
Read: Job 42:7–10

After Job had prayed for his friends, the Lord made him prosperous again and gave him twice as much as he had before.
Job 42:10

Job's friends played an important role in his life. When they heard of his suffering they visited him and spent seven days and seven nights with him sitting on the ground without saying a word (Job 2:13). When they started talking, Job was not always very pleased with their advice. He had too many 'whys' of his own.

Then God himself reprimanded Job's friends and commanded them to bring a sacrifice before him. He told them that Job would pray for them, and that he would accept Job's prayer (Job 42:7–8).

The Lord did not answer Job's 'whys', but as soon as Job looked away from himself and started praying for his friends, this prayer not only benefited his friends but also himself. The Lord changed Job's circumstances but only after Job had started praying for his friends and he even blessed him more than before.

How often do you pray for your friends? Sometimes we are so wrapped up in our own problems and our 'whys' that we often forget to pray for our friends. Make a point of praying for your friends daily from today.

Heavenly Father, thank you for my friends. I am sorry that I pray so rarely for my friends. Help me to commit each one of them to you regularly. Amen.

15 August
Pray for your family
Read: Nehemia 1:4–10

> *O Lord, God of heaven, the great and awesome God ... let your ear be attentive and your eyes open to hear the prayer your servant is praying before you day and night for your servants, the people of Israel. I confess the sins we Israelites, including myself and my father's house, have committed against you.*
> Nehemia 1:5–6

Nehemia really took prayer seriously. The Lord therefore heard his prayers and Nehemia succeeded in building the wall around Jerusalem in record time. When Nehemia started praying, he first of all confessed the sin of his people, his own sin and the sin of his family.

Although it is important to pray for your country and your people regularly, you also have to confess your own sin and the sin of your family before God. Consider whether there are any relatives of yours who desperately need your prayers right now because they are not obedient to the Lord. Then pray for them by name, confess their sin before the Lord and ask him to forgive them.

Perhaps he also wants you to go to them to persuade them to turn away from their sin.

> *Heavenly Father, when I consider your holiness, I once again become aware of my own sinfulness and the sinfulness of my family. Please forgive us and help us to turn away from our sin and commit ourselves to serving you. Amen.*

16 August
Pray for your children and grandchildren
Read: Job 1:1–5

> *When a period of feasting had run its course, Job would send and have them (his sons and daughters) purified. Early in the morning he would sacrifice a burnt offering for each of them ... This was Job's regular custom.*
> Job 1:5

Job was a father who had the interests of his children at heart. When he noticed that they had been partying too much, he would sacrifice a burnt offering for them – this implies that he pleaded with God for his children and asked forgiveness for the sins they might have committed.

Parents and grandparents can still have a tremendous spiritual effect on their children. Paul also wrote to Timothy and stressed the influence his mother and grandmother had had on his spiritual life (2 Timothy 1:5): 'I have been reminded of your sincere faith, which first lived in your grandmother Lois and in your mother Eunice and, I am persuaded, now lives in you also.'

Your children and grandchildren are surrounded by temptations. They are confronted with things like alcohol, drugs and immorality from a very tender age. They need your prayers every day. Pray for them that God will make them happy and keep them from the evil one.

Heavenly Father, I once again want to pray for my children and grandchildren. You know the temptations they face daily – please keep them and forgive their sins. Amen.

17 August
Pray for spiritual maturity
Read: 2 Corinthians 13:9–13

Our prayer is for your perfection.
2 Corinthians 13:9

Paul prayed faithfully for 'his children in the faith'. When he wrote to the church in Corinth, he assured them that he was praying daily for their spiritual maturity. He asked them to turn away from wrong things so that he would not have to reprove them! He also requested them to pursue spiritual maturity, to accept his reproof, to be one in spirit and live in harmony. Should they do so, the love of God would be with them (verse 11).

If you work with people on a spiritual level, if you are a Sunday school teacher or a leader of a cell group, or if you attend church outreaches regularly, remember to pray faithfully for those you are working with. Pray particularly that they should become spiritually mature, and that the Lord himself will complete the work he has started in their lives. When we do much for God, we have to ask much of God, we have to be praying people, writes a certain Payson *(Christen en gebed,* p. 18).

Let this be true of you too!

Heavenly Father, thank you for the privilege of being a worker in your vineyard. I pray for every person I have shared you with, that they will become spiritually mature so that they will come to know you better every day. Amen.

18 August
Prayer means dependency
Read: Psalm 127

*Unless the Lord builds the house, its builders labour in vain ...
In vain you rise early and stay up late, toiling for food to eat –
for he grants sleep to those he loves.*
Psalm 127:1–2

Only when you truly realise that you can do absolutely nothing without God, you have the right attitude to pray. 'Blessed are the poor in spirit, for theirs is the kingdom of heaven,' Jesus said in his beatitudes (Matthew 5:1–2).

God makes it possible for you to pray. God comes ever closer to you when you take a step towards him. Everything is in vain if he does not help you, the psalmist wrote.

When you pray, you should be like a beggar standing beseechingly before God's throne of grace. Someone who knows that you could not have succeeded without the Lord' help. Someone who knows that everything you possess has been received from God. However, when you pray, you may also confess, like Paul, that you can do everything through him who gives you strength (Philippians 4:13).

Heavenly Father, I want to confess that I am totally dependent on you. Thank you that I know that everything I have has been received from you. Thank you that I may kneel before you, begging for your blessing. Amen.

19 August
Present your requests to God
Read: Philippians 4:1–9

Do not be anxious about anything, but in everything, by prayer and petition, with thanksgiving, present your requests to God.
Philippians 4:6

Wouldn't it be wonderful if all your requests could be fulfilled immediately and you could, at the same time, be rid of all your anxietes? All of us have dozens of things we would like to have and many things which cause anxiety. In his letter to the church in Philippi, Paul gives excellent advice as to how to have your dreams come true and how to be rid of your anxieties: tell God about them!

Although prayer should in the first place revolve around praising and honouring God, you may make your anxieties and desires known to God at the same time. Although God already knows all about you, he wants you to talk to him – just as you like listening when your children are talking to you.

When you pray, you may share everything you have in your heart with God with confidence – and entrust it to him. Once you have learnt to share your dreams and problems with God, you will discover that your anxieties will disappear – that you will no longer be anxious about so many things because you have a Father in heaven who cares for you.

Heavenly Father, thank you that I may bring all my anxieties and worries to you for the umpteenth time and leave them with you, knowing that you will provide. Amen.

20 August
Carry each other's burdens
Read: Galatians 6:2

Carry each other's burdens, and in this way you will fulfil the law of Christ.
Galatians 6:2

A believer who loves his neighbour will be willing to bear such a person's burdens. The burdens which Paul referred to may be anything which makes life difficult for them, such as illness, financial or family problems.

One of the very best ways of carrying the burdens of others is to pray for them. When my children were still at school and university, they regularly asked the prayer chain of our church to pray for them when they had to write tests and exams – and they also assured me time and again how much the prayers had meant to them.

When you pray for others who have problems, they find that their burdens are lifted. When my husband had a heart attack some years ago, the whole congregation prayed for us. I could literally sense the prayers, and this made me much calmer than I would have been without them.

If you are aware of a particular person who is experiencing major problems at the moment, do not postpone carrying that person's burdens by praying for him or her.

Heavenly Father, I pray for everyone who has to carry heavy burdens. For those with financial problems, for the sick and for people who are discouraged and sad. Please strengthen them. Amen.

21 AUGUST
Pray for the right guidance
Read: Psalm 25

Show me your ways, O Lord, teach me your paths.
Psalm 25:4

All of us at times need guidance. Throughout the Bible we also read that God gives his children the right guidance and points them in the right direction by his word.

You may also ask God for this guidance like the psalmist often did. David had no doubts about this: 'Who, then, is the man that fears the Lord? He will instruct him in the way chosen for him,' he wrote in Psalm 25:12. You may claim this promise for yourself, provided you study the six words which read: the man who fears the Lord. The Lord will give you the right guidance only when you love him, obey his word carefully and serve him faithfully.

However, God's guidance no longer occurs by signs and wonders as in the Old Testament times. Today God guides his children by his Holy Spirit and his word. 'Your word is a lamp to my feet and a light for my path,' David said in Psalm 119:105.

Study your Bible so that you will be able to make use of that light when you are looking for the right guidance again.

Heavenly Father, I pray that you will show me daily how I should live. Please point me in the right direction by the light of your word. Amen.

22 August
Remain in Jesus
Read: John 15:7–16

---

*If you remain in me and my words remain in you,
ask whatever you wish, and it will be given you.*
John 15:7

Jesus asked his disciples to go out and bear fruit for him (John 15:16). In order to bear this fruit, they had to remain in him and his words in them. Then Jesus promised them that they would be able to ask anything they wished and it would be given them. There is no way the branch of a vine is able to grow and bear grapes unless it is grafted into the vine. It is likewise impossible for a Christian to bear fruit and receive answers to his prayers unless he remains in Jesus.

Two conditions for answer to prayer appear in our verse: If you remain in me, and my words remain in you. If you have an intimate relationship with Jesus, you will actually know his will for your life; and if you permit his message to shape your life and thoughts, you will be able to ask anything knowing that you will receive what you have asked, because your prayer requests will always be in line with God's will.

Lord Jesus, I want to live close to you and make your words part of my life, so that my prayer requests will always be according to your will, and so that I will bear much fruit for you. Amen.

23 August
Pray simply
Read: Matthew 6:5–14

And when you pray, do not keep on babbling like pagans.
Matthew 6:7

Simplicity is one of the most important requirements for a blessed prayer life. All of us have been in prayer meetings where people literally 'kill' the prayer meeting with their long drawn-out prayers! The Authorised King James version uses the expression 'vain repetition'. Some people think they can impress not only others but also God with their eloquence.

Unfortunately it does not work that way. Your Father already knows what you need before you even ask him, Jesus himself said (Matthew 6:8). You therefore do not have to feel inferior if you cannot pray 'eloquently' or pray long prayers like other Christians. All you need to do is simply to talk to God: praise him because he is great and wonderful, confess your sin, thank him for all his blessings poured out on you and tell him about your husband and children, about what you have to do today, about the things you fear and the things that fill you with joy.

You will soon discover that it is quite simple to talk to God – and that he is always there to listen to your prayer.

Heavenly Father, thank you that I do not have to pray complicated or eloquent prayers to communicate with you – that I merely have to talk to you the way a child would talk to its Father. Amen.

24 August
Pray for the needs of others
Read: Luke 11:5–13

Though he will not get up and give him the bread because he is his friend, yet because of the man's boldness he will get up and give him as much as he needs.
Luke 11:8

Here Jesus told his disciples in a parable what prayer meant. In the story he told them, it is interesting to note that the man's initial request for bread was refused by his friend. However, when he persevered, he eventually gave him what he needed. God's willingness to give to those who keep on asking is the focal point of this parable.

When we pray for others we do not always receive exactly what we are asking and when we want it, Andrew Murray wrote. However, God gives us the assurance that if we keep on asking, the Lord will eventually answer our prayers for those we are interceding for (*With Christ in the school of prayer*, p. 64).

If any of your friends are currently in distress and need your help, pray for them. God will answer your prayers at the right time, but be patient, keep on asking and also be willing to wait on God for an answer.

Heavenly Father, I want to pray for all those in need. Make me willing not only to pray, but also to help them. Thank you for your willingness to answer my prayer requests. Amen.

25 August
Pray for open doors
Read: Colossians 4:2–6

And pray for us, too, that God may open a door for our message, so that we may proclaim the mystery of Christ, for which I am in chains. Pray that I may proclaim it clearly, as I should.
Colossians 4:3–4

Paul's whole ministry underlined the importance of prayer. He often asked churches to pray for him when he was proclaiming the word or when he was a prisoner. He believed that the success of his ministry was closely linked to others praying for him. In our verses for today, he requested the Colossians to pray for him that, where he was at that time, he would have positive opportunities to proclaim the gospel. By their participation in his ministry they then became involved in what he was doing.

Have you ever considered the possibility that the fact that we are not praying enough in our congregations could be one of the reasons for our churches being so powerless? How often do you personally pray for 'open doors' so that Jesus' gospel can be proclaimed in the world? Do you make use of the prayer opportunities in your own congregation such as the Week of Prayer at the beginning of the year and the prayer meetings at Pentecost? Try to join those who regularly intercede for the preaching of the gospel in future.

Heavenly Father, please forgive me for having done so little about proclaiming your kingdom in the world to date. Help me to make the best possible use of the opportunities for prayer in my own congregation in future. Amen.

26 August
Be holy!
Read: Hebrews 12:14–17

Make every effort to live in peace with all men and to be holy.
Hebrews 12:14

If you want God to answer your prayer requests, you will in turn have to be willing to live the way he asks you to. The Holy God expects his children to be holy too. Christians are called to holiness in several passages of Scripture. In Leviticus 11:45 the Lord told his people in the words of Moses: 'I am the Lord who brought you up out of Egypt to be your God; therefore be holy, because I am holy.' God's children are predestined to conform to the likeness of his Son, Paul wrote to the church in Rome (Romans 8:29). This is the crux of sanctification: that we should become more like Jesus every day.

We have repeatedly heard that sin is a very important factor which prevents God from listening to our prayers. If you still cherish sin in your life, you have not yet responded to God's command for holiness. Just remember: being holy does not mean sinless perfection, but that you will be set aside for God, and that sin will no longer rule you.

Heavenly Father, please enable me to live in holiness as you are holy so that I will become more like Jesus every day. Amen.

27 August
Pray for forgiveness
Read: Luke 15:11–24

I will set out and go back to my father and say to him: Father, I have sinned against heaven and against you. I am no longer worthy to be called your son.
Luke 15:18–19

The parable of the lost son is the most beautiful illustration of God's unconditional forgiveness. The son who had squandered his inheritance in a foreign country, decided to return home to ask his father's forgiveness. He realised that he had not only sinned against his father but also against God (verse 18). The father responded in a surprising way: when he was still a long way off, his father saw him, ran towards him, embraced and kissed him and organised a feast to celebrate his joy because his son had returned home. Before the son could even say a word, his father showed him that he was forgiven unconditionally.

God does this with every child of his who is convicted of sin, returns to God and confesses his sin. He is immediately willing to forgive us time after time. Use this illustration when you are convicted of sin: God is waiting impatiently for you to return and he wants to forgive all your sin unconditionally.

Heavenly Father, I want to return to you once again to apologise for sinning against you. Thank you for being willing to forgive me time after time when I confess my sin. Amen.

28 August
Serve God by prayer
Read: Luke 2:3, 6–8

*She was eighty-four. She never left the temple
but worshipped night and day, fasting and praying.*
Luke 2:37

This is a wonderful character reference of the prophetess Anna! Although she was already advanced in years, her place in the temple was never empty, and she served God day and night, fasting and praying. Anna could have had many excuses for no longer serving the congregation, but she was absolutely faithful to her Lord. Her whole life was one of service, commitment and persevering prayer. 'Next to worshipping God, service is the most important objective of prayer. Prayer is true religion, service to God,' Dr Hennie Conradie writes (*ABC van die gebed*, p. 33).

Prayer is also the special service to the glory of God which each of us can perform, even when we are no longer young, even when we are ill, even when we can do nothing else. And when people pray, God listens.

Perhaps you are no longer young, either, and perhaps your circumstances are such at present that, in your own eyes, you do not mean much to others. Then you can still serve God by praying for others. Serve God like Anna by interceding for others every day.

*Heavenly Father, you know there is not much I can still do for you.
Thank you that I can still pray for other people. Show me who needs
my prayers the most today. Amen.*

29 AUGUST
What you do for God lasts for ever
Read: 1 Corinthians 15:58

Therefore, my dear brothers, stand firm. Let nothing move you.
Always give yourselves fully to the work of the Lord,
because you know that your labour in the Lord is not in vain.
1 Corinthians 15:58

At the beginning of his second letter to the church in Corinth, Paul wrote that he was urging them as fellow-workers of God to see to it that they did not receive God's grace in vain (2 Corinthians 6:1).

In 1 Corinthians 15:58 Paul asked that the church in Corinth should stand firm, not allow anything to move them, always give themselves fully to the work of the Lord because they knew that their labour in the Lord was not in vain. 'Since you know that in the Lord your labour cannot be lost,' reads the NEB version of this verse. Our prayers and the things we do for God's kingdom are never wasted, even if we only see the fruit of those prayers and our labour in God's kingdom years later.

You can also be a fellow worker in God's kingdom by praying.

You may also claim this promise – that your effort in God's service will never be in vain. When you pray, the Lord will answer your prayers and reward your prayer effort.

Heavenly Father, thank you for the assurance that nothing I do for you is ever wasted. Help me to work for you with my whole heart and please give me fruit on my work for your kingdom. Amen.

30 August
Fellow workers by prayer
Read: 2 Corinthians 1:3–11

> ... *as you help us by your prayers. Then many will give thanks on our behalf for the gracious favour granted us in answer to the prayers of many.*
> 2 Corinthians 1:11

In 2 Corinthians 1:8–10 Paul gave a detailed account of exactly how much he and his fellow workers suffered in Asia. However, the description of their disasters ended in a testimony: They were under great pressure, far beyond their ability to endure, so that they despaired even of life. However, this happened that they might learn not to rely on themselves but on God. They believed that he would continue to deliver them (verses 8–10). The Corinthian believers were contributing by praying for them, Paul wrote in verse 11. Their prayers were not only a tremendous blessing to Paul and his fellow workers but also to many others.

Paul regarded himself as part of a body whose sympathy and prayer support he could rely on. In the work of the kingdom, the prayers of the churches were just as real to him as the power of God, Andrew Murray wrote (*With Christ in the school of prayer*, p. 115).

Are your prayers a blessing to those around you?

Heavenly Father, thank you that I may be a fellow worker in your kingdom by means of prayer. I pray that my prayers will be a blessing to others so that they will thank you. Amen.

31 August
Before you pray for others
Read: Psalm 139:19–24

Search me, O God, and know my heart; test me and know my anxious thoughts. See if there is any offensive way in me, and lead me in the way everlasting.
Psalm 139:23–24

In this psalm, the psalmist asked God to search his heart to see if he was perhaps heading in the wrong direction. Before we can intercede for others before God, we should check whether the communication channel between God and us is open.

Evelyn Christenson says that a group in their church decided to start praying for the congregation on a regular basis. However, God gave them Psalm 66:18 as guideline: If they still cherished sin in their hearts, God would not listen. This verse made them realise that God could only use them as intercessors once they had confessed each sin before him (*A journey into prayer*, p. 17).

If you want to become a serious intercessor after you have studied the daily readings for this month, you should also ask the Lord to search your heart and see whether you are perhaps going in the wrong direction by concealing the sin in your life from him.

Heavenly Father, forgive me for having prayed for others so many times while I have tried to conceal the sin in my own life from you. Please search my heart and point out my sin to me. Amen.

SEPTEMBER

Prayers from the Bible

The prayers prayed in the Bible have remained fresh and new down the years. When we study these prayers we can still be inspired by them and learn precious lessons in prayer from them. We may also use the prayers to talk to God ourselves. For example, if you are happy, praise God by reading one of David's psalms of joy; if you are discouraged, go to Jeremiah; if you want to intercede for your loved ones, follow Paul's example. These Biblical prayers verbalise practically every emotion God's children still experience every day.

God answered some of the prayers, while others were not answered, because he had another, better plan for those who had prayed. However, a silver thread runs through the prayers of these prayer warriors in the Bible: they had an intimate relationship with their Lord, and they had the confidence to discuss anything with him.

By analysing the prayers of men of God like Abraham, Moses, David and Paul, you can learn a great deal about prayer – and you can also enrich your own prayer life by them.

1 September
Humble yourself
Read: Genesis 18:22–33

*The men turned away and went towards Sodom,
but Abraham remained standing before the Lord.*
Genesis 18:22
*Now that I have been so bold as to speak to the Lord,
though I am nothing but dust and ashes ...*
Genesis 18:27

When Abraham's visitors returned to Sodom and Gomorrah, the Lord remained standing with Abraham – as if he were waiting for Abraham to speak to him. And Abraham did not disappoint God. However, before he started talking to God, Abraham realised his own insignificance before the Lord. This is the right attitude everyone who prays should have. Abraham's heart was also filled with love for the people in Sodom and Gomorrah, therefore he was willing to pray for them. 'This is intercession, not to continue hammering stubbornly on a door that has been shut, but to plead with God for his own glory. God is waiting to see whether we are willing to look around with eyes filled with love and to pray. Perhaps we do not pray because we do not love,' DJS wrote in the column on spiritual values (*Die Burger*, 22 January 2000).

When you pray, it would be good if you would always, like Abraham, remember that the God to whom you are praying is great and omnipotent and that you yourself are insignificant. Ask God to give you love in your heart for others to be able to pray for them.

*Lord, forgive me for praying so much more for my own needs
than for the deliverance of others. Teach me to intercede for others
like Abraham. Amen.*

2 September
Abraham prays for Sodom and Gomorrah
Read: Genesis 18:16–22

Abraham approached him and said: 'Will you sweep away the righteous with the wicked? What if there are fifty righteous people in the city. Will you … not spare the place for the sake of the fifty righteous people in it?'
Genesis 18:23–24

The ungodly people in Sodom and Gomorrah deserved to be destroyed by God. God confided in Abraham and told him what he was planning to do to the sinful cities. However, Abraham dared to plead with God for the godless people in Sodom and Gomorrah again and again. By repeatedly praying for them, he was not praying against the will of God. It was after all God's will that all men should be saved. He was being drawn into God's universal plan of mercy, step by step. To him it was unthinkable that a city could be destroyed while even a small handful of righteous people were living there. He therefore pleaded with God to save them if there were only fifty, only forty-five, only forty, thirty, twenty righteous people to be found. When it became clear that there were not even ten righteous people, Abraham gave up.

You could learn from Abraham to plead with God for others with confidence. However, like Abraham, you also have to learn to submit when the time is right.

Lord, make me concerned about others like Abraham was, and willing to plead for them with you. Thank you that I know that you always do what is right. Amen.

3 SEPTEMBER
Moses' prayer
Read: Exodus 15:1–18

The Lord is my strength and my song; he has become my salvation. He is my God, and I will praise him, my father's God, and I will exalt him. The Lord will reign for ever and ever.
Exodus 15:2, 18

God manifested his wonderworking power time and again in the life of his servant Moses. God delivered his people from Egypt in such a way that nobody could doubt that he was indeed the only God. However, God not only delivered his people from slavery, he also sustained them in the desert for forty years. To this Lord Moses sang a song in Exodus 15. He praised God as his strength and salvation, as the victor in battle, as the One who rules for ever.

God is still able to work miracles in your life the way he did for his people then. He is still the faithful God of the Covenant who keeps all the promises in his word. The God who promises you his strength and protection every day of your life. Like Moses you should praise God for who he is and for what he does for you.

Lord, I praise you as the God who is still my strength and my protection. Thank you for still guiding me the way you guided Moses. I praise you because you rule for ever. Amen.

4 September
Joshua asks for a miracle
Read: Joshua 10:12–15

*On the day the Lord gave the Amorites over to Israel,
Joshua said to the Lord in the presence of Israel: 'O sun, stand still over
Gibeon, O moon, over the Valley of Aijalon.'*
Joshua 10:12

In the passage of Scripture for today we read that Joshua asked God an impossible sign and God answered Joshua's prayer: he made the sun stand still for a whole day so that his people could defeat the Amorites. 'There has never been a day like it before or since, a day when the Lord listened to a man! Surely the Lord was fighting for Israel!' we read in Joshua 10:14.

Sometimes the Lord allows miracles to happen when his children pray, as he did when Joshua asked that the sun and the moon should stand still so that Israel could win the war. Today we would definitely not ask the Lord to make the sun stand still, yet the Lord is still the same omnipotent God as he was in Joshua's time. He can still work miracles. He still controls nature. Do you have Joshua's faith to ask him to perform a miracle for you? He will also allow you to have the victory over your personal crises if you ask him. He is on your side, so you can never be anything but victorious!

*Heavenly Father, thank you for being omnipotent, for loving me
and for still being able to perform miracles. I praise you that,
with you, I am always on the winning side. Amen.*

5 September
Solomon's prayer
Read: 1 Kings 8:22–24, 39, 56–57

Praise be to the Lord, who has given rest to his people Israel just as he promised. Not one word has failed of all the good promises he gave through his servant Moses.
1 Kings 8:56

After Solomon had completed the temple, he prayed a moving prayer before the Lord. In this prayer he praised God for his faithfulness, he asked the Lord to watch over the temple day and night, and he also interceded for the people before the Lord. He thanked God for giving them a country, and for always keeping all his promises. He also prayed that God's people would always be willing to live according to his will and obey his commands and that he would answer the prayers prayed to him in the temple.

From Solomon you can learn to thank the Lord for everything he gives you by his grace. You should not fail to remind the Lord of his promises either. Ask him in your own prayer to enable you to live according to his will and to obey his law. He will do this for you by his Holy Spirit.

Heavenly Father, I praise you for your incomparable greatness. Thank you that I may be your temple where you live, and that I have the assurance that you will also fulfil every promise in your word for me. Amen.

6 September
The prayer of a sinner
Read: 2 Chronicles 33:1–2, 10–13

In his distress he sought the favour of the Lord his God and humbled himself greatly before the God of his fathers. And when he prayed to him, the Lord was moved by his entreaty and listened to his plea; so he brought him back to Jerusalem and to his kingdom. Then Manasseh knew that the Lord is God.
2 Chronicles 33:12–13

King Manasseh of Israel was a terrible atheist – he rebuilt the idolatrous altars in Israel and worshipped idols himself. He even sacrificed his own sons to idols. When the Lord sent the king of Assyria to take him captive, Manasseh suddenly remembered the God of Israel and pleaded for mercy before the Lord.

Instead of punishing him as he deserved, we read that the Lord had mercy upon him. He not only answered the godless Manasseh's emergency prayer, he also allowed him to return to Israel and reinstated him as king!

To us it would appear as if the disobedient Manasseh got off very lightly! However, this is a beautiful illustration of God's infinite mercy when his children pray and ask for forgiveness.

If you have strayed from the Lord lately, ask him to forgive you as he forgave Manasseh. He is always willing to do so.

Heavenly Father, your mercy on sinners is infinite!
Thank you that you hear my prayers time and again
when I ask you to forgive my sins. Amen.

7 September
The prayer of Nehemiah
Read: Nehemiah 1:4–11

O Lord, let you ear be attentive to the prayer of your servant and to the prayers of your servants who delight in revering your name. Give your servant success today by granting him favour in the presence of this man.
Nehemiah 1:11

When Nehemiah heard that the citizens of Jerusalem were suffering and that the walls of Jerusalem were broken down, his heart was touched. He decided to ask the king's permission to go to Jerusalem to help his people. However, before Nehemiah went to the king, he approached the Lord. He prayed that the Lord should answer his prayer and that the king would be sympathetic. The rest is history. The king gave him permission, Nehemiah travelled to Jerusalem and, with the help of the Lord, he succeeded in rebuilding the walls of Jerusalem in record time, despite tremendous resistance.

'We can achieve more by our prayers than by all our labour. Prayer can achieve anything, it can achieve everything God can do!' writes Onbekende Christen *(Christen en gebed,* p. 14).

If, like Nehemia, you can master the secret of praying before doing, you will save yourself many failures. If you want to do something for the Lord again, consult him first and ask him to bless your plans with success.

Heavenly Father, thank you for the lesson that I should pray before I act. Teach me to talk to you before I tackle anything. Amen.

8 September
Prayers in emergencies
Read: Nehemiah 2:1–8

The king said to me, 'What is it you want?' Then I prayed to the God of heaven ... and because the gracious hand of my God was upon me, the king granted my requests.
Nehemiah 2:4, 8

Although Nehemiah had asked the Lord's counsel and assistance before he went to the king, his courage failed him when the king asked him plainly what he wanted. In the presence of the king, Nehemiah prayed an emergency prayer to the Lord. He then submitted his request to the king, and afterwards testified: 'Because the gracious hand of my God was upon me, the king granted my request' (verse 8).

God's children do not always have to pray long prayers when they are alone. We may talk to God at any time of the day or night – also by means of a quick prayer in emergencies. The Lord already knows what you need as well as what you want to ask him. He also listens when you use the hot line for emergency prayers. You may be linked to God all day long by means of quick prayers – also when you are travelling by car or experiencing a crisis at work. God is always there for you – you have a hot line to him.

Heavenly Father, thank you that I may also communicate with you by means of quick prayers. I praise you for always being accessible to me. Amen.

9 September
Seek God
Read: Job 23:1–5

If only I knew where to find him; if only I could go to his dwelling!
I would state my case before him and fill my mouth with arguments.
I would find out what he would answer me, and consider what he would say.
Job 23:3–5

Prayer is always a search for God. When Job was really suffering, he tried to find God's dwelling. In the midst of loss, pain, sorrow and illness, Job's prayer was not that the Lord should restore his wealth or heal him, but that he would answer his prayers. He succeeded in holding on to God in the midst of his despair.

Although Job did not receive answers to all the questions he wanted to ask God, God gave Job a peep into his glory by showing him the works of his hands. Job then acknowledged God's omnipotence and his own inability.

Unlike Job, it is much easier for us to get in touch with God. By his death on the cross, Jesus enables you to talk to God in prayer directly with the assurance that he answers as well as listens, even when you are not always aware of it. Furthermore, by his Holy Spirit God himself lives in you and you have him with you every day – ready to listen to your prayers.

Holy Spirit, thank you for living in me and for always being there
when I want to talk to you. Although there are still many unanswered
questions in my life, I know you love me and care for me. Amen.

10 September
You do not have to remain silent
Read: Job 23:10–17

Yet I am not silenced by the darkness,
by the thick darkness that covers my face.
Job 23:17

Job felt terribly wronged by all the disasters which had struck him, and he had the courage to tell God as much. Although he knew God was far greater than he was and that he could never oppose God, he nevertheless stated his case before God, knowing full well that he could not change his circumstances by doing so. 'He does whatever he pleases,' Job said (Job 23:13). Eventually God answered Job's prayer, and he blessed him even more than before (Job 42:10).

It is a mistake to remain silent when things happen in your life which you cannot understand. It is good to tell God exactly how you feel: tell him you cannot understand him, that you feel bitter and wronged. Eventually you will discover, like Job, that God will change your circumstances or give you the strength to handle your negative circumstances by his power.

Heavenly Father, thank you that you do not expect me to remain silent when I am disappointed in you. Thank you for listening, even when my prayers are lamentations! Please change my circumstances so that I will be able to praise you again. Amen.

11 September
When hearsay becomes seeing …
Read: Job 42:1–6

> *Then Job replied to the Lord: 'I know that you can do all things …*
> *My ears had heard of you but now my eyes have seen you.'*
> Job 42:2, 5

In Job 42 Job acknowledged God's omnipotence – he put away his 'whys' without insisting on answers. The Lord taught Job a precious lesson for life: his suffering became the glasses through which he could see God. Although he had served the Lord before, he had never met him face to face. His knowledge of God had only been hearsay, but now Job discovered that God was much greater than himself, and his hearsay knowledge of God was changed into an encounter with God himself.

Job ultimately admitted that he had tried to talk about things he had not understood. He realised that it was always a mistake to question the works of God and he confessed his guilt before the Lord.

All of us experience things in life which we cannot explain and which we cannot reconcile with God's love for us. We often become better acquainted with God personally by these negative things. Your problems may be the glasses through which you are able to see God face to face.

> *Heavenly Father, forgive me for so often questioning you and teach me*
> *that I get to know you better by the suffering and pain. Amen.*

12 September
You make people rejoice!
Read: Psalm 65

Praise awaits you, O God, in Zion; to you our vows will be fulfilled. You crown the year with your bounty, and your carts overflow with abundance.
Psalm 65:1, 11

Of all the prayer warriors in the Bible, David is probably the one with whom we can most easily identify. Practically every human need is brought before God in the psalms, and you could therefore choose the words of any psalm and quote them to God directly.

Psalm 65 is a song of praise to the God who makes all people rejoice, who deserves to be praised, who answers our prayers and cares for us day after day. The reasons why the psalmist wanted to praise God is spelled out clearly: forgiveness of sin, the awesome deeds with which God responded to the prayers of his people, God's faithful care for their land – he made it fertile so that his children could enjoy abundance.

God does not bless Israel only. He is still meeting the material needs of his children. We also gather the fruit of his abundance in nature – everything we have comes from God's hand. You have even more reason to praise him than his people Israel, because he not only looks after you – he also sent his Son so that you can have eternal life. Should you need anything at the moment, you may ask him for it with confidence.

Heavenly Father, thank you that you meet my needs every day – that you not only look after me, but provide me with your abundance. Amen.

13 SEPTEMBER
Call to God
Read: Psalm 119:145–152

I call with all my heart; answer me, O Lord … I call out to you; save me … I rise before dawn and cry for help; I have put my hope in your word.
Psalm 119:145–147

When the psalmist talks to God here, it is obvious that he spends much time in prayer. He calls to God 'before dawn' (verse 147) and lies awake all night while he meditates on God's word (verse 148). He urgently pleads with God to answer his prayer. His worst fear is not physical suffering but that his commitment to the word of the Lord could be severed. His desire is to be delivered from his circumstances so that he could get to know the Lord even better. He also told the Lord about his enemies who are drawing closer. Yet he was positive that God was still nearer to him than his enemies.

You may also hold on to this promise personally: the Lord is always closer to you than your crises. You may talk to him before dawn and late at night and tell him of your problems. Nothing can ever separate you from his love for you.

Heavenly Father, thank you that I may call to you day and night and tell you about all my problems. I praise you for the assurance that you are always closer to me than my problems. Amen.

14 September
Look to heaven!
Read: Isaiah 38:14

I cried like a swift or thrush, I moaned like a mourning dove. My eyes grew weak as I looked to the heavens. I am troubled; O Lord, come to my aid!
Isaiah 38:14

This striking prayer by King Hezekiah teaches us that when we are suffering, we have to look to the Lord. As a result of his illness, King Hezekiah was in such a desperate situation that he complained to God that his eyes were growing weak looking up to the heavens! He also prayed earnestly that the Lord should deliver him from his suffering. However, in the end he was able to testify that the Lord had spoken to him personally through his illness.

Most people who had to suffer a serious illness can testify that they were able to hear God's voice more clearly than before because of their illness. In Isaiah 38:15 Hezekiah testified: 'I will walk humbly all my years because of this anguish of my soul.' Even if the consequences of your illness will haunt you all your life, as in Hezekiah's case, you should listen carefully to God's voice when you are suffering.

Learn to look away from your own suffering and look up to heaven …

Lord, although this illness is very difficult for me, I have to confess that it has taught me to look up to you and see your hand in my life. Thank you that I can experience your help daily. Amen.

15 September
Suffering is good for you
Read: Isaiah 38:17–22

Surely it was for my benefit that I suffered such anguish. In your love you kept me from the pit of destruction; you have put all my sins behind your back.
Isaiah 38:17

Suffering and illness often make us move back to God. This was also true in King Hezekiah's case. Although he had served God faithfully at first, he gradually became very complacent. He no longer needed God as much as before, because he was so prosperous. However, then God intervened and Hezekiah became seriously ill.

Fortunately Hezekiah knew who to turn to in a crisis. He prayed earnestly that the Lord should heal him again. And Hezekiah's prayer was answered. After his illness we are introduced to another Hezekiah. He experienced his suffering as a lesson and admitted that the suffering had been good for him, that it had once again taught him that God loved him and had saved him from death and had forgiven his sin.

Suffering is good for you, although no-one enjoys suffering. Although you may experience illness and suffering negatively, you could benefit from it: in times of suffering you realise all too well that only God can help and heal you. Suffering also teaches you to be sympathetic towards others.

Heavenly Father, I now realise that you have been teaching me valuable lessons by means of my negative experiences. Thank you that these experiences have also taught me to feel for others. Amen.

16 September
A song of praise to the Creator
Read: Jeremiah 10:12–16

---

*But God made the earth by his power; he founded the world
by his wisdom and stretched out the heavens by his understanding ...
for he is the Maker of all things.*
Jeremiah 10:12, 16

The prophet Jeremiah was actually known for his lamentations, but here he sang a beautiful song of praise to the Creator of the world. Jeremiah here compared the omnipotence and insight of the God of Israel with the worthless idols that were sometimes worshipped by God's people. He once again realised his own insignificance compared to God's greatness, his own lack of understanding compared to God's wisdom.

Whenever you go for a walk and see the miracles in nature, you should sing a song of praise as Jeremiah sang to the Creator God. When you look at all the things God has made, you should once again become aware of God's unfathomable omnipotence and insight – and at the same time realise your own insignificance. Never become blasé about the beauty of nature or forget to praise God for it. When you look at the sun setting over the sea again or at a bunch of flowers from your garden, praise God in the words of Jeremiah.

*Heavenly Father, I praise you for having made the earth by your power,
for having established the world by your wisdom. When I consider the
work of your hands, I know your are omnipotent. Thank you that you
love me even though I am so unworthy. Amen.*

17 September
Jeremiah's prayer in a time of crisis
Read: Jeremiah 15:15–20

Why is my pain unending and my wound grievous and incurable?
Will you be to me like a deceptive brook, like a spring that fails?
Jeremiah 15:18

To me this prayer by Jeremiah is one of the most moving in the Bible. The prophet had reached the stage where his suffering had become so severe that he felt he could no longer rely on the Lord. All of us experience times in our lives when we could pray this prayer with Jeremiah.

Fortunately Jeremiah (and perhaps you) only feel as if God is far away. In verse 20 God promised Jeremiah that he would be with him to help and rescue him. This promise applies to all God's children even today. Even in times when you personally feel as if you can no longer rely on God, he is still listening to you, and he is with you to help and rescue you. Perhaps he only wants you to wait for his answer for a little while right now.

Heavenly Father, forgive me that today I also feel as if you are not listening to my prayers, as if I cannot rely on you. Thank you for your promise that you are with me, that you yourself will deliver me. Amen.

18 September
Daniel's prayer
Read: Daniel 9:4–9

O Lord, the great and awesome God, who keeps his covenant of love with all who love him and obey his commands.
Daniel 9:4

Daniel used to kneel in front of his window three times a day to praise, worship and thank God (Daniel 6:11). It is also obvious from his prayer in Daniel 9 that he was used to talking to the Lord. His respect for the Lord becomes obvious in the salutation of his prayer: he addressed God as 'the great and awesome God' and acknowledged him as the God who kept his Covenant with Israel and who kept his promises.

Daniel was honest with God and did not try to conceal his own sin and the sin of his people, but confessed it openly: 'We have not obeyed the Lord our God … all Israel has transgressed your law,' he said in verses 10 and 11. He then pleaded with God to forgive his own sin and the sin of his people.

And God always responds when his children confess their sin sincerely: in verse 23 the angel told Daniel that God had answered him as soon as he began to pray.

When you confess your sin before God, he is always willing to listen to your confession and to forgive you just as he did in Daniel's case.

Heavenly Father, like Daniel, I want to plead with you to forgive my sin. Thank you for the assurance that you are always willing to do so. Amen.

19 September
Jonah's selfish prayer
Read: Jonah 2:1–10

From inside the fish Jonah prayed to the Lord his God. He said:
'In my distress I called to the Lord, and he answered me.'
Jonah 2:1–2

Jonah refused to obey the Lord's command but when he had been inside a fish for three days and three nights, he realised very well that only God could save him from that predicament. From inside the fish Jonah prayed to God, and God answered the prayer of his disobedient child. God's incredible mercy on sinners is illustrated in this prayer. God is willing to listen to us, and to answer our pleas, even when we are disobedient and even when our prayers are sometimes very selfish.

Jonah was rather selfish. When the people of Nineveh turned to the Lord and the Lord decided not to punish them, Jonah prayed that the Lord should let him die (Jonah 4:3). The Lord nevertheless remained merciful.

You may pray when you are desperate, but guard against praying only when you are desperate. However, it is wonderful that God continues to listen and answer you, as he did in Jonah's case.

Heavenly Father, I confess that my prayers are sometimes just as selfish as Jonah's prayers. Forgive me for so easily praying when I am desperate while I neglect you when all is well. Amen.

20 September
Jonah inside the fish
Read: Jonah 2:1–9

When my life was ebbing away, I remembered you, Lord, and my prayer rose to you, to your holy temple. But I, with a song of thanksgiving, will sacrifice to you. What I have vowed I will make good. Salvation comes from the Lord.
Jonah 2:7, 9

In the meantime Jonah learnt a lot. Although his circumstances had not yet changed, his prayer had changed him. Inside the fish he discovered that he could do absolutely nothing about his circumstances. He was completely helpless, but he realised the Lord could nevertheless help him. After he had prayed, Jonah even managed to sing a song of praise to the Lord. He also promised to bring a sacrifice to the Lord and to keep his promises to God in future. Only then did the Lord command the fish to vomit Jonah onto dry land.

When you pray to God in a desperate situation, you will probably discover that you will be able to praise the Lord, although your negative circumstances may remain unchanged. Eventually the Lord will deliver you the way he delivered Jonah – at the right time.

Heavenly Father, thank you that I can also manage to sing you a song of praise while I am in a crisis situation because I have shared this crisis with you. I praise you for always helping me. Amen.

21 September
Mary's prayer
Read: Luke 1:46–55

And Mary said: 'My soul glorifies the Lord and my spirit rejoices in God my Saviour, for he has been mindful of the humble state of his servant.'
Luke 1:46

Mary was a remarkable young woman. She had just been informed by the angel that she, although unmarried, would conceive a son whom she had to call Jesus. He would be the Son of the Most High, and would reign over the house of Jacob for ever, the angel told her (Luke 1:30, 32–33).

Mary was prepared to accept the great responsibility the Lord had given her immediately: 'I am the Lord's servant. May it be to me as you have said,' she said to the angel. And instead of bemoaning her fate, she sang a song of praise to the Lord. In the first part of the song, she praised God for his tremendous mercy on her and in the second part she praised him for the mighty deeds he had done for Israel in the past.

Perhaps the Lord has also given you a major responsibility which is a heavy burden to you at the moment. Praise him for it. His mercy is still available to you, and he will help you, by his power, to honour your responsibilities. 'When you make yourself available to God unconditionally, he uses you to turn the world around,' writes *Die Bybellennium* (p. 1248).

Heavenly Father, please make me willing, like Mary, not only to do the things you ask of me, but also to be willing to sing you a song of praise. Amen.

22 September
Zechariah's prayer
Read: Luke 1:67–79

Praise be to the Lord, the God of Israel, because he has come and has redeemed his people. He has raised up a horn of salvation for us …
Luke 1:68–69

While Zechariah, the high priest, was burning incense at the altar, an angel appeared before him. The angel promised Zechariah that he would soon have a son and told him that he was to be called John.

After John's birth, Zechariah was filled with the Holy Spirit and he sang a beautiful song of praise to God's glory. In this song of praise he prophesied the birth of the Saviour. He prophesied that Jesus would shine on those living in darkness and in the shadow of death and guide our feet into the path of peace (Luke 1:78–79).

We are living about 2000 years after the prophet Zechariah, we know the story of Jesus' birth and his death on the cross, but how often do we praise God for the birth of the Saviour? Thank God regularly in your prayers that his Son has made it possible for you to have eternal life, that Jesus came to take away the darkness of your sin and give you the light of life.

Heavenly Father, today I want to praise you for the birth of my Saviour. Thank you for sending your Son so that I can have eternal life because he has paid for all my sins on the cross. Amen.

23 September
Prayer of the Pharisee
Read: Luke 18:9–12

The Pharisee stood up and prayed about himself:
'God, I thank you that I am not like other men – robbers, evildoers,
adulterers – or even like this tax collector.'
Luke 18:11

On listening to the prayer of the Pharisee, we understand why Jesus called the Pharisees hypocrites and whited sepulchres! Selfishness and pride are qualities of Pharisees – they think they are better than all other people, and do not even hesitate to tell God so! They are insensitive to their own sin and always right in their own eyes.

In this prayer there is no suggestion of any of the features of every sincere prayer. There are no elements of humility, confession of sin or praise. The Pharisee is only concerned with himself while he prays and he does not pray in order to communicate with God, but to be noticed by others. He is perfectly self-righteous, but God is not interested in such prayers.

What is your position? Do you also sometimes feel you are slightly better than other Christians? Be on your guard against the 'yeast of the Pharisees', Jesus warned in Matthew 16:6 – particularly when you pray! Take care that your prayers always include humility, confession of sin and praise.

Heavenly Father, I confess that my prayers are also often selfish because I tend to think only of myself and fail to humble myself, confess my sins and praise you. Please forgive me. Amen.

24 September
Prayer of the tax collector
Read: Luke 18:13–14

But the tax collector stood at a distance. He would not even look up to heaven, but beat his breast and said, 'God, have mercy on me, a sinner.'
Luke 18:13

Quite unlike the proud Pharisee, the tax collector in the parable was deeply conscious of his own sinfulness. He did not try to list his good deeds before the Lord and did not compare himself with others either, but he humbly beseeched God to have mercy on him.

Although the Pharisees were regarded as important people by the Jews at the time and everybody looked down upon the tax collectors because they collected tax for the Romans, and many accumulated wealth for themselves in this way, God saw the two praying men in a different light. The tax collector, and not the Pharisee, received mercy in his eyes. 'I tell you this man, rather than the other, went home justified before God,' Luke wrote (Luke 18:14).

Be careful that you do not think like the Pharisee that you can buy God's mercy by being 'good'. Also guard against looking down on others. You are right with God only once you discover that you have nothing to offer him, and that his goodness towards you is mercy only.

Lord, I admit that I have nothing to offer you in exchange for your mercy. Please forgive my sin as you forgave the tax collector. Amen.

25 September
Remember me, Lord!
Read: Luke 23:39–43

Then he said, 'Jesus, remember me when you come into your kingdom.' Jesus answered him, 'I tell you the truth, today you will be with me in paradise.'
Luke 23:42–43

Two criminals were crucified on either side of Jesus. The one insulted him, but the other one prayed a beautiful prayer: 'Jesus, remember me when you come into your kingdom.'

The condemned man stretched out his hand to Jesus. This faith is without any works, without any conditions, but its reward is God's mercy. In fact, the dying criminal's faith is greater than that of Jesus' disciples – those who had walked and worked with him for three years. Their hope and expectation of his kingdom were devastated by his crucifixion while the criminal still believed Jesus could save him.

And Jesus did not disappoint him – he promised him that he would be with him in paradise that very day.

Mercy turns even hardened criminals into God's children! Even if you do not deserve God's mercy, even if you are a hardened criminal, you may stretch out your hand to Jesus like the condemned criminal. He never turns anybody away.

Lord Jesus, thank you that you did not die for good people, but for sinners like me. I praise you for your great mercy which includes me as well. Amen.

26 SEPTEMBER
Paul's prayers for the Ephesians
Read: Ephesians 1:15–22

I keep asking that the God of our Lord Jesus Christ, the glorious Father, may give you the Spirit of wisdom and revelation, so that you may know him better. I pray also that the eyes of your heart may be enlightened in order that you may know the hope to which he has called you, the riches of his glorious inheritance in the saints.
Ephesians 1:17–18

It is not so easy to pray for the needs of others. Paul succeeded in doing that here excellently. He was interceding for the believers in Ephesus, and asked God to give them three things: wisdom, revelation so that they would be able to know him and insight so that they could know the riches of his glorious inheritance awaiting them. Paul was not keeping his prayers secret either, he told the Ephesians about them to strengthen their faith.

Like Paul, you can learn to ask God for specific things for the people you are praying for. If you cannot do this well yet, start using Paul's recipe straight away, and pray for God's wisdom, knowledge and insight for your loved ones. Then tell them that you have prayed for them, and what you have asked God.

Lord, I am sorry that my prayers for others are still so vague. Teach me to intercede for others like a Paul, and to ask your wisdom and insight for them. Amen.

27 September
The power of his love
Read: Ephesians 3:14–17

I pray that out of his glorious riches he may strengthen you with power through his Spirit in your inner being, so that Christ may dwell in your hearts through faith. And I pray that you, being rooted and established in love, may have power ...
Ephesians 3:16–17

Paul prayed this beautiful prayer while he was in prison. He assured the church in Ephesus that he was interceding for them before God faithfully. He also prayed that God would give them the power to be strengthened in their inner being. Paul explained in verse 17 how one can obtain this inner strength: it would be given to them when Christ dwelled in their hearts and they were rooted and established in love. This verse means that you can receive God's power only when you are in a living relationship with him.

All of us need God's inner power in our lives. This power does not depend on outward circumstances, it comes from the heart. It gives you the courage to master your physical as well as your spiritual problems. Jesus wants to make his wonderworking power available to you every day. By means of this power you can do all things, provided you believe in Jesus and live God's love daily.

Lord Jesus, thank you for your wonderworking power which you make available to me every day. Please help me to pass on your love to those who cross my path. Amen.

28 September
This is what your love should look like
Read: Ephesians 3:18–21

That you .... may have the power, together with all the saints, to grasp how wide and long and high and deep is the love of Christ, and to know this love that surpasses knowledge – that you may be filled to the measure of all the fulness of God.
Ephesians 3:18–19

In Ephesians 3:18–19 Paul gives a description of Jesus' love for us. 'May you have the power ... to grasp how wide and long and high and deep is the love of Christ, and to know this love that surpasses knowledge ...' was his prayer for the church in Ephesus.

And this is exactly what your love for others should be like! This unselfish, unique love can only be realised in your life if God's love has already become a reality in your life. This love is a love which acts, a love which should be lived out in your relationship with others.

To live like this you need God's power – and Paul described the greatness of this love in verse 20: God is able to do immeasurably more than all we ask or imagine! By yourself you will never succeed, but by the supernatural power of the Holy Spirit in your life, he wants to make it possible for you to love like Jesus.

Heavenly Father, teach me to love others with the love of Jesus. Thank you for the assurance that I will be able to love like this because your Holy Spirit will enable me to do so. Amen.

29 September
Paul's prayer for the Philippians
Read: Philippians 1:4, 9–10

*In all my prayers for all of you ... And this is my prayer:
that your love may abound more and more in knowledge
and depth of insight, so that you may be able to discern what is best ...*
Philippians 1:4, 9–10

Here Paul prayed for the spiritual growth of the church in Philippi. They already had love, but their love still had to increase in knowledge and depth of insight.

Christians' love for one another should be characterised by understanding, knowledge of God's plan of redemption. This love also needs depth of insight so that we will be able to discern between right and wrong. Love which is supplemented by understanding and depth of insight always involves discernment. Paul also assured them that God who began a good work in them would carry it on to completion so that their love for God and one another would increase and they would be ready when Jesus returned.

Consider carefully whether your love for others does not perhaps need knowledge and depth of insight, and ask God to give you these qualities. It is very important that you will put your priorities straight so that you will know how to discern between important and less important things. Then you will be able to claim the promise: God will carry the good work which he began in you on to completion until the day Jesus returns.

*Heavenly Father, I pray that you will supplement my love
with your knowledge and depth of insight so that I will be able
to discern what is best. Amen.*

30 September
Prayer for holiness
Read: Colossians 1:9–14

For this reason, since the day we heard about you,
we have not stopped praying for you.
Colossians 1:9

The tremendous success of Paul's ministry was probably due to the fact that he used to pray faithfully and regularly for the churches where he worked and that he also relied on their prayers for him. In this passage of Scripture (Colossians 1:9–11), Paul described the road to holiness in detail:

Paul prayed for the following eight aspects for the church:

- that they would have all spiritual wisdom and understanding;
- that they would know the will of God;
- that they would live a life worthy of the Lord and please him in every way;
- that they would bear fruit;
- that they would grow in the knowledge of God;
- that they would be strengthened with all power according to his glorious might;
- that they would always thank God joyfully; and
- that they would have a hope for the future – because they would one day share in the inheritance of the saints in the kingdom of light.

See to it that justice will be done to these eight pleas in your own life so that you, will become more and more like Jesus.

Heavenly Father, I pray that you will give me wisdom and insight to know your will, to live the way you want me to live and to bear fruit for you to persevere with patience, to thank you joyfully and to have a hope for the future. Amen.

October

Prayer is a joy

Praise is one of the most important elements of prayer – and unfortunately also an element which most of us neglect. We have to praise God when we pray. Praising makes us forget our own problems and focuses our attention on God – it shifts our perspective from earth to heaven.

Make a point of praising God for everything that fills you with joy, for his infinite mercy and love for you and also for the fact that, eventually, he will make all things, even your current pain and suffering, work together for an eternal glory.

Gratitude always involves praise. If you have a grateful heart, you realise the magnitude of God's love and mercy for you personally, and you cannot but praise him for this.

One of the most beautiful songs of praise is found in Revelation 5:12–14:

> Worthy is the Lamb, who was slain, to receive power and wealth and wisdom and strength and honour and glory and praise! To him who sits on the throne and to the Lamb be praise and honour and glory and power, for ever and ever!

If you lack the words to praise God when you pray, learn to use the words in your Bible.

1 October
God's presence brings joy!
Read: Psalm 105:1–11

Glory in his holy name; let the hearts of those who seek the Lord rejoice. Look to the Lord and his strength; seek his face always.
Psalm 105:3–4

Psalm 105 is actually a history lesson. By means of this psalm the psalmist outlined the wonderful way in which God had kept and protected his people in the past. He described how each of their needs had been met and how they were delivered from Egypt. In the first verses of the psalm, the people were called to praise the Lord for all the mighty deeds he had done for them. According to the psalmist, those who seek the presence of the Lord are people who always have joy in their hearts.

You will probably be able to testify first-hand that God's presence in your life fills you with joy. 'You will fill me with joy in your presence,' it says in Acts 2:28. When you study God's word, and you hear his voice, when you answer him by praying and consider all the wonderful things he has done for you personally in the past, a song of praise will bubble forth spontaneously! Go to God right away and tell him that his presence in your life fills you with joy every day!

Lord, I praise you for the bubbling joy which I experience in your presence. Thank you that this is a joy of the heart, and that no-one can take it away from me. Amen.

2 OCTOBER
Prayer is a joy
Read: 2 Chronicles 15:8–15

They sought God eagerly, and he was found by them.
So the Lord gave them rest on every side.
2 Chronicles 15:15

King Asa undertook to let his people return to the Lord, and the people were immediately prepared to listen to him. They brought sacrifices for their sins and entered into a covenant to obey the Lord in future. This return to the God of the Covenant brought great joy to the Israelites. They sought the Lord eagerly, and when people draw near to God, he draws near to them. God allowed himself to be found by them, and he gave them rest on every side, reads our verse.

Prayer is seeking God. Unfortunately prayer is not always a joy to all of us. We neglect our prayer time because we are so busy, and although we pray, we see it as work instead of looking forward with joy to communicating with God. If your prayer time is not yet a joy to you, it is not too late to start doing something about it. Merely ask the Lord to make it a joy to you to talk to him. Approach God in prayer – he wants you to find him and he wants to offer you his rest during a stressful day.

Heavenly Father, forgive me for sometimes regarding prayer as a burden rather than a joy. Teach me to seek you with joy, and please give me your joy in exchange for my anxieties. Amen.

3 OCTOBER
The source of your joy
Read: Psalm 37:1–7

Delight yourself in the Lord and he will give you the desires of your heart.
Psalm 37:4

People who live close to the Lord are people who live with joy in their hearts because they know that the God whom they worship will meet all their needs. God is the real Source of our joy – lasting joy is always anchored in him.

David knew the secret of lasting joy: 'The Lord is my shepherd, I shall not be in want,' he wrote in Psalm 23:1. If you endeavour to live close to the Lord, he will give you everything you need, and even spoil you with those things you would like to have.

If this has not yet happened in your life, you should consider your relationship with the Lord for a change. Then do what the psalmist recommends in Psalm 37:5, 'Commit your way to the Lord; trust in him and he will do this.' People who hold on to God every day and trust in him, may be assured that the Lord will give them the things they really need. God is a caring Father who loves his children and who wants to meet all their needs.

Heavenly Father, I want to entrust my life to you and trust you to give me everything I need. Thank you for the promise that you will give me the desires of my heart if I delight myself in you. Amen.

4 October
Prayer as a song of praise
Read: Psalm 66:8–20

I cried out to him with my mouth; his praise was on my tongue.
Psalm 66:17

Not everything in the life of the psalmist was always plain sailing. 'For you, O God, tested us; you refined us like silver. You let men ride over our heads; we went through fire and water,' he wrote in verses 10 and 12. However, whenever he started calling to the Lord during those times of trouble, he discovered a song of praise on his lips. And it did not take long before this song of praise rolled from his lips: 'I cried out to him with my mouth; his praise was on my tongue,' he testified in the verse for today.

If you would also be still with the Lord – even in the midst of difficult times – and have fellowship with him, you will always be so impressed by his greatness and majesty that you will practically have no choice but to worship and praise him for his lasting love for you.

When you experience troubled times again, the best advice is to pray: when you think about God instead of your problems, you will soon be able to sing a song of praise to God again.

Heavenly Father, thank you for teaching me to pray when I am in the wilderness so that my communication with you will inspire me to sing you a song of praise again. Please make this possible for me now. Amen.

5 OCTOBER
Praise the Lord for all his benefits
Read: Psalm 103:1–7

Praise the Lord, O my soul; all my inmost being, praise his holy name.
Praise the Lord, O my soul, and forget not all his benefits.
Psalm 103:1–2

In this psalm which is often read after the Communion service, the psalmist praises the Lord for all his benefits.

Some time ago I was talking to one of my friends who was going through a bad patch just then. I wanted to know what her secret was – how she could remain full of joy and happiness despite the many things that were going wrong in her life. I still remember her answer very well: 'When problems pile up, I simply start counting my blessings,' she said. 'And then I thank the Lord for each of them.'

This is a wonderful recipe – continue praising the Lord, in times of trouble as well: Keep a record of all his benefits and thank him for each of them! Do try this when you experience difficult times again. When you start counting your blessings, you cannot but praise God.

Heavenly Father, I am sorry that I do not count my blessings more often and keep a record of all the mercy which you pour out on me daily. Please help me to be more grateful in future. Amen.

6 OCTOBER
Praise the Lord for his love and compassion
Read: Psalm 103:1, 8–13

Praise the Lord, O my soul; all my inmost being, praise his holy name ...
He does not treat us as our sins deserve or repay us according to our
iniquities. For as high as the heavens are above the earth,
so great is his love for those who fear him.
Psalm 103:1, 10–11

The psalmist jotted down a whole list of reasons why he wanted to praise God. God is compassionate and gracious. He forgives us our sins. Although man's life is as transitory as a flower of the field, he gives us his eternal love and righteousness. He cares for us every day as a Father would for his children.

His compassion for us is one of the most important reasons why God's children should praise him with 'all their inmost being'. Although God is holy and hates sin, he loves sinners. He does not punish us for our sins, but sent his Son into the world so that the penalty for our sin could be paid by his blood shed on the cross. We cannot fail to praise him for his infinite love – a love which is as vast as the distance between heaven and earth.

Always praise the Lord with all your inmost being when you kneel in prayer!

Heavenly Father, I want to praise you with all my inmost being
for your infinite love for me, for the fact that you have forgiven all
my sin and have compassion on me like a father on his child. Amen.

7 OCTOBER
Praise as sacrifice
Read: Hebrews 13:10–16

Through Jesus, therefore, let us continually offer to God a sacrifice of praise – the fruit of lips that confess his name.
Hebrews 13:15

God's children should offer praise to him as a sacrifice. When all is well, we praise God involuntarily. However, praising the Lord is not always easy. We just do not feel like it every day! Sometimes our negative circumstances and difficult personal crises make us complain to God rather than praise him.

When the writer to the Hebrews said that praise is a sacrifice which we should offer to God, he meant that we should praise God even when it is difficult to do so. Sacrificing is never easy or pleasant, but God expects his children to bring him praise as a sacrifice; praise which will cost us, praise despite problems and crises in our own lives.

These sacrifices of praise are defined in Hebrews 13:16: 'And do not forget to do good and to share with others, for with such sacrifices God is pleased.' By reaching out to others and helping them in such a way that you will actually feel it as a sacrifice yourself, you praise God. Make a point of often bringing God a sacrifice of praise by your attitude and by helping others.

Heavenly Father, today I want to bring you a sacrifice of praise, although all is not well with me at the moment. Help me to do good to others and to be openhanded. Amen.

8 OCTOBER
Praise God for his creation!
Read: Psalm 66:1–8

Shout with joy to God, all the earth! Sing the glory of his name; make his praise glorious! Say to God, 'How awesome are your deeds!'
Psalm 66:1–3

In Psalm 111:2 the psalmist wrote, 'Great are the works of the Lord; they are pondered by all who delight in them.' The psalmists often praised God when they looked at creation: 'When I consider your heavens, the work of your fingers, the moon and the stars which you have set in place, what is man that you are mindful of him?' David asked in Psalm 8:3–4. In Psalm 19 he confessed: 'The heavens declare the glory of God; the skies proclaim the work of his hands' (verse 1).

The more you look at and read about the wonder of nature, the more you are impressed by God's omnipotence and majesty. And when you look at creation you once again discover your own insignificance and you are amazed about the fact that such a great God has compassion on you.

Praise God for his creation when you see the colours at sunset, when the moon rises behind the mountain, when you hold a newborn baby in your arms or look at the flickering stars at night.

Heavenly Father, I praise you for your creation, for everything you have made so exceedingly beautiful. You are great and do marvellous deeds! Amen.

9 OCTOBER
Know that the Lord is God ...
Read: Psalm 100

> *Know that the Lord is God. It is he who made us, and we are his; we are his people, the sheep of his pasture. Enter his gates with thanksgiving and his courts with praise; give thanks to him and praise his name ...*
> Psalm 100:3–4

In this psalm, the psalmist gave God all praise and honour. He acknowledged his greatness and omnipotence, his wonderful creation. For this reason he thanked him, and he praised and honoured his holy Name.

When you pray, you should always realise that you are deeply indebted to God, and that you should be grateful to him. You belong to him because he created you and delivered you from sin.

Five aspects which you could praise him for are underlined in the psalm:

- He is God, the only living God.
- He is your Creator – he not only made everything in nature, he also made you.
- He is your Owner – everything in heaven and on earth belongs to him.
- He is your Lord and King. You belong to his people, and should acknowledge his kingship over your life.
- He is your Shepherd – your benefactor who cares for you and guides you every day.

Praise him now for all five!

> *Heavenly Father, I praise you because you are God. I praise you as the Creator of all things, I praise you because everything in heaven and on earth belongs to you, I praise you as my Lord and King and as my Shepherd who guides me every day. Amen.*

10 October
Praise and thanksgiving go hand in hand
Read: Psalm 100

*Shout for joy to the Lord, all the earth. Worship the Lord with gladness …
Enter his gates with thanksgiving and his courts with praise;
give thanks to him and praise his name.*
Psalm 100:1, 2, 4

In this psalm the psalmist praised and thanked the Lord simultaneously. The reason for the enthusiastic praise and thanks to God is found in verse 5: 'For the Lord is good and his love endures for ever; his faithfulness continues through all generations.'

You should be giving thanks to God. 'Always give thanks to God the Father for everything, in the name of our Lord Jesus Christ,' Paul wrote to the church in Ephesus (Ephesians 5:20).

Unfortunately not all God's children are equally grateful. However, when we pray we usually thank God for things like food, clothes and health. However, there are still so many things which God gives us in his mercy but which we assume as our right.

Learn to praise and thank the Lord for various things. Thank him for those things which you have never thanked him for before: for the birds in the garden, the first flowers of spring, for his infinite love and goodness to you personally.

*Lord, make me so grateful that I will praise and thank you
for something new every day. Thank you that you love me,
that your faithfulness towards me and my people endures
from generation to generation. Amen.*

11 OCTOBER
Praise God in your old age
Read: Psalm 71:1–8

I will ever praise you. I have become like a portent for many, but you are my strong refuge.
Psalm 71:6–7

'Do not cast me away when I am old,' verse 9 of this psalm reads. The psalmist was therefore no longer young, but he still praised the Lord. 'I have become a marvel for many' (American Standard version), he said in our verse, so physically he was still strong.

As you grow older, you sometimes feel you have fewer things to be happy about! Most elderly people think back to the days when they could drive for hours without being stiff after the journey; when they were able to run upstairs, two steps at a time, without a burning sensation in the chest; when they were able to read fine print without glasses …

It is true that ageing does have many negative aspects but, as they grow older, God's children can still retain their joy of life like the psalmist in Psalm 71. If you are already a senior citizen, you may claim God's promise in Isaiah 46:4: 'Even to your old age and grey hairs, I am he who will sustain you. I have made you and I will carry you; I will sustain you and I will rescue you.' This gives you more than enough reason to praise the Lord!

Heavenly Father, I praise you for having cared for me and kept me all my life. Thank you that you are also holding and carrying me now that I am older. Amen.

12 OCTOBER
Praise the Lord every day
Read: Psalm 71:6–14

From my birth I have relied on you; you brought me forth from my mother's womb. I will ever praise you. My mouth is filled with your praise, declaring your splendour all day long.
Psalm 71:6, 8

In this beautiful psalm of praise, the aged psalmist who had experienced God's care from a tender age, asked God to be close to him in his old age. He testified that he had experienced God's help and protection from birth. His relationship with the Lord had therefore come a long way. In verses 6 and 8 he also undertook to praise the Lord at all times, to sing his praises every day.

Your thoughts determine your whole life. You can also decide that you will not allow a single day to pass without your having praised the Lord. 'I will praise the Lord …' the psalmist wrote. 'I will sing praise to my God as long as I live' (Psalm 146:1–2).

My husband firmly believes that one should start each day with a psalm of praise. Then every day will be a day of victory for you, he says! Would you like to follow this advice? Before you do Bible study or pray, read one of your favourite psalms of praise and praise the Lord in those words. Do it even when you do not feel like it.

Lord, I want to make a habit of praising and thanking you every day of my life. Thank you that there are so many reasons for doing this. Amen.

13 OCTOBER
God is with you!
Read: 1 Chronicles 16:7–27

The Lord made the heavens. Splendour and majesty are before him; strength and joy in his dwelling-place.
1 Chronicles 16:26–27

Here Asaph and his people were singing a beautiful song of praise to the glory of God. By means of this song they wanted to express their exuberant gratitude towards the Lord as well as their reverence and awe.

This God whom you worship is the same God to whom Asaph had sung a song of praise. He is still incomparably great and wonderful. He is the Lord who made the heaven and the earth, the sea and everything in it, and who cares for his creation every day. Majesty and splendour are before him – there is no-one like him. In his presence his children are filled with the power and joy which emanate from him.

One of the reasons why you may be full of joy every day is the fact that you always have the Lord with you. 'With joy you will draw water from the wells of salvation. Shout aloud and sing for joy, people of Zion, for great is the Holy One of Israel among you,' the prophet Isaiah wrote (Isaiah 12:3, 6). When you pray, you should also praise God's greatness like the Israelites of old and be filled with joy because you always have him with you.

Heavenly Father, I want to praise you because you are incomparably great and good. Thank you that I may be full of joy because you are my God who is always with me. Amen.

14 OCTOBER
Praise God, for his love endures for ever
Read: Psalm 118:1–9; 28–29

> *You are my God, and I will give thanks; you are my God, and I will exalt you. Give thanks to the Lord, for he is good; his love endures for ever.*
> Psalm 118:28–29

In Psalm 118 the psalmist praised God for his love which endures for ever. (In Psalm 136 this chorus is repeated 36 times!) One of the most important things we have to praise God for is his unconditional, infinite, incomprehensible love for us. We are assured of God's love in so many passages in the Bible that we should never doubt it. He has proved this love by sending Jesus to the world to pay the penalty for our sin on the cross. If you ever doubt God's love, only look at Jesus.

Paul described the greatness of this love beautifully in Ephesians 3:18 and 19 when he prayed for the church in Rome: 'May you have power to grasp how wide and long and high and deep is the love of Christ, and to know this love that passes knowledge.'

'For I am convinced that nothing can separate us from the love God has for us. Not death, not life, not angels, not ruling spirits, nothing now, nothing in the future, no powers, nothing above us, nothing below us, or anything in the whole world will ever be able to separate us from the love of God that is in Christ Jesus our Lord' (Romans 8:38, *The Everyday Bible*). Don't you want to praise God for such a love?

Heavenly Father, I want to praise you for your incomprehensible love which you have manifested in Jesus. Thank you that nothing can ever separate me from your love. Amen.

15 October
What God's love looks like
Read: Hosea 11:1–8

I led them with cords of human kindness, with ties of love …
How can I give you up, Ephraim? How can I hand you over, Israel?
… My heart is changed within me; all my compassion is aroused.
Hosea 11:4, 8

God's relationship with his people Israel clearly reflects his love. He looked after them and protected them like a father. Even when they rejected him time and again and deserved to be destroyed, he could not bring himself to do so, because his love for them was too deep. He was prepared to forgive them time after time.

Humanly speaking it is practically impossible for us to imagine God's love because it differs totally from our human love. God's love is a love in spite of our shortcomings and sins, a love which expects nothing in return: God loves you as you are. You do not have to do anything to earn or deserve that love.

God wants to guide you with care and love every day as he did for Israel. His love for you is so strong that he did not even hesitate to sacrifice his Son to prove it. You may walk into the outstretched arms of God with all your problems and fears. His love is always available to you – in abundance!

Heavenly Father, although I cannot understand your love for me, I accept it with joy. Thank you that your love for me is new every morning and that you envelop me in that love every day. Amen.

16 October
Praise the Lord when you lie awake!
Read: Psalm 63:7–8

O God, you are my God, earnestly I seek you;
my soul thirsts for you, my body longs for you ...
Psalm 63:1

From this psalm it is obvious that David and the Lord had a special relationship. The three verbs seek, thirst and long used in verse 1 express the psalmist's continuous longing for the Lord. God's faithful love meant more to him than life itself, and he therefore wanted to praise God. Even when he was lying awake at night, he would think about God's goodness and he would sing about God's protection. 'My soul cling to you; your right hand upholds me' he confessed in verse 9.

We live in difficult times. Sometimes we lie awake at night (like the psalmist) and we worry about our many anxieties. It would be far better when we lie awake to think about God's goodness rather than about our problems. If we remain close to God, he will protect and support us. Remember to praise him for it, because praise is the most perfect response you can give God in exchange for his love and protection for you.

Heavenly Father, thank you that I, when I cannot sleep, can think of you instead of my problems. Like the psalmist I want to remain close to you so that your hand can support me every day. Amen.

17 OCTOBER
Praise the Lord for his word
Read: Psalm 119:111, 162

I will follow your rules for ever. They make me happy. I am as happy over your promises as if I had found a great treasure.
Psalm 119:111, 162 (The Everyday Bible version)

God's word was very precious to the psalmist. This whole psalm is one long song of praise about God's word and his law. 'Blessed is the man … his delight is in the law of the Lord. He is like a tree planted by streams of water, which yields its fruit in season and whose leaf does not wither,' reads Psalm 1:1–3.

During a service a missionary with the Open Doors Society told the congregation how a colleague once handed a beautiful leather-bound Bible to a pastor in China during a cottage meeting. To his surprise the pastor started tearing out pages from the Bible and handing them to his parishioners. No-one there possessed a Bible. Those pages torn out of the Bible were their greatest treasure on earth.

We are inclined to take our Bibles for granted because we are so used to reading from it every morning and evening. Always remember: your Bible is a treasure – the living word of God through which he speaks to you personally.

Praise him for it every day.

Heavenly Father, I want to praise you for your word through which you speak to me personally every day. Help me always to realise that my Bible is an immeasurable treasure. Amen.

18 October
Praise God for his protection
Read: Psalm 62:3–9

He alone is my rock and my salvation;
he is my fortress, I shall not be shaken. My salvation
and my honour depend on God; he is my mighty rock, my refuge.
Psalm 62:6–8

God is often described as a rock and a refuge in the psalms: a safe place where his children can find shelter in dangerous circumstances knowing that he will keep them safe and give them rest. For this reason the psalmist felt safe despite his negative physical circumstances.

During the border war in Angola a book was written about supernatural ways in which soldiers were protected on the border. God is the great Protector. He undertakes to keep his children safe, therefore we do not have to fear anything. You can also be sure that God will protect you when you are in danger. And his protection is all-encompassing – he is always with you. 'He will command his angels … to guard you in all your ways; they will lift you up in their hands, so that you will not strike your foot against a stone,' the psalmist wrote in Psalm 91:11–12.

Even when God's children are indeed killed in dangerous situations, they have the assurance that he himself will be with them in the valley of the shadow of death and that they will be with him in heaven for ever.

Heavenly Father, thank you that I can rely on your protection
when I am in danger. I praise you because you have been a rock
and a refuge to me so often in the past. Amen.

19 October
Praise the Lord for health and vitality
Read: Jeremiah 17:14–18

Heal me, O Lord, and I shall be healed; save me and I shall be saved, for you are the one I praise.
Jeremiah 17:14

Jeremiah was very unpopular with the people of the Lord, because he did not hesitate to proclaim the word of the Lord to them. The curse which Jeremiah proclaimed to the people involved himself as well and he therefore asked God to examine his words and motives and heal him so that he would be able to praise him again.

Sometimes we first have to lose something before we can estimate its true value. Health is one of the things we easily take for granted. When my husband had a heart attack at the age of 34, I suddenly realised that health is not to be taken for granted but that it is a privilege which we should praise God for every day. He is the One who heals us – he gives health and vitality. If you have been ill and have now recovered again, praise him – if you enjoy good health, praise him even more.

Unfortunately not all ill people get well again. If you are still ill – despite your having asked the Lord to heal you – ask yourself what the Lord wants to teach you. You can be a radiant witness for him even while you are ill.

Heavenly Father, thank you that you can heal the sick. Today I am praying for all the sick. Please heal them again, if it is your will. Amen.

20 October
Praise God for the effect of his lessons for life
Read: Psalm 119:67–75

I know, O Lord, that your laws are righteous, and in faithfulness you have afflicted me. May your unfailing love be my comfort, according to your promise ...
Psalm 119:75–76

The psalmist realised that the time of trouble had been to his advantage because he had strayed from God in times of prosperity. However, as a result of the suffering he was now more obedient than before. 'Before I was afflicted I went astray, but now I obey your word,' he said in verse 67. In verse 71 he also confessed, 'It was good for me to be afflicted so that I might learn your decrees.'

Perhaps it does not sound right to you that suffering could be good for you, but if you have already experienced it first-hand, you will be able to underline the psalmist's opinion. God teaches us some of our most valuable lessons in times of trouble. We then realise his love anew and experience his presence physically every day. We grow as Christians through suffering and pain – and for that reason suffering is practically always worthwhile. While we suffer, we are comforted by knowing that God is with us, and that he will deliver us again as he promises in his word.

Heavenly Father, the suffering in my own life has been far from pleasant, but you know that it has brought me closer to you. Thank you for valuable lessons for life which I was able to learn during my own times of trouble. Amen.

21 October
Praise and thank God when you pray
Read: Ephesians 5:15–20

*Sing and make music in your heart to the Lord,
always giving thanks to God the Father for everything.*
Ephesians 5:19–20

Most of us find it easy to praise and thank the Lord when all is well. However, it is a different matter altogether to praise the Lord when everything goes wrong, to thank him when you cannot see anything to be grateful for!

Paul wrote to the church in Ephesus that they should be willing to thank the Lord in all circumstances – even for those things which, humanly speaking, they could not be grateful for. Those who are able to do this have learnt the lesson that the Lord can eventually make all things – even the negative things – work together for good for his children. They also know that when they are at their weakest, others can clearly see the power of the Lord in their lives.

For this reason, Paul said, he delighted in weaknesses, in insults, in hardships, in persecutions, in difficulties, for Christ's sake (2 Corinthians 12:10).

Do you have a difficult situation in your own life at the moment? Dare to praise and thank God in the midst of it. You will then discover that he will turn the hurt in you into a plus!

*Heavenly Father, help me to praise you in times of trouble
and to thank you for the things which I would rather change. Amen.*

22 October
Rejoice in the Lord!
Read: Isaiah 61:10–11

I delight greatly in the Lord; my soul rejoices in my God.
For he has clothed me with garments of salvation and arrayed me
in a robe of righteousness, as a bridegroom adorns his head like a priest,
and as a bride adorns herself with her jewels.
Isaiah 61:10

In this beautiful song of praise, the prophet Isaiah praised the Lord for the deliverance he had brought about for his people. God promised to enter into an eternal covenant with them and to bring them back from their exile and rebuild their cities. The prophet rejoiced about this like a bridegroom adorned like a priest and a bride adorned with her jewels.

One of the happiest days in one's life is certainly one's wedding day. Everything is organised to highlight the happiness of the bride and groom: the triumphant notes of the organ, the festive flowers, the joy on the faces of the guests, the delicacies … It is not mere coincidence that the relationship between God and his church is compared to the relationship between a bride and her bridegroom.

Can you honestly say that your relationship with God is like the relationship between a bride and her bridegroom? Are you truly glad that you belong to God, that he has delivered you and washed you with his blood? Then you should live in such a way that those around you will be able to see this joy in your life and give God the glory.

Lord, thank you that I may be your bride. Help me to live in such a way
that the joy in my life will show others that I belong to you. Amen.

23 October
Always be joyful!
1 Thessalonians 5:16–24

Be joyful always; pray continually; give thanks in all circumstances, for this is God's will for you in Christ Jesus.
1 Thessalonians 5:16–18

Lasting joy, persevering prayer and consistent gratitude are not merely a voluntary choice made by some Christians – it is commanded by God himself. Nothing gives God more joy than his children's prayers of praise. It is his will that his children should always rejoice, that they pray continually and that they be grateful in all circumstances. God does not want his children to be depressed, and not one of his children has reason for endless depression, writes Onbekende Christen (*Christen en gebed*, p. 112). We are therefore called to rejoice in numerous passages in the Bible.

Are you giving thanks in all circumstances yet – even in situations which you would rather have otherwise – even for the things with which you cannot come to terms? This joy should not be linked to your circumstances or your emotions. Humanly speaking, this is impossible, but God will make it possible if you ask him for this in prayer.

Heavenly Father, I just cannot always be happy and grateful and pray continually. Please help me to do so. Amen.

24 October
Praise the Lord in times of crisis
Read: Acts 16:22–31

About midnight Paul and Silas were praying and singing hymns to God, and the other prisoners were listening to them.
Acts 16:25

The people of Philippi threw the innocent Paul and Silas into prison after they had been flogged and beaten. Instead of their trying to prove their innocence or of insisting, like Job, that the Lord should explain why they had to suffer, Paul and Silas were praying and singing in prison! This spontaneous testimony was much more valuable than their sermons before their imprisonment. Their strange conduct showed the other prisoners that they were different – they were therefore listening to them, Luke said. God also listened to them – and he sent an earthquake which shook the foundations of the prison and flung open the prison doors.

What do you do when you are sometimes treated unjustly? Your response will clearly show who rules your life! You will obviously not find it easy to pray and sing songs of praise, yet if you will still be able to praise God in the midst of crises, you will not only reach others by your testimony, but God will also help you time and again the way he helped Paul and Silas.

Heavenly Father, make me a positive witness for you, even in difficult situations, so that people will be able to see by my actions that I love you. Amen.

25 October
Praise God for today!
Read: Psalm 118:24–29

This is the day the Lord has made; let us rejoice and be glad in it.
Psalm 118:24

'Yesterday is a cancelled cheque, tomorrow is a promise. Today is cash in your hand, use it,' reads an anonymous saying (*Vonkelvreugde*, p. 65). Every new day is a gift from God. An opportunity for you to sort out the blunders of yesterday, and carefully plan for tomorrow. If you think about it, you only have today – yesterday is already in the past, and tomorrow is still in the future. But you have today. Twenty-four hours which you can use in a positive way to glorify God and to serve your fellow man.

Praise God for the opportunities which he sends you every day. Do not postpone until tomorrow anything you can do today. Live today to the full. If you can do anybody a favour, do it immediately.

The secret of happiness is to notice and cherish even the slightest cause for joy. Not to look forward to tomorrow so much that you forget about today, not to be so worried about the mistakes made yesterday that you allow today to pass unnoticed.

Praise the Lord for every day!

Heavenly Father, I praise you for today. Thank you for twenty-four hours which I can use positively to glorify you and to help others. Amen.

26 October
Joy after suffering
Read: 1 Peter 4:12–19

Dear friends, do not be surprised at the painful trial you are suffering, as though something strange were happening to you. But rejoice that you participate in the sufferings of Christ, so that you may be overjoyed when his glory is revealed.
1 Peter 4:12–13

Here Peter wrote that Christians should not be surprised at the difficult times in their lives, they should actually expect them! If you are suffering, you have to rejoice, because this suffering is the proof that you will one day participate in Jesus' glory when he returns. However, to rejoice in suffering is in conflict with our human nature. We would prefer to ask God why he is permitting the suffering in our lives. Like Job and Jeremiah we are looking for reasons for the suffering and for answers to our whys.

If your child were killed in an accident, or your fiancé shot during an armed robbery, it is perfectly natural to be angry with God. You may also tell him this. In such situations it is also no use when others tell you that everything happens for a purpose.

James also wrote about trials. These trials are God's way of testing you until you are spiritually mature, he said (James 1:2–4). Just hold on to God, trust him to give you joy again after the suffering.

Heavenly Father, at the moment I am disappointed in you – you could have prevented my crisis but you didn't. Forgive me and restore my joy after the suffering. Amen.

27 OCTOBER
Hold on to God in times of crisis
Ecclesiastes 7:8–15

When times are good, be happy; but when times are bad, consider: God has made the one as well as the other. Therefore, a man cannot discover anything about his future.
Ecclesiastes 7:14

God's children must praise him for days of prosperity, but in days of adversity, they should still hold on to him. God allows adversity in our lives although it is never his will. By means of adversity he wants to teach us to rely totally on him, even if we cannot see what will happen to us in future.

Job knew this secret: he had lost everything – his possessions, his children and his health – yet he could still say: 'The Lord gave and the Lord has taken away; may the name of the Lord be praised' (Job 1:21).

While I was writing this daily reading, a friend phoned to tell me that two Christian students had been raped. Her son was battling to come to terms with what had happened to his young friends. What could she say to him? I don't know either, I said to her. We are living in an imperfect world and such things happen. We have no instant answers or easy solutions. We do not understand how God can permit such things.

Fortunately we do not need answers. God is the Answer. He loves us. He will comfort us. We have to cling to this.

Heavenly Father, thank you that I do not have to understand everything that happens in the world. Thank you that I merely have to hold on to you and your love for me and that I can rely on your comfort. Amen.

28 October
Praise the Lord all your life!
Read: Psalm 146

Praise the Lord, O my soul. I will praise the Lord all my life;
I will sing praise to my God as long as I live.
Psalm 146:1–2

Here the psalmist declared his intention to praise the Lord all his life. People rely on many things (and people), but unfortunately things and people often disappoint you. The only Person who will never disappoint you is the Lord. He will never leave you in the lurch, he is absolutely faithful. Over the centuries he has proved himself to be the faithful God of the Covenant who helps, protects and keeps his children.

God has compassion particularly on people who are really in need: the oppressed, those who are starving, the strangers and orphans and widows. If you need help and protection, you may call out to God with confidence. If you feel discouraged, you can hope in him. 'Blessed is he whose help is the God of Jacob, whose hope is in the Lord his God,' the psalmist wrote (verse 5).

Don't you want to praise God, with the psalmist, for his goodness all your life?

Heavenly Father, I praise you for your goodness to me.
I want to praise you all my life because you are absolutely faithful.
Thank you that I may rely on you all the days of my life. Amen.

29 October
Praise God for his church
Read: Ephesians 1:18–23

The church ... is his body, the fulness of him
who fills everything in every way.
Ephesians 1:23

Sometimes we are very disgruntled with our church, our own congregation. We then go elsewhere to find that which we want but cannot find in our own church. We also attach great value to a church building. If you have doubts about your church at the moment, ask yourself: who is the church? The answer to this question is: YOU. 'You are the body of Christ, and each one of you is a part of it,' Paul wrote to the church in Corinth (1 Corinthians 12:27–28). Ephesians 2:20 reads, 'You are built on the foundation of the apostles and prophets, with Christ Jesus himself as the chief cornerstone.' The believers are actually the house of God, the church building is merely their venue.

Although the church here on earth will never be perfect, it is still the church of Christ. If you are dissatisfied with your church and your congregation, you should begin with yourself. As a member of that church you have a specific task which you should perform in your congregation.

Are you doing this? Then you may praise God for his church!

Heavenly Father, forgive me for being so critical about our church
and congregation. Help me to understand that I am your church,
and that I therefore have to accept my responsibilities. Amen.

30 October
Praise Jesus, the Lamb of God
Read: Revelation 5:8–14

Worthy is the Lamb, who was slain, to receive power and wealth and wisdom and strength and honour and glory and praise.
Revelation 5:12

In Revelation 5 the 24 elders and the 4 living creatures sing a beautiful song of praise to the glory of Jesus, the Lamb of God. 'He is worthy to receive the power and the wealth, the wisdom and the strength, the honour and glory and praise. To him belongs all praise and honour, glory and power for ever and ever.'

We are so used to thanking Jesus that he has delivered us, that we often forget who he is. Jesus is God himself. All the angels worship him. Through him God created the world, he is the radiance of God's glory and the exact representation of God's being. His throne will last for ever and ever. God himself anointed him as King. He will always remain the same and his years will never end (see Hebrews 1:2, 3, 6, 8, 9 and 12).

And this Jesus was willing to become a human being for you, to die the cruellest death imaginable to pay the penalty for your sin. When you pray again, use the above attributes of Jesus to praise him!

Lord Jesus, I praise you as the Lamb of God who is worthy to receive all glory and honour. Thank you that you who are so great and glorious were prepared to die on a cross for my sins. Amen.

31 OCTOBER
Praise God on his throne
Read: Revelation 5:9–14

To him who sits on the throne and to the Lamb be praise and honour and glory and power, for ever and ever.
Revelation 5:13

The whole creation joins in to praise God in this 'new song' which the living creatures and the elders sang. Everything created by God praises him by singing:

> To him who sits on the throne and to the Lamb be praise and honour and glory and power, for ever and ever!

We should still praise God whenever we kneel to pray. Glorifying God should form the substance of our prayers.

Are you able to praise God in all circumstances yet? You probably already know that, despite the critical state of your circumstances here on earth (as in the case of the persecuted Christians to whom John's letter was addressed), God is still on his throne, and he controls a master plan for the world. Regardless of what happens, he is still in control.

If you believe this with your whole heart, it is easy to continue praising God, even if you are battling at the moment.

Lord God, I praise you who are sitting on the throne. You are worthy to receive all praise and honour, all glory and power, for ever and ever. Thank you for the promise that you are still in control. Amen.

November

Answer to prayer

Answer to prayer can be quite a difficult issue. Sometimes God's answer to our prayer requests differs completely from what we have asked. Sometimes God answers 'yes' immediately, and at other times his answer is an unequivocal 'no'. However, this 'no' is always a 'no' for our own good. 'The day of the NO has been recorded in God's book. And all the days that lie ahead as well. As God knows the script for the days and years to come, as he writes and reads them long before we reach them, today might perhaps be the day of the NO. It is not the echoing of a NO in an empty space where God no longer exists. It is the NO of a Father who ultimately wants to give us something better than that which we ask him for in our short-sightedness,' writes Maretha Maartens (*Gebed kan my lewe verander,* p. 19).

However, you may be sure of one thing: God hears every prayer presented to him. And he answers all of them – in what is the very best way for you personally, even if his answer often differs from your original request. 'Before they call I will answer; while they are still speaking I will hear,' the prophet Isaiah wrote (Isaiah 65:24).

Hold on to this promise whenever you pray to God!

1 November
God answers promptly!
Read: Daniel 9:17–23

As soon as you began to pray, an answer was given, which I have come to tell you, for you are highly esteemed.
Daniel 9:23

After Daniel's moving prayer that the Lord should forgive the sin of his disobedient people, he received an answer immediately. God sent the angel Gabriel to assure Daniel that his prayer of supplication had been heard. Daniel did not have to wait long for the Lord's answer. Daniel himself testified: 'While I was still in prayer, Gabriel, the man I had seen in the earlier vision, came to me in swift flight about the time of the evening sacrifice' (Daniel 9:21). The angel then also explained to Daniel the meaning of the passage of Scripture he was reading.

The Lord is always ready to answer his children's prayers. However, the answers do not always come as quickly as in Daniel's case. If you pray and the answer to your prayer is delayed, follow the advice of the psalmist in Psalm 131:5: 'I wait for the Lord, my soul waits, and in his word I put my hope.'

If you are willing to wait patiently for God, and trust him during the waiting period, he will answer your prayer request in his own time and in his own way.

Heavenly Father, forgive me for wanting an answer to my prayer requests immediately. Please make me willing to wait for you when you do not answer me immediately as in Daniel's case. Amen.

2 November
God's timing
Read: Isaiah 49:8–14

---

*Zion said, 'The Lord has forsaken me, the Lord has forgotten me.' (verse 14)
This is what the Lord says: 'In the time of my favour I will answer you, and in the day of salvation I will help you.' (verse 8)*
Isaiah 49:8, 14

God's people had been taken into exile and they felt as if God had forgotten them. Fortunately that was not the case. The Lord promised that he would hear their prayers and save them, but that this deliverance would come according to his timing.

Sometimes we also feel God's answer to our prayers has being delayed for a long time and we then wonder whether he has forgotten us! In such a case it would be good to bear in mind that our timing differs totally from God's. 'With the Lord a day is like a thousand years, and a thousand years are like a day,' Peter wrote (2 Peter 3:8).

You therefore cannot expect God to answer your prayers within a specific period of time, but you may indeed claim Isaiah 49:8 for yourself. God will answer your prayers at a time he deems fit. Have courage when you pray and God's answer is delayed. Perhaps today is not yet God's time to answer your prayer request.

Heavenly Father, make me willing to wait calmly until you answer my prayer according to your own timing. Thank you for the promise that you will eventually help me. Amen.

3 November
When God says 'no'
Read: 2 Samuel 12:13–23

David pleaded with God for the child. He fasted and went into his house and spent the nights lying on the ground. On the seventh day the child died.
2 Samuel 12:16, 18

After the prophet Nathan had reprimanded King David about his adultery with Bathsheba, and God's punishment had been announced, David and Bathsheba's little boy became seriously ill. David prayed earnestly that God should heal the child, but God did not hear David's pleas – the child died on the seventh day.

By means of this 'no', God wanted to teach David that he regarded sin as a serious matter. It is interesting to note that David accepted God's 'no' immediately. He went home, washed himself and asked for food. Then God proved his forgiveness by blessing David and Bathsheba with another son.

Sometimes the Lord does not answer your prayer requests either, but he always pours out his mercy in a special way on everyone who prays to him. If God does not answer your prayer request of the moment, first of all check whether or not God is trying to teach you a valuable lesson for life by this 'no' as in David's case.

Lord, help me to accept your 'no' answers in my life like David. Thank you that I know that you will never withdraw your mercy from me. Amen.

4 NOVEMBER
God is near when you pray
Read: Psalm 145:17–21

The Lord is near to all who call on him, to all who call on him in truth.
Psalm 145:18

In the Hebrew text the first letter of each line of Psalm 145 forms the letters of the alphabet. 'This is an indication that the psalmist wanted to sing God's praise in a comprehensive way. We could say that God's goodness is praised from A to Z ,' writes *Die Bybellennium* (p. 705). And one of the promises made in this psalm is that the Lord is near to all who call on him.

We often feel God is far away when our lives are struck by incomprehensible disasters. David also experienced this: 'Why, O Lord, do you stand far off? Why do you hide yourself in times of trouble?' he asked in Psalm 10:1. Should you ever feel as if God is far off during a time of crisis, know that he is near when you call to him. He lives in you by his Holy Spirit. It is therefore impossible for your prayers not to reach him. 'Come near to God and he will come near to you' (James 4:8). For this you could sing his praise 'in an all-embracing manner' like the psalmist in Psalm 145!

Heavenly Father, I praise you for being near to all who call on you in truth. Thank you for the assurance that you can never be far from me because your Spirit lives within me. Amen.

5 November
God hears your prayers
Read: Psalm 116:1–11

I love the Lord, for he heard my voice; I believed therefore I said, 'I am greatly afflicted.' And in my dismay I said, 'All men are liars.'
Psalm 116:1, 10–11

When the psalmist was in trouble, the Lord heard his prayer, and helped him. Even when he was sometimes on the point of losing all hope, and he realised that he could not rely on anybody, his faith in God still kept him going. He testified that God had delivered him from death and wiped away his tears (verse 8).

Some of the most difficult situations to come to terms with is when people we have trusted leave us in the lurch. We cannot even really blame them, because we also frequently disappoint people who rely on us. However, God is absolutely reliable. He listens when you pray. He keeps each of his promises. You may believe in him in all circumstances, even in your greatest crises, because he will always help you. You can rely on his help with confidence, even when you are standing all alone.

Heavenly Father, thank you for the promise that you are absolutely faithful, that you will hear my pleas and always help me. Help me to believe in you despite the circumstances, even in my greatest crises. Amen.

6 November
God is planning something better for you
Read: Hebrews 11:35–39

These were all commended for their faith, yet none of them received what had been promised. God had planned something better for us ...
Hebrews 11:39–40

Apart from those people in whose lives God performed miracles as a result of their faith, we also hear of another group of people in Hebrews 11: Those believers who received no reward during their life on earth. Although they had faith in God, for example Noah, Abraham and Moses, they did not receive what had been promised. There was no sign of the miracles characteristic of the lives of other heroes of the faith. God planned something better for them, said the writer to the Hebrews. They could look forward to a heavenly life despite their difficult times on earth.

When you are also struggling and on the point of losing hope, when you pray and God does not seem to hear, claim this promise for yourself: God is planning something better for you. Something which might mean even more to you than the answer to your prayers, that is, a place in heaven where all God's children will one day gather. For that reason you should be able to look away from your earthly problems because they will eventually result in 'an eternal glory that far outweighs them all ... and is eternal' (2 Corinthians 4:17).

Heavenly Father, thank you for the assurance that when you do not answer my prayers according to my wishes, you have something better in store for me, a glory which far outweighs everything else and which is eternal. Amen.

7 November
Courage for the discouraged
Read: Psalm 10:1, 16–18

You hear, O Lord, the desire of the afflicted; you encourage them, and you listen to their cry.
Psalm 10:17

Psalm 10 starts as a lamentation. At the beginning of this psalm the psalmist was deeply discouraged. He felt as if the Lord was far away from him in his trouble, as if he was far off and not listening to his pleas. However, at the end of the psalm the lamentation turned into a song of praise. Now the psalmist praised the Lord because he had heard the cries of the discouraged and given them fresh hope.

Like the psalmist, all of us experience times when we feel totally despondent and we feel as if God is far away and not listening to our prayers. If you really feel discouraged and hopeless, go to God with confidence. He is aware of you and he hears your prayers – even if you feel he is not hearing you at the moment. He will give you fresh courage and energy at the right time.

'I will refresh the weary and satisfy the faint,' God promised in the words of the prophet Jeremiah (Jeremiah 31:25). He wants to do this for you today. Trust him to do so!

Heavenly Father, you know how tired and discouraged I am today, how I also feel as if you are far away. Please give me new courage and energy as you promise in your word. Amen.

8 November
Tell God about your need
Read: Psalm 142

*I cry aloud to the Lord; I lift up my voice to the Lord for mercy.
I pour out my complaint before him; before him I tell my trouble.*
Psalm 142:1–2

The psalmist poured out his distress before God in prayer and told him exactly why he was so depressed. He pleaded with him to intervene in his crisis because he knew that the Lord not only knew what he was going through, but also that he was the only One who could help him.

If you are also going through a crisis, call to God for help and tell him of your despair. He loves you and wants to help you. However, if you want God to listen to your prayer requests, you have to learn to be specific. Tell God in detail about the things which trouble you, about everything which is causing anxiety. Should something happen to you which you cannot reconcile with God's love for you, remember that God's love can never be measured against your personal pain. 'God's love is measured against a cross. What happened on Golgotha can never be made undone. God's Son died there alone so that you will never be without God in your despair,' writes Johan Smit (*Here, leer my bid*, p. 145).

Heavenly Father, please forgive me for sometimes allowing disasters to make me doubt your love. Thank you for the assurance that I may take my distress to you with confidence. Amen.

9 November
God listens
Read: Psalm 6

My soul is in anguish. How long, O Lord, how long?
Turn, O Lord, and deliver me; save me because of your unfailing love.
Psalm 6:3–4

When he wrote this psalm the psalmist was despairing and ill and could no longer face the gnawing pain and the grief which accompanied him daily. 'I am worn out from groaning; all night long I flood my bed with tears,' he said in verse 6. However, once he had shared his pain and grief with God, he discovered that 'The Lord has heard my cry for mercy; the Lord accepts my prayer' (verse 9).

All of us experience times of grief and illness in our lives. Times when we feel we have reached the end of our tether and we cannot handle the persistent pain any longer. In these times we start doubting the love and mercy of God and it is easy to become depressed. However, God is always there for you, he listens when you pray.

If you experience difficult times again, take your grief to God with confidence. He wants to take care of you, and help and comfort you as he did in the case of the psalmist. Like the psalmist you will also eventually be able to testify that the Lord answered your prayer after he had heard your cry.

Heavenly Father, thank you that you always listen when I am ill and in despair and I bring my distress to you. Please hear my prayer and grant that all will be well with me again. Amen.

10 November
God wants to deliver you
Read: Psalm 118:5–23

*In my anguish I cried to the Lord, and he answered by setting me free.
The Lord has done this, and it is marvellous in our eyes.*
Psalm 118:5, 23

In this psalm the Lord was praised for the mighty deeds he had done in the past. The psalmist testified that he had called to the Lord in his despair and that the Lord had delivered him. He knew no fear, because the Lord was with him. With the Lord on his side, he did not have to fear people either. He could rely on the help of the Lord at all times. God intervened and delivered him from his enemies. In verse 23 he then glorified God for his deliverance: 'The Lord has done this, and it is marvellous in our eyes.'

As you have the Lord with you, you do not have to fear people either. With God on your side, you are always a winner. If you do in fact sometimes land in a crisis situation, ask the Lord's help. He will always hear your prayer and help you. However, remember to give him the glory like the psalmist.

*Heavenly Father, you are also my strength and my shield!
Thank you for hearing my prayers and delivering me from many
crisis situations. I want to glorify you for this. Amen.*

11 November
God gives strength
Read: Isaiah 40:27–31

*He gives strength to the weary and increases the power of the weak.
Even youths grow tired and weary, and young men stumble and fall;
but those who hope in the Lord will renew their strength.
They will soar on wings like eagles; they will run and not grow weary ...*
Isaiah 40:29–31

God who does not grow weary, promises to give his children new strength when they need it. At times when Jesus was very weary, he used to spend all night in prayer with his Father and his strength was then renewed to continue his work. When you pray, you are sometimes physically aware of God strengthening you and giving you new energy.

Henri Nouwen writes that the praying person not only says 'I can't do it and I don't understand it,' but also, 'Of myself, I don't have to be able to do it and of myself, I don't have to understand it' (*Circles*, p. 34). If you are at present even more exhausted than usual, if you are discouraged and in despair, talk to God about it. He wants to offer you his wonderworking power, he wants to strengthen and protect you.

Prayer can do the impossible because the God we worship is a God of miracles. And this is the promise: God will renew the strength of his children. Ask him for this strength in prayer so that you will also be able to soar on wings like eagles, and run without growing weary!

*Heavenly Father, I pray that you will make your wonderworking
power available to me so that I will be able to do the things
expected of me. Amen.*

12 November
God's perspective
Read: Acts 17:22–29

The God who made the world and everything in it is the Lord of heaven and earth ... And he is not served by human hands, as if he needed anything, because he himself gives all men life and breath and everything else.
Acts 17:24–25

God does not always answer our prayers the way we expect, and we therefore often say we do not understand God. Trying to understand God with our puny human minds is in any case futile. He is so much greater than we are. He made the world and everything in it, he does not need anything from us, because he gives life and breath to all.

Should God therefore remain silent again without answering your most fervent prayer requests – which appear so logical and in line with his will – stop judging God according to your human criteria. 'We need to see prayer from God's perspective,' Evelyn Christenson writes. 'We should try to see the big picture of what God's overall plan might be and how each little and big request with his answer fits into his sovereign purpose' *(Journey into prayer,* p. 51).

God looks from above and you look from below. He sees the complete picture of the puzzle of your life while you can only see one piece at a time. Trust him therefore to provide the right answer!

Heavenly Father, forgive me for sometimes questioning you because your answers to my prayers differ so much from what I want. Teach me to see prayer from your perspective. Amen.

13 November
Reconciled with God
Read: Psalm 65:5

Blessed are those you choose and bring near to live in your courts!
Psalm 65:4

When he wrote this psalm, the psalmist had already confessed his sins. 'To you our vows will be fulfilled. O you who hear prayer, to you all men will come. When we were overwhelmed by sins, you forgave our transgressions,' he confessed in verses 1–3. Thereupon he experienced a deepening of his relationship with God.

Forgiveness of sin always reconciles us to God. When the barrier of sin between us and God, which prevents him from hearing us, is torn down, the relationship between man and God is restored. Like the psalmist we can now approach God in the temple because we have been reconciled to God.

The rest of the psalm is also a song of praise about God's abundant provision – if you are reconciled to God, he provides your physical needs. 'You crown the year with your bounty, and your carts overflow with abundance,' the psalmist said in verses 10–11.

Jesus has already paid for your sins on the cross so that you can be reconciled to God. Reconcile yourself to God so that you can share in his abundance!

Heavenly Father, I praise you for sending Jesus so that my sin could be forgiven. Thank you that I may now enjoy your abundance. Amen.

14 November
God can still storms
Read: Psalm 65

[You] who formed the mountains by your power, having armed yourself with strength, who stilled the roaring of the seas, the roaring of their waves and the turmoil of the nations.
Psalm 65:6–7

God is so mighty that he stabilises the mountains by his power, stills the roaring of the sea and also the turmoil of the nations. God not only controls nature but also history. Here the psalmist referred to the turmoil of war – in their skirmishes with other nations, God invariably gave his people victory.

Usually all of us experience some kind of 'turmoil' in our lives which God can still for us. Perhaps your problem is stress or fear. You may leave all your problems in God's hands with confidence. No power on earth is stronger than he is. Regardless of your present circumstances, God is stronger than all of them – he is still in control. He can also put an end to the violence and bloodshed which is so prevalent in our society today.

Tell him about your personal 'turmoil' – he wants to still the storms in your life if only you would entrust them to him.

Heavenly Father, thank you for you omnipotence, that you not only control the storms in nature but that you can also still the storms in my life. Please do this for me. Amen.

15 November
God never withdraws his promises
Read: Psalm 89:1–9, 34

I will not violate my covenant or alter what my lips have uttered.
Psalm 89:34

Throughout the history of Israel, God proved himself as the God of the Covenant who never withdrew any of the promises he had made. Although his people broke the covenant time after time and served pagan idols, God always forgave them again.

When you pray, you may be very sure of this: God is serious about every promise made in the Bible and you may remind him of those promises when you pray. Underline and memorise your favourite promises and repeat them to the Lord. He is faithful – he never promises anything he is not prepared to honour. God's promises are like a crowbar which opens the storehouse of his mercy by force, writes Joni Eareckson *(Seeking God,* p. 77).

Sometimes incomprehensible things happen in your life which result in your doubting God's promises. In these wilderness times you can either stare blindly at the disasters which have hit you, or decide to hold on to God and his promises. If you can manage to do the latter, you will always discover that God is still holding you, even when you feel he has forgotten you.

*Heavenly Father, I praise you for your faithfulness
and for keeping all your promises. Please enable me to keep
the promises I have made you. Amen.*

16 November
God heals
Read: Psalm 30

O Lord my God, I called to you for help and you healed me. O Lord, you brought me up from the grave; you spared me from going down into the pit.
Psalm 30:2–3

God can do all things – it is therefore perfectly within his power to heal the sick. In Psalm 30 the psalmist said that he had called to God during his illness, and that God healed him. While Jesus was on earth, he demonstrated this attribute of God – he restored hearing to the deaf, made the paralysed walk again, restored sight to the blind and healed many sick people. However, Paul (who also healed many people) wrote that he had to leave his sick friend Trophimus in Miletus (2 Timothy 4:20).

God therefore does not heal all sick people, because he wants to test us when we are sick. If you can remain a radiant witness despite your sickness, others who look at you will be able to see that you are different because you belong to God.

Are you sick at present? Then you may ask God to heal you. He will most probably do so. However, if you are not healed, try to remain a witness even when you are sick.

Heavenly Father, I pray that you will help me to be a witness for you here on my sickbed so that others who look at me will be able to see that I belong to you. Amen.

17 November
You may pray for health
Read: Exodus 15:22–27

If you listen carefully to the voice of the Lord your God and do what is right in his eyes, if you pay attention to his commands and keep all his decrees, I will not bring on you any of the diseases I brought on the Egyptians, for I am the Lord, who heals you.
Exodus 15:26

God promised his people that he would keep them from all the diseases which he had brought on Egypt, provided they obeyed his commands. 'I am the Lord, who heals you,' he assured them.

A short while ago one of my friends died of a rare neurological disease although the congregation prayed for her healing for years. The Lord did not answer those prayers, although it was within his power to heal Anneli. However, the way she lived while she was ill made far more people aware of God than would have been the case had she been well.

Nothing prevents you from asking the Lord to heal you or your loved ones when they are sick, as long as you remember that the Lord sometimes uses your illness to make you a more impressive witness for him. Sometimes you have to come to terms with his answer to your prayer.

Heavenly Father, I pray that you will heal me if it is your will, but if not, I ask that you will use this illness to your honour and glory. Amen.

18 November
Repentance and turning away from sin are required
Read: 2 Chronicles 7:14, 12–20

If my people, who are called by my name, will humble themselves and pray and seek my face and turn from their wicked ways, then I will hear from heaven and will forgive their sin and will heal their land.
2 Chronicles 7:14

Here God promised King Solomon that he would answer his prayer and protect the place where the temple had been built. However, before God undertook to hear his people's prayers, he made a provision: they first had to humble themselves before him, confess and turn away from their sins – only then he committed himself to listening to them, to forgiving their sins and to healing their land. He also told Solomon in verses 19–20 that he would uproot them from their land and destroy the temple if they turned against him again.

Before you start praying and submitting requests to God, you should likewise be prepared to change. Only when you are willing to humble yourself before God, to confess your sins and also turn away from those sins, will God commit himself to listening to your prayers. God loves you just as much as he loved his people, and just as his love made him listen to them and meet their needs, he will do this for you, too.

Heavenly Father, please change me so that I will acknowledge my inability before you, confess my sins and be prepared to turn away from them. Please hear my prayer. Amen.

19 November
God will answer!
Read: Jeremiah 33:1–9

*Call to me and I will answer you and tell you great
and unsearchable things you do not know.*
Jeremiah 33:3

God promised the prophet Jeremiah that he would do various things for his people, provided they called to him again: He undertook to rebuild their city and heal his people, give them children again as in the past, and cleanse them from their sin (Jeremiah 33:6–8). Should the other nations see these things, they would honour and glorify God for them.

When you pray, God promises not only to listen to you but also to answer your prayers. You should in turn be willing to listen to God's answer because prayer is not merely making your requests known to God, or talking to God, but also listening to God. If you are willing to do so, you will definitely hear God's voice speaking to you – he wants to tell you about the 'great and unsearchable things you do not know'. Concentrate on listening to his voice whenever you kneel to talk to him.

*Heavenly Father, I want to call to you in prayer but I also want to
listen to your voice. Thank you for answering me and for talking to me
whenever I pray. Amen.*

20 November
Call upon him
Read: Psalm 91:11–16

He will call upon me, and I will answer him; I will be with him in trouble,
I will deliver him and honour him.
Psalm 91:15

'Fear not,' is the subject of Psalm 91. God undertakes to protect his children in dangerous situations, to be there for them, to assist them in their distress and to hear their prayers when they call to him. However, these promises apply to his children only, to those who know him, who obey him and who communicate with him.

Our congregation has prayer chains which pray for various subjects every morning. From my own experience I can testify that the Lord really works miracles when this group of believing women agree in prayer. We discover time and again that he answers our prayers – minor as well as major requests.

My children have also discovered that all is well in their lives when the prayer chain prays for them. Before one of them takes an important decision, applies for a job or when they are in the midst of a crisis, they immediately phone me and ask that the prayer chain pray for them. We can testify first-hand that God's promise in Psalm 91:15 is still valid: When his children call upon him, he hears their prayers.

Heavenly Father, I praise you for answering the prayers of your
children and for being with them in crisis situations. Thank you
that we as a family have also had first-hand experience of this
on several occasions. Amen.

21 NOVEMBER
When God does not answer
Read: Psalm 22:1–5, 22–25

My God, my God, why have you forsaken me? Why are you so far from saving me ... O my God, I cry out by day, but you do not answer, by night, and am not silent.
Psalm 22:1–3

Here the psalmist was in the deepest despair: he felt God had forsaken him and was no longer listening to him. His lamentation reminds us of Jesus' cry on the cross (Matthew 27:46). However, unlike Jesus who was truly forsaken by God, the psalmist merely felt as if God was far away and was not responding. A few verses later he in fact said: 'I will declare your name to my brothers; in the congregation I will praise you' (verses 22–23).

All believers at times feel as if God has forsaken them. Richard Foster describes this feeling of being forsaken by God beautifully: 'We do everything we know. We pray. We serve. We worship. We live as faithfully as we can. And still there is nothing ... nothing! It feels as if we are "beating on heaven's door with bruised knuckles in the dark"' *(Prayer,* p. 17).

Should you some day again experience the feeling of being forsaken by God, know that it is impossible. God will answer your prayer – when it happens, testify to other believers about his goodness!

Heavenly Father, at present I feel as if you have forsaken me and as if you are not listening to my prayers. Thank you for the assurance that this is impossible and that you are still there for me. Amen.

22 November
Power in agreeing in prayer
Read: Matthew 18:15–20

Again, I tell you that if two of you on earth agree about anything you ask for, it will be done for you by my Father in heaven. For where two or three come together in my name, there am I with them.
Matthew 18:19–20

Jesus himself promised that he would be present wherever his children would meet to pray and agree about a certain matter. He also promised that this agreement in prayer had great power, that his Father would grant these prayer requests. When a congregation reaches out to their fellow members in love and prayer, and agree about the matters they are submitting to God, God himself will confirm their action and answer their prayers.

Perhaps churches are losing members and people are falling away increasingly because Christians have forgotten or are too busy to pray together. The vitality of a congregation can be measured against the number of members who attend the prayer meetings. We are convinced that the lukewarmness in the spiritual life of many churches and congregations can be ascribed to inadequate prayer meetings or the total lack of opportunities for prayer, writes Onbekende Christen *(Christen en gebed,* p. 111).

Are you pulling your weight in your congregation by attending their prayer meetings faithfully?

Heavenly Father, I confess before you that I often fail to attend prayer meetings in my church because I find it difficult to pray with others. Teach me the importance of agreeing in prayer. Amen.

23 November
Stop worrying!
Read: Matthew 6:25–34

If that is how God clothes the grass of the field, which is here today and tomorrow is thrown into the fire, will he not much more clothe you, O you of little faith?
Matthew 6:30

God's children do not have to worry, Jesus assures us in his beatitudes. Just as God looks after the birds, wild animals and flowers, he will also meet the needs of each of us. Are you anxious about anything at present? Tell God about your problems and trust him to solve them. He already knows exactly what you need even before you can ask him. He will also give you everything you cannot do without, provided you undertake to set him first in your life.

We cannot push away our worries with our minds, writes Henri Nouwen. If you want to worry, worry about that which is worth the effort. Worry about larger things than your family, your friends or tomorrow's meeting. Worry about the things of God: truth, life and light! When you do this, you enter into communion with the One who is there to give you what you most need. And so worrying is turned into prayer, and your feelings of powerlessness are turned into a consciousness of being empowered by God's Spirit … (Nouwen: *The only necessary thing,* p. 165).

Heavenly Father, thank you for the privilege of being able to turn my anxieties into prayer and for the promise that you will then equip me with power. Amen.

24 November
Do not fear
Read: 1 John 4:13–21

There is no fear in love. But perfect love drives out fear, because fear has to do with punishment. The one who fears is not made perfect in love.
1 John 4:18

If we believe that Jesus is the Son of God and we have the same love for one another that he has for us, this love is perfected in us in the absence of fear for the day of judgment, John wrote. His great love for us is the very reason why we do not have to fear God's judgment. God's perfect love in our lives casts out all fear still present in our lives.

The greatest block in the spiritual life is fear. As long as we are afraid of God, we cannot pray, writes Henri Nouwen *(The only necessary thing*, p. 167).

Most of us have many fears in our hearts: we fear the day of judgment and we also fear today. In fact, we fear so many things that our trust often disappears. However, Jesus came to teach us the extent of God's love for us. This love relationship has no room for fear.

God offers you his unconditional love in exchange for your many fears, but he expects a fearless love from you in return.

*Heavenly Father, I praise you for your immeasurable love for me.
This love which puts an end to each of my many fears.
I now want to offer you my love in return. Amen.*

25 November
The reason why you pray
Read: Psalm 5

Give ear to my words, O Lord, consider my sighing. Listen to my cry for help … In the morning, O Lord, you hear my voice; in the morning I lay my requests before you and wait in expectation.
Psalm 5:1, 3

The psalmist prayed to God knowing that God was listening to him because he loved him.

Your main reason for praying is not to make your numerous prayer requests known to God, but because God loves you and wants to listen to you. Make enough time for God, even if you sometimes find it difficult to talk to him.

Prayer continues to be very difficult for me, writes Henri Nouwen. Still, every morning when I walk in the garden being in the presence of God, I know that I am not wasting my time. … We must pray not first of all because it feels good or helps, but because God loves us and wants our attention *(The only necessary thing,* p. 171).

You sometimes pray and nothing happens. Perhaps you feel God is not listening to your prayers. Yet, if you persevere in prayer, you will in due course discover that God is in fact listening and answering – although he sometimes does this in unexpected ways. Make time to be still in God's presence. Prayer is never a waste of time – even if you only realise this much later.

Heavenly Father, please help me to spend more time talking to you so that I can experience your love and presence in my life every day. Amen.

26 NOVEMBER
When God's promises are not fulfilled
Read: Exodus 5:22–24

Moses returned to the Lord and said, 'O Lord, why have you brought trouble on this people? Is this why you sent me? Ever since I went to Pharaoh to speak in your name, he has brought trouble upon this people, and you have not rescued your people at all.'
Exodus 5:22–23

Moses did exactly what God had asked him to do at the burning bush, but the Pharaoh refused to cooperate! Just then the Israelites appeared to be in a worse position than ever before and they were very disappointed in Moses, which was to be understood.

Moses must have been very confused. To him it seemed as if God was not keeping his promises. However, God wanted Pharaoh to resist him and refuse to let the Israelites go. This was the only way Israel as well as Egypt would realise that he was the only God, and that he had the power to deliver his people despite their hopeless circumstances.

Sometimes you also feel as if the Lord is not keeping his promises to you personally. He promises to protect you and you are attacked in your home; he promises to care for you and you lose your job. Although we do not understand these things they might be happening to us because God wants to reveal his omnipotence to us. Don't you want to give him a chance to do this in your life?

Heavenly Father, I do not understand why bad things happen to me while you promised to be with me. Thank you for the assurance that you will never forsake me. Amen.

27 November
Selfish prayers
Read: 1 Peter 2:11–17

Dear friends, I urge you, as aliens and strangers in the world, to abstain from sinful desires, which war against your soul.
1 Peter 2:11

God's children are aliens and strangers on earth. However, although we are actually citizens of heaven, we are still sinners. Here Peter explains the basic principles for Christians, that is, that they should not submit to their innate sinful desires because these sinful desires could destroy life. Sometimes these desires are so important to you, that you might even ask God to make them come true!

It is therefore possible to pray wrongly. When you pray that your sinful desires should be fulfilled, God will not answer your selfish prayers. However, if you learn to organise your desires in such a way that they are in line with God's will for your life, God will give you the things you desire.

Pray that God himself will show you which of your prayer requests are still sensual and selfish and ask him to guide your prayers along the right channels by his Holy Spirit.

Heavenly Father, forgive me for so often having asked you things relating to my selfish, innate tendencies. Please teach me to request the right things from you. Amen.

28 November
Should God cover his eyes
Read: Isaiah 1:15–20

---

*When you spread out your hands in prayer, I will hide my eyes
from you; even if you offer many prayers, I will not listen.
Your hands are full of blood; wash and make yourselves clean.*
Isaiah 1:15–16

These words of the Lord in this passage of Scripture are quite alarming: when his disobedient people prayed, he would cover his eyes and ears to their prayer requests should they continue in their sin. No matter how much they prayed, he would refuse to hear their prayers.

These words still apply to each one of us, even today. If you have had the experience of praying without anything happening, you should perhaps consider your own life for a change. Are you perhaps cherishing sin in your life which makes the Lord deaf to your pleas?

Several passages of Scripture spell out to us that sin prevents the Lord from listening to us. Perhaps it is time that you clean up your life. Accept the invitation in Isaiah 1:18: 'Come now, let us reason together, says the Lord: Though your sins are like scarlet, they shall be as white as snow; though they are red as crimson, they shall be like wool.'

*Heavenly Father, forgive me for often having been the cause of your
closing your eyes and ears to my prayer requests. Please wash me so that
I will be whiter than snow. Amen.*

29 November
Prayer brings peace
Read: Philippians 4:2–9

Do not be anxious about anything, but in everything, by prayer and petition, with thanksgiving, present your requests to God. And the peace of God, which transcends all understanding, will guard your hearts and your minds in Christ Jesus.
Philippians 4:6–7

The *Collins English Dictionary* defines peace as 'a state of harmony between people or groups, absence of mental anxiety, a state of harmony, stillness or serenity'. It means harmony, unity and reconciliation with your fellow man as well as with God. Paul wrote to the church in Philippi that when you make your desires known to God, he will give you the peace of God which will guard your hearts and minds.

Pray for the peace of Jesus in your life by verbalising everything which makes you anxious, everything you cannot understand, everything you desire and then taking them to God. However, this peace is possible only if the Lord is close to you (verse 5). With him on your side you do not have to fear anything, you may remain calm – even in the midst of danger – God will protect you and act on your behalf.

For this reason you sometimes kneel beside your bed with your heart filled with anxiety, and a short while later rise again from your knees with a smile. Are you worried at the moment? Tell God about it, so that he can give you his peace in exchange for your anxiety.

Heavenly Father, I now want to give you all my anxieties. Please give me your peace which transcends all understanding instead. Amen.

30 November
A God of miracles
Read: Psalm 118:5–9, 21–23

I will give you thanks, for you answered me; you have become my salvation. The Lord has done this, and it is marvellous in our eyes.
Psalm 118:21, 23

The husband of one of my friends had cancer, and she prayed for his healing. The doctor had assured her that only a miracle could save her husband. Today he is healed – the miracle did indeed happen! And only God could have done this.

Sometimes we ask God for things which are so impossible that we actually cannot believe that God can answer our prayers! However, we must never lose sight of the fact that we worship the God who is a God of miracles. He can do all things, nothing is impossible for him. He made the sun stand still and his people passed through the sea on dry ground. He can still do the impossible in your life.

Continue believing in him when you pray, even if your circumstances at present seem absolutely hopeless. God can still perform miracles like he did in Bible times – if you pray and cling to your faith in him, you will soon be able to testify with the psalmist: 'The Lord has done this, and it is marvellous in our eyes!'

Heavenly Father, give me more faith so that I can pray with confidence and believe that you can still perform miracles as in the past. Amen.

DECEMBER

The power of prayer

Prayer has tremendous power. In fact, our spiritual power and productivity depend on our prayers. Jesus emphasised this power in prayer when he promised: 'You may ask me for anything in my name, and I will do it' (John 14:14). God is omnipotent – he can do anything. However, sometimes we limit his power because we pray too little and our faith is too weak.

'For you are their glory and strength, and by your favour you exalt our horn (sovereign),' the psalmist wrote (Psalm 89:17). When his children pray, God's wonderworking power is released in the world. Even although God can do anything he wants to, he prefers to work through the prayers of his children, because God's power works through you when you pray. Through that power which works in us when we pray, we will also discover time and again that God can do even more than we ask or imagine (Ephesians 3:20).

Perhaps you have not yet experienced the power of prayer in your own life. It is my prayer that, after the daily readings for this month, God's power will really be released in your life by prayer.

1 December
God's power works through his Son
Read: John 14:1–11

Don't you believe that I am in the Father, and that the Father is in me? The words that I say to you are not just my own. Rather, it is the Father, living in me, who is doing his work.
John 14:10

In John 14 Jesus talked to the disciples as people who had worked with him for three years – they were ready to take over his work on earth and expand his kingdom by proclaiming the gospel.

He and the Father were One, Jesus said. God's power worked through him. They merely had to look at the things he did: how the sick were healed and how even the dead were raised, then they would know very well that the power of God was at work. Without the wonderworking power of God, these things would be impossible.

God's power is obtained by prayer. Whenever Jesus himself needed special power, he would draw aside to pray. God equipped his Son with power when he had fellowship with his Father.

When you need special power at times, you may ask God with confidence to give it to you. He promised in his word that he would do so.

Heavenly Father, today I want to ask you to give me more power in my life so that I will glorify you by what I do like Jesus did. Amen.

2 December
Do the same things as Jesus did
Read: John 14:12–14

I tell you the truth, anyone who has faith in me will do what I have been doing. He will do even greater things than these, because I am going to the Father.
John 14:12

Jesus told his disciples that he was going to his Father. On earth he was sometimes hampered by his human limitations but in heaven he is God himself, with God's wonderworking power. Jesus made an incredible promise to his disciples: if they had faith in him, they would do what he had been doing. They would furthermore be able to do even greater things. He also works through every believer the way God worked through his Son. His power is now available to all of us.

This promise is still valid for you as well – if you pray and believe even you will do greater things than Jesus did. And prayer is the only way you will be able to obtain this power.

However, Jesus' promise is intended only for those who want to promote God's kingdom and glorify his Name. When you therefore pray in his Name, you should also be willing to go forth in his Name and work for him.

Lord Jesus, I now want to claim your incredible promise for myself. Help me to be able to do the things which you did, and make me willing not only to pray but also to work. Amen.

3 December
Equipped with power
Read: Acts 10:34–43

> *You know ... how God anointed Jesus of Nazareth with the Holy Spirit and power, and how he went around doing good and healing all who were under the power of the devil, because God was with him.*
> Acts 10:38

In his speech in the house of Cornelius, the Gentile, Peter said that God showed no favouritism, but that he accepted from any nation those who feared him and did what was right (verse 34). He told them about Jesus' ministry on earth, of his crucifixion and his resurrection from the dead. Jesus was able to perform so many miracles because God had filled him with the Holy Spirit and with power. By means of this speech, Peter destroyed the barrier between Jews and non-Jews.

While Peter was still talking, the Holy Spirit fell on those who were listening to him (verse 44).

If you belong to God, you have already been anointed with the Holy Spirit. 'Don't you know that you yourselves are God's temple and that God's Spirit lives in you?' Paul asked the church in Corinth (1 Corinthians 3:16). God also lives in you by his Holy Spirit, and he himself will equip you for each task you want to do for him.

Heavenly Father, thank you for the miracle of your living in me by your Holy Spirit, and that you equip me for all my responsibilities day by day. Amen.

4 December
Near the source of power
Read: Luke 5:12–16

… crowds of people came to hear him and to be healed of their sicknesses. But Jesus often withdrew to lonely places and prayed.
Luke 5:15–16

Jesus' ministry on earth must have been very exhausting. Crowds of people followed him continually and each of them had an urgent request which he had to attend to. But Jesus was able to handle everything, because he knew where he could be 'refuelled' for the task God had entrusted to him. 'But Jesus often withdrew to lonely places and prayed,' Luke wrote.

Jesus knew that his heavenly Father was his source of power and that he could only obtain the necessary power for his demanding earthly ministry if he remained close to that source of power.

If Jesus has to withdraw to obtain the power of God in his life, we need to do so even more. Withdraw regularly so that God can equip you with his power. Martin Luther often said that he spent one hour a day in prayer, but when he had an extraordinarily full programme he needed two hours with God.

If you need more power today, ask God to give it to you. Pray that God will give you the necessary power for the demands made on you every day, and make time for more prayer on the days when you will need even more power!

Heavenly Father, thank you for equipping me with your divine power whenever I make time to withdraw to spend time with you. Please do it now as well. Amen.

5 December
God's power is infinite
Read: Ephesians 1:15–23

I pray that you may know ... his incomparably great power for us who believe. That power is like the working of his mighty strength, which he exerted in Christ when he raised him from the dead and seated him at his right hand in the heavenly realms.
Ephesians 1:19–20

You release the power of God by prayer. However, have you ever considered the vastness of this power? Paul described it to the church in Ephesus when he was interceding for them before God: The power of God which he uses in each person who believes in him is the same power he used in Jesus to raise him from the dead!

As Jesus ultimately defeated Satan on the cross, he is now in control of all things. All power in heaven and on earth now belongs to him, and God makes this same power available to you. As his power is available to you, you do not have to fear anything on earth – not even the devil himself! Like Paul, you can now say with confidence: 'I can do everything through him who gives me strength' (Philippians 4:13).

Do you live in such a way that people who look at you see God's power in the things you do?

Heavenly Father, thank you for the assurance that I can do anything because you are with me and you give me the power. Help me to live in such a way that others will see your power in my life. Amen.

6 December
The mighty strength of God's power
Read: Ephesians 1:20–22

> *That power is like the working of his mighty strength,*
> *which he exerted in Christ when he raised him from the dead*
> *and seated him at his right hand in the heavenly realms,*
> *far above all rule and authority, power and dominion,*
> *and every title that can be given ... And God*
> *placed all things under [him] ...*
> Ephesians 1:19–22

When God raised Jesus from the dead and seated him at his right hand in the heavenly realms, it was the final proof of the vastness and greatness of God's power. He seated his Son far above all rule and authority. Jesus now rules as King with his Father! To them be all power for ever and ever. And he uses this same power in every believing child of his!

In the midst of the greatest temptations, you can therefore believe that God will make all things work together for your good because he has totally defeated Satan by resurrecting his Son. You therefore no longer have to fear temptations either because you have God and his immeasurable power on your side. And this power is inherent in prayer.

'Prayer is the conduit through which power is brought from heaven to earth,' writes William Law (Foster: *Prayer*, p. 253). Call on this power when you need it.

> *Heavenly Father, I praise you for the vastness of your power which*
> *I may obtain by praying. Please give me that power in my own life.*
> *Amen.*

7 December
Prayer and faith
Read: Hebrews 11:1–6

Without faith it is impossible to please God, because anyone who comes to him must believe that he exists and that he rewards those who earnestly seek him.
Hebrews 11:6

Prayer and faith are inseparable. If you ask God for something without faith, he will not give it to you. James wrote that everyone could pray and ask God for wisdom, but he added: 'But when he asks, he must believe and not doubt, because he who doubts is like a wave of the sea, blown and tossed by the wind. That man must not think he will receive anything from the Lord' (James 1:6–8).

If you therefore pray without believing that God will answer your prayers, you will definitely not receive God's power in your life. Without faith it is impossible to please God. Read Hebrews 11 to see what God did in the lives of people who believed in him. If you do not believe, it is impossible to do God's will or pray in line with God's will. If you lack power, ask God to give you more faith!

Heavenly Father, forgive me for so often praying without really believing that you will give me the things I ask. Please give me more faith so that I will be able to please you. Amen.

8 December
The power of prayer
Read: James 5:13–18

The prayer of a righteous man is powerful and effective.
James 5:16

The word which is translated here as 'power' is the Greek word *dunamis* from which our word dynamite has been derived.

On studying the life of Jesus one realises the tremendous power in prayer. We can also achieve more in God's kingdom by praying than by doing. However, then our prayers must not be selfish. Our prayers should be focused totally on God and his honour. What James wants to say here is not that the power is actually in the prayers of the righteous, but in the God to whom the prayer is addressed.

Prayer is never a personal achievement. God must always have the glory for the effect which follows on the prayer of the righteous. And if we also pray in this way, our prayers in fact make things happen. Elijah prayed like this and it stopped raining for three and a half years. Then he prayed again, and the heavens were opened to release rain.

When you pray, your prayer must be focused on God and his will – then you will find that your prayers really have power.

Heavenly Father, I praise you for the dynamic power inherent in prayer. Help me to base my prayers on you and your honour and glory and not on my own desires. Amen.

9 December
Fervent and righteous
Read: James 5:13–17

Is any one of you in trouble? He should pray ...
The prayer of a righteous man is powerful and effective.
James 5:13, 16

God wants us to be available to him. Before we start praying and swamping God with our requests, we should first of all ask God what he is planning for us, what he wants us to do, where he wants to send us. 'We work, we struggle, we plan until we are utterly exhausted, but we have forgotten to plug into the source of power. And that source of power is prayer – the fervent prayer of a righteous person that is powerful and effective,' writes Evelyn Christenson *(Journey into prayer,* p. 20).

Note the type of person whose prayer is powerful: *the fervent prayer of a righteous man.* For your prayers to be really powerful, you should pray fervently, and live a righteous life. It also means that your relationship with God will be right. It also means that you will have to turn away from those sins which you cherish and smooth your relationship and attitude with regard to others.

If you are struggling at the moment, tell God about it in prayer. However, you should also check whether you are praying fervently enough and living righteously.

Heavenly Father, teach me to pray fervently. And if I pray
and you do not answer me, help me to double check whether
my relationship with you is right. Amen.

10 December
God changes his mind
Read: 2 Kings 20:1–11

Hezekiah turned his face to the wall and prayed to the Lord, 'Remember, O Lord, how I have walked before you faithfully and with wholehearted devotion and have done what is good in your eyes.'
2 Kings 20:2–3

Praying in faith always makes a tremendous difference. When the Lord decided that King Hezekiah should die, Hezekiah was very distressed. He pleaded with God to extend his life and God heard his cry. He sent his prophet to the king with the promise: 'Go back and tell Hezekiah, the leader of my people, "This is what the Lord, the God of your father David, says: I have heard your prayer and seen your tears; I will heal you. On the third day from now you will go up to the temple of the Lord"' (2 Kings 20:5).

Prayer has a remarkable effect, not only in the case of major human catastrophes, but also in personal illness and other crises. When such things happen to you, you may pray like Hezekiah, with full confidence that the Lord will hear and answer you. God knows all about you, he also knows when you are suffering. And your faithful prayer could make him change his mind!

Heavenly Father, it is incredible to know that you could change your mind when people pray. Thank you that you hear my prayers when I am ill or when I have problems. Amen.

11 December
Power through prayer
Read: Daniel 10:12–21

'Do not be afraid, O man highly esteemed,' he said. 'Peace! Be strong now; be strong.' When he spoke to me, I was strengthened and said, 'Speak, my lord, since you have given me strength.'
Daniel 10:18–19

When Daniel saw the vision, he lost all his strength. 'I had no strength left, my face became deathly pale and I was helpless' (Daniel 10:8). However, God sent an angel to strengthen Daniel. This angel came in answer to Daniel's prayers, but Daniel said to him: 'How can I, your servant, talk with you, my lord? My strength is gone and I can hardly breathe' (verse 17). Then the angel touched him and told him to be strong. When he spoke to Daniel he was strengthened by God and he could listen to the angel's message.

His conversation with the angel gave Daniel new strength. The same is true of God's children when they talk to him. In Psalm 138:3 the psalmist said, 'When I called, you answered me; you made me bold and stouthearted.' God always keeps the promises in his word. He answers prayer and gives the one who is praying new strength. If you are tired or discouraged again, be still before the Lord and let him equip you with his power.

Heavenly Father, thank you that I have so often in the past experienced that you give me new power when I pray. Today I need that power more than ever. Please equip me with your power. Amen.

12 DECEMBER
Prayer can change your life
Read: Acts 9:10–15

The Lord told him, 'Go to the house of Judas on Straight Street and ask for a man from Tarsus named Saul, for he is praying.'
Acts 9:11

When the Lord sent Ananias to Saul, he was not keen to go. 'Lord,' Ananias answered, 'I have heard many reports about this man and all the harm he has done to your saints in Jerusalem' (verse 13). We can understand why Ananias was hesitant – Saul did indeed have many Christians persecuted. However, at that moment this Saul whom Ananias feared was praying ...

Saul's prayer changed his whole life. He not only received a new name – Paul – but the former zealous persecutor of Christians became the greatest missionary of all times. He became the person God revealed to Ananias, the person chosen by God to carry his name before the Gentiles and their kings and before the people of Israel (verse 15).

Prayer can also change your life. The more you pray, the closer you move towards God, the better you get to know him, and the more he will equip you with his power to do the things for him for which he has chosen you.

Heavenly Father, thank you that prayer has changed so many people. Please change me, too, so that I will come to know you better, and equip me to do the work for you which you have specially chosen for me. Amen.

13 December
The secret of Paul's success
Read: 2 Timothy 4:16–18

But the Lord stood at my side and gave me strength, so that through me the message might be fully proclaimed and all the Gentiles might hear it.
2 Timothy 4:17

When Paul heard God's call on the road to Damascus, the first thing he did was to pray. The secret of the tremendous success of Paul's ministry was also his persevering prayer life. Paul never acted before he had prayed, he prayed faithfully for everybody he came in contact with, and also requested the Christians to pray for him regularly so that he might fully proclaim the word.

Paul gave God all the glory for his success. He wrote to Timothy that God was at his side and had given him strength so that he could fully proclaim his message to the Gentiles. 'My message and my preaching were not with wise and persuasive words, but with a demonstration of the Spirit's power,' he said in 1 Corinthians 2:4.

By means of God's help and the power the Holy Spirit will give you, you can also answer your calling. This Lord who called you into his service, will also provide the assistance and strength you will need to answer your calling.

Heavenly Father, I pray that you will be with me every day and that you will provide me with the necessary power by the Holy Spirit to enable me to answer my calling in your kingdom. Amen.

14 December
God can do even more!
Read: Ephesians 3:14–21

Now to him who is able to do immeasurably more than all we ask or imagine, according to his power that is at work within us, to him be glory ...
Ephesians 3:20–21

God is omnipotent and strong and he works in our lives with that same power. He can and will do things for us which we can never even imagine. We may therefore pray with confidence and ask him to reveal his power in our lives. *Do not pray for an easy life, pray to be stronger people; do not pray for tasks which match your strength, pray for enough strength to complete your work successfully,* writes Joni Eareckson *(Seeking God,* p. 123).

Whatever you want to ask God when you pray, you may be assured of one thing: he can do much more than you can ask or imagine. There is nothing which you want to ask him that he cannot do. He is omnipotent, nothing is impossible with him. Dare to expect the impossible from him – he will not disappoint you. If you claim God's wonderworking power for yourself personally, you will find that you will be more than a conqueror in all circumstances.

Heavenly Father, I praise you for being able to give me much more than I can ask or imagine. Give me the boldness and the faith to ask much of you. Amen.

15 December
Prayer is as powerful as God himself
Read: Ephesians 3:14–20

Now to him who is able to do immeasurably more than all we ask or imagine, according to his power that is at work within us, to him be glory ...
Ephesians 3:20–21

Believers throughout the centuries have acknowledged the tremendous power of prayer. 'God does nothing except in answer to prayer,' John Wesley wrote. Martin Luther agreed: 'Prayer is a tremendous power, because God has committed himself to it,' he said. You cannot believe exactly how powerful prayer is and what it can achieve unless you learn by experience (both quotations from *A life of prayer,* p. 29).

We have numerous illustrations in the Bible of the miracles God performed in response to the prayers of his children. When Joshua prayed, he made the sun stand still, when Hezekiah prayed, he made the shadow move back ten steps, when Elijah prayed he sent fire from heaven to burn up the sacrifice on the altar.

God's power is still the same as in biblical times. He is still powerful to do more than you can ever ask him for. Do not, therefore, hesitate to claim his power in your prayers.

Heavenly Father, you are awesome! Thank you that you have repeatedly made your power available to your children in answer to prayer. Thank you that I may still rely on that power. Amen.

16 December
Strength in dangerous times
Read: Habakkuk 1:2–3, 17–19

How long, O Lord, must I call for help, but you do not listen? Or cry out to you, 'Violence!' but you do not save? ... The sovereign Lord is my strength; he makes my feet like the feet of a deer, he enables me to go on the heights.
Habakkuk 1:2, 3:19

The prophet Habakkuk was dismayed about the current injustice in his country, and about God's apparent disinterest, and rightly so. It seemed to him as if God was not listening to his pleas for help, as if God did not care that his people were being destroyed by the enemy. He prayed fervently that the Lord should help them.

The Lord answered Habakkuk's lamentation. He promised that he would intervene and help his people. At the end of the book Habakkuk prayed a beautiful prayer in which he recalled how God had delivered them in the past. Although his circumstances had not yet changed, he declared that he would nevertheless rejoice in the Lord, because the Lord was his strength, and enabled him to pass through danger safely.

God is still perfectly in control. He can intervene in your negative circumstances and give you the strength to understand that he will eventually make all things work together for your good. In times of danger he is there to keep you safe and to protect you. Trust in him!

Heavenly Father, I praise you for everything you have done for me in the past. Please give me strength for today to be safe in dangerous situations. Amen.

17 December
The power of persevering prayer
Read: Acts 12:5–17

> *So Peter was kept in prison, but the church was*
> *earnestly praying to God for him.*
> Acts 12:5

While Peter was in prison, the believers were praying for him in the home of Mary, the mother of Mark. And God heard their unanimous prayers. We have already seen that prayer avails much! An angel visited Peter in prison, the chains fell off his wrists and Peter followed the angel out of prison.

He immediately decided to go to Mary's house himself where they were still praying for him. When the servant girl opened the door, she could hardly believe that it was Peter. When she told the other believers about it, they at first said she was crazy, and then that it was probably Peter's spirit! (Acts 12:15).

What is so ironical is that God had answered the prayers of the believers, and Peter was delivered from prison miraculously, but the believers couldn't believe what had happened!

Don't be as unbelieving as Peter's friends when you pray and God makes the impossible possible for you!

Heavenly Father, thank you that you still do the impossible
when your children agree in prayer. Give me more faith
to believe that you keep each of your promises. Amen.

18 December
Be strong in the Lord!
Read: Ephesians 6:10–11

---

*Finally, be strong in the Lord and in his mighty power.
Put on the full armour of God ... And pray in the Spirit on all
occasions with all kinds of prayers and requests.*
Ephesians 6:10–11, 18

In Ephesians 6 Paul explained to the church in Ephesus exactly what they had to do to ward off the attacks of the devil and be strong in the Lord. Firstly, they were not to try to tackle him in their own power, but had to rely on God and his mighty power. Then they had to put on the armour of God: they had to put on the belt of truth, the breastplate of righteousness, fit their feet with the readiness that comes with the gospel of peace, take the shield of faith, and put on the helmet of salvation. As offensive arms, Paul suggested the sword of the Spirit, the word of God.

However, the armour of God will function only if it is put on prayerfully. Each Christian is faced with attacks by Satan daily. You can resist them only if you undertake to live prayerfully every day, if you will rely totally on God's power and get to know your Bible so well that you will know exactly how to use the sword of the Holy Spirit.

In this way you should be able to trump the devil every time! This is possible, because God's power is far greater than his.

*Heavenly Father, thank you that I may rely on your
strength, armour and sword to defeat the devil.
Help me to live prayerfully every day. Amen.*

19 December
Prayer, part of your armour
Read: 1 Thessalonians 5:14–24

Pray continually ... May God himself, the God of peace, sanctify you through and through. May your whole spirit, soul and body be kept blameless at the coming of our Lord Jesus Christ.
1 Thessalonians 5:17, 23

Although the devil has much power, and we can see that power in the world every day, the devil is actually a defeated foe. He is powerless against the weapon of prayer. Here Paul warned the church in Thessalonica to pray continually and to ask God to protect them spirit, soul and body until the coming of Jesus.

'I am convinced that my prayer is more than the devil himself. People nevertheless refuse to see the great wonders or miracles and admit that God is working on my behalf. If I were to neglect praying only one single day, I would lose a considerable part of the fire of faith,' Martin Luther wrote (*Krag deur gebed*, p. 96).

No-one who is involved in warfare against the devil can therefore afford not to pray. Do you pray daily that the Lord will keep you from temptation? If not, it is time that you pay more attention to prayer. Without prayer you will never win the battle against the devil.

Heavenly Father, forgive me for praying so little in my daily struggle against the devil. Please deliver me from the evil one. Amen.

20 December
Power and the Holy Spirit
Read: Acts 1:1–8

But you will receive power when the Holy Spirit comes on you;
and you will become my witnesses in Jerusalem,
and in Judea and Samaria, and to the end of the earth.
Acts 1:8

The disciples were not at all equal to the tremendous task Jesus had commissioned them to do. However, Jesus promised that they would receive the necessary power when the Holy Spirit was poured out on them so that they would be able to be his witnesses.

When the Holy Spirit was poured out on the first day of Pentecost, he indeed gave the group of timid followers of Jesus a supernatural power. The change brought about in their lives was illustrated best in the life of the impetuous Peter. The same timid disciple who had denied Jesus three times, testified fearlessly before thousands of people with the result that about 3 000 were converted.

'For God did not give us a spirit of timidity, but a spirit of power, of love and of self-discipline,' Paul wrote to Timothy when it seemed to him that Timothy's zeal for the gospel was beginning to fade (2 Timothy 1:7). The Holy Spirit wants to fill your life with his power and fill you with power, love and self-discipline when your enthusiasm sometimes starts flagging. Will you allow him to do so?

Holy Spirit, I want to claim your power, love and self-discipline
in my life. Make me a powerful witness for you. Amen.

21 December
Not by might nor by power
Read: Zechariah 4:1–8

So he said to me, 'This is the word of the Lord to Zerubbabel: "Not by might nor by power, but by my Spirit," says the Lord Almighty.'
Zechariah 4:6

Israel was in dire straits in the days of Zechariah. The work on the temple had come to a halt because the people lacked motivation. In chapter four the prophet saw a vision of a lampstand with two olive trees. An angel explained to him the message for Zerubbabel (the governor in Judea at the time): that he would not succeed in building the temple by might or by power but by the Spirit of the Lord. The Holy Spirit would give the governor the power to do the work but he himself would not be able to be idle either, he would have to be willing to start the work.

By means of this verse, God wants to tell you that his work in the world will not depend on human initiative and motivation, but will be completed by the powerful working of his Spirit in Christians. Pray that God will enable you by his Spirit to do the work which he has planned specially for you.

Heavenly Father, I am sorry that I often tackle your work in my own power. Thank you for the message that I will not succeed by might or by power, but by the working of your Holy Spirit. Amen.

22 DECEMBER
Strength together with the command
Read: Isaiah 49:1–7

… I am honoured in the eyes of the Lord and my God has been my strength – he says: … I will also make you a light for the Gentiles, that you may bring my salvation to the ends of the earth.
Isaiah 49:5–6

God gives an important command to his people Israel who have been delivered from exile: they had to proclaim the message of God's deliverance to the ends of the earth. They were not only to reassure their own people of God's love and faithfulness, but reach out much further so that they would become a light for the Gentiles. However, God promised that he himself would give them the strength to carry out this extremely important command.

God is still sending out his children into the world, he still gives them commands to obey, but at the same time always provides the strength and equipment to do so.

Perhaps God has a special assignment for you today and you do not feel like doing it. Know this: God does not expect you to tackle his work in your own strength because then failure is guaranteed. He himself will provide you with the strength you need. All he asks of you is willingness to be used by him.

Heavenly Father, I am sorry that I am so scared to obey your instructions. I now know that you yourself will give me the strength to obey them. Make me willing to be used by you. Amen.

23 December
All authority in heaven and on earth
Read: Matthew 28:16–20

All authority in heaven and on earth has been given to me.
And surely I am with you always, to the very end of the age.
Matthew 28:18, 20

Just as God had expected Israel to take salvation to the nations, Jesus in turn asked his disciples to do the same. He was sending them into all the world to make disciples of all nations, baptise them in the Name of the Father and of the Son and of the Holy Spirit and teach them to obey everything he had commanded them. At the same time, however, he assured them that he had been given all authority in heaven and on earth and that he would be with them to the very end of the age.

The disciples were often present when Jesus demonstrated this supernatural power: in nature, over sickness, even over death. In that power, with the promise of Jesus' support every day, they did the impossible: they proclaimed the gospel over the whole of the ancient world.

If you experience days again when your own strength is flagging, pray that Jesus will reveal his supernatural power in your life. Always remember: All authority in heaven and on earth has been given to him and he is with you, every day of your life.

Lord Jesus, you are so great! Thank you that you want
to offer me your power too, and that you have promised
to be with me all the days of my life. Amen.

24 December
God gives you his power
Read: 2 Peter 1:3–10

His divine power has given us everything we need for life and godliness through our knowledge of him who called us by his own glory and goodness.
2 Peter 1:3

When Peter wrote about the calling and predestination of the Christian, he said that the divine power had given us everything we needed for life and to serve him. Christians should therefore do everything possible to get to know Jesus better, and prove by their daily lives that God had called and predestined them.

What a glorious message! God wants to give you everything you need to live and to serve him. He has called you and predestined you to be his child. He makes his glory and power available to you personally. By faith in Jesus, you are adopted into God's family and you may be assured, even now, of one day being with him in heaven.

But remember: God's power can only be revealed in your life if you know him, if you are willing to obey his voice and his commands. Always live in such a way that your life will prove that you have been called and predestined by God.

Heavenly Father, you are so great, and you have given me everything I need by your divine power. Help me to live in such a way that my life will always show that I belong to you. Amen.

25 December
Power and protection
Read: Psalm 84

> *For the Lord God is a sun and shield; the Lord bestows favour and honour; no good thing does he withhold from those whose walk is blameless.*
> Psalm 84:11

In Psalm 84 the psalmist expressed his yearning to be in the temple, the place where he could meet God. He emphasised the fact that those who trusted in the Lord were blessed, that they found their strength in him and loved going to the temple. When they travelled through deserts, God provided fountains for them, when they sowed, he gave rains at the right time. At the end of the psalm, the psalmist said that the Lord bestowed power and protection, grace and honour on those who lived close to him.

'Blessed are those who dwell in your house; they are ever praising you,' the psalmist wrote in verse 4. They also go 'from strength to strength' (verse 7). If you want to experience God's power, favour and protection in your life, you should also be prepared to live close to God and meet in his house regularly.

Heavenly Father, thank you that your house is also my home, and that I can experience your power, favour and protection in my own life every day. Keep me close to you. Amen.

26 December
Power to endure
Read: Colossians 1:9–14

Being strengthened with all power according to his glorious might so that you may have great endurance and patience.
Colossians 1:11

In the passage of Scripture for today, Paul gave the Colossians a blueprint of how a Christian should walk in holiness. He described in detail what the lives of Christians should look like from day to day: they had to know the will of God, live to his glory, bear fruit for him and increase in the knowledge of God. This knowledge would help them to live the way God wanted them to live.

However, walking in holiness every day is not so easy. Many Christians give up after a while, because they try to walk in their own strength. Paul writes that this is not necessary if they were to look for strength in the right place. By his wonderful power, God himself would give them the courage to endure with patience in all circumstances.

God also wants to provide you with the power to walk in holiness in order to endure and persevere. If your own strength starts flagging, rely on God's power. He has all the authority and the glory for ever!

Heavenly Father, I praise you for providing me with the necessary power and endurance day by day to be able to persevere in the race of faith to the end. Amen.

27 December
Power in Jesus' Name
Read: Luke 10:1–17

After this the Lord appointed seventy-two others and sent them two by two ahead of him to every town and place where he was about to go. The seventy-two returned with joy and said, 'Lord, even the demons submit to us in your name.'
Luke 10:1, 17

Jesus sent out seventy-two disciples to the towns where he himself was about to go. He equipped them with his power and asked them to demonstrate the kingdom of God by doing the things they had seen him do. They also had to tell the people that the kingdom of God was very near. The seventy-two disciples returned with a beautiful testimony: 'Lord, even the demons submit to us in your name.'

The power of the Name of Jesus enabled the disciples to perform the same miracles as Jesus himself. 'I have given you authority to trample on snakes and scorpions and to overcome all the power of the enemy; nothing will harm you,' Jesus told them in Luke 10:19.

Jesus' Name still has the same power as when he was on earth. When you ask things of God in his Name, he will give it to you, provided it is in line with his will.

Heavenly Father, thank you that I may pray in the Name of Jesus with confidence, and that you hear my prayers because he paid the penalty for my sin on the cross. Amen.

28 December
A different kind of fasting
Read: Isaiah 58:3–10

Is not this the kind of fasting I have chosen ... Is it not to share your food with the hungry and to provide the poor wanderer with shelter – when you see the naked, to clothe him, and not to turn away from your own flesh and blood?
Isaiah 58:6–7

In Bible times people often fasted while they were praying fervently. Believers still believe that their prayers are strengthened by fasting. However, whereas fasting referred to in Scripture meant abstaining from food for a period of time, God himself said in the words of the prophet Isaiah that the fasting he expected from us was that we should feed the hungry and have mercy on those in need. True fasting is therefore not what you are abstaining from, but that which you do for people in need.

If you 'fast' by caring for other people and really helping them, God gives you a beautiful promise: 'Then your light will break forth like the dawn ... Then you will call, and the Lord will answer; you will cry for help, and he will say: Here am I ... The Lord will guide you always; he will satisfy your needs ...' (Isaiah 58: 8, 9, 11).

Heavenly Father, open my eyes to the needs of others so that you will answer when I call, so that you will lead me every day and meet my needs. Amen.

29 December
Prayer and suffering
Read: 2 Timothy 1:8–12

That is why I am suffering as I am. Yet, I am not ashamed, because I know whom I have believed, and am convinced that he is able to guard what I have entrusted to him for that day.
2 Timothy 1:12

Paul wrote this letter to Timothy because his zeal for the ministry seemed to be waning. The persecution of the Christians at the time might have been a possible reason for this. Paul asked Timothy to bear his part of the suffering with the power God would give him. He [God] had saved Timothy and also called him to be committed to him. Paul also testified that he himself was suffering continually (he was writing the letter while he was in prison), but that did not deter him because he had put his trust in God.

If you are in a tight spot, you will always find refuge with God. He is still a rock, a refuge for his children where they can always find safety. If your problems, therefore, force you to your knees again, that would be the very best place for you to find solutions to your problems. Trust God to give you solutions, or to give you strength to be able to handle the problems.

Heavenly Father, thank you for being my refuge, a rock where I can find shelter when the world becomes too difficult for me. Please help me with this problem which is threatening to overwhelm me today. Amen.

30 December
Fix your eyes on Jesus
Read: Hebrews 12:1–3

Let us run with perseverance the race marked out for us.
Let us fix our eyes on Jesus, the author and perfecter of our faith ...
Hebrews 12:1–2

Athletes who do not fix their eyes on the finishing line, but who run while looking over their shoulders from time to time, have no chance to win the race. Life is a race, a race which we can only complete if we fix our eyes on Jesus, the author and perfecter of our faith, the writer to the Hebrews wrote.

The same is true of us if we look at our problems in times of trouble instead of at Jesus. Joni Eareckson said that she received a letter from a certain Ted Smith in which he wrote: 'Many believers gaze at their problems and glance at the Lord. But I tell you to gaze at the Lord and glance at your problems *(Seeking God,* p. 27).

If problems arise in your life again, it always helps to look away from your problems before they make you discouraged and to look up at God. When you pray, it is likewise as important to focus correctly. Focus on Jesus – and not on the problems. You will always find help there.

Lord Jesus, help me to look away from my many problems and look up at you. Thank you for the promise that I merely have to focus on you when I need help, strength and advice. Amen.

31 December
God bless you
Read: Numbers 6:24–26

The Lord bless you and keep you; the Lord make his face shine upon you and be gracious to you; the Lord turn his face towards you and give you peace.
Numbers 6:24–26

The Mosaic blessing is probably the most beautiful prayer to use in blessing anybody at the end of an old year and the beginning of a new year. During the past year we have reflected on prayer. In the year that lies ahead, you may also be assured that, when you pray, the Lord will bless and protect you. You may be assured that he will answer all your prayers and give you his peace on the uncharted course of the new year which lies ahead.

In the original Hebrew the name of the Lord (Yahweh) appears in every line of the above blessing. He promised to save his people and protect them and hear their prayers. God embraces all his people in this blessing – everybody is included in this blessing.

God's way of doing is still the same. By his blessing he wants to be present in your life as well. If you experienced the blessing of the Lord during the past year, you may also expect it in the year that lies ahead.

Heavenly Father, thank you that you blessed and protected me during the past year, that you were merciful to me, that you heard my prayers and gave me peace. Please do this for me in the year that lies ahead too. Amen.

BIBLIOGRAPHY

COURSE:
Conradie, Dr Hennie: *ABC van die gebed*, Bybelkor, Wellington, 1981.

BOOKS:
Bounds, EM: *Krag deur gebed*, Hart Uitgewers, Posbus 353, Kempton Park, 1976.
Die Bybel in praktyk, CUM, Vereeniging, 1993.
Die Bybellennium, CUM, Vereeniging, 1999.
Cedar, Paul: *A life of prayer*, Victor Books, Colorado Springs, 1995.
Christenson, Evelyn: *Journey into prayer*.
Eareckson Tada, Joni: *Seeking God*, Word U.K. Ltd, Struik Christian Books, 1991.
Foster, Richard: *Prayer*, Struik Christian Books, Cape Town, 1992.
Maartens, Maretha: *Gebed kan jou lewe verander*, Lux Verbi, Cape Town, 8th Impression 1993.
Murray, Andrew: *With Christ in the school of prayer*, Whitaker House, Springdale, 1981.
Nouwen, HJ: *Circles*, Darton, Longman and Todd, London, 1988.
Nouwen, HJ: *The only necessary thing*, Darton, Longman and Todd, London, 2000.
Onbekende Christen: *Die Christen en gebed*, NG Kerk Uitgewers, Cape Town, 1981.
Smit, Johan: *Abraham-avontuur*, NG Kerk Uitgewers, Cape Town.
Smit, Johan: *Trefferwoorde van Jesus*, Struik Christian Books, Cape Town, 1996.
Smit, Nina: *Vonkelvreugde*, Carpe Diem Uitgewers, Vanderbijlpark, 1999.